TECHNIQUES OF NOVEL WRITING

Techniques
of
Novel Writing

Edited by
A. S. BURACK

Publishers • THE WRITER, INC. • Boston

"Novel Writer's World," by Margaret Forster. Reprinted by permission of
John Cushman Associates, Inc. Copyright © 1968 by Margaret Forster.
"How to Keep the Reader on the Edge of the Chair," by Joan Aiken. Copy-
right © 1973 by Joan Aiken.

ooB4448

U.S. Library of Congress Cataloging in Publication Data

Burack, Abraham Saul, 1908–
 Techniques of novel writing.

 1. Fiction—Technique. I. Title.
PN3365.B83   808.3'3   72–95433
ISBN 0–87116–000–5

MANUFACTURED IN THE UNITED STATES OF AMERICA

CONTENTS

PREFACE   ix

GENERAL

1 PLANNING AND WRITING A
   NOVEL   *David Westheimer*   1
2 ELEMENTS OF SUCCESSFUL
   NOVEL WRITING   *Frank G. Slaughter*   13
3 LETTER TO AN UNPUBLISHED
   NOVELIST   *B. J. Chute*   19
4 THE INTUITIVE FICTION
   WRITER   *Janice Elliott*   25
5 FLASHBACKS AND FLASH-
   FORWARDS   *Eugene Mirabelli, Jr.* 31
6 TELLER OF TALES   *Mary Stewart*   39
7 BUILDING READER
   IDENTIFICATION   *Alfred Coppel*   48
8 GETTING TO TIMBUKTU   *Cecilia Bartholomew*   54
9 HOW TO WRITE A NOVEL   *John Braine*   67
10 THE UNIQUE/UNIVERSAL IN
   FICTION   *Joyce Carol Oates*   71
11 HOW PEOPLE SOUND   *Marjorie Lee*   78
12 AN INTERVIEW WITH EVAN
   HUNTER—ED MCBAIN   *Evan Hunter*   85
13 THE LURE OF "I," THE
   TYRANNY OF "HE"   *R. F. Delderfield*   92
14 MAKE IT HAPPEN   *Rosemary Gatenby*   97

15 BALANCING PLOT AND CHARACTER   *Elizabeth Cadell*   105

16 THE FACTS OF FICTION   *Monica Dickens*   110

17 A TIME TO LIVE, A TIME TO WRITE   *Sylvia Wilkinson*   119

18 "I LOVED THE WAY YOU DESCRIBED AUNT MARY . . ."   *Evelyn Hawes*   126

19 NOVEL WRITER'S WORLD   *Margaret Forster*   131

20 EVERY NOVEL IS LIKE ANOTHER PLANET   *Hannah Lees*   137

21 THE CORNERSTONE OF THE NOVEL   *Anton Myrer*   145

SPECIAL FIELDS

22 "I COULDN'T PUT IT DOWN"   *Phyllis A. Whitney*   155

23 THE DETECTIVE NOVEL   *Catherine Aird*   164

24 WHEN YOU WRITE HISTORICAL FICTION   *Norah Lofts*   172

25 THE ELUSIVE PLOT   *Dorothy Eden*   181

26 WRITING THE CAREER NOVEL   *Marjorie Mueller Freer*   186

27 PLOTS AND PEOPLE IN MYSTERY NOVELS   *Hillary Waugh*   193

28 SCIENCE FICTION: SHORT STORY AND NOVEL   *Harry Harrison*   201

29 I LIVE MY NOVEL   *Amelia Walden*   207

30 THE THRILLER IS A NOVEL   *Ellis Peters*   213

31 WRITING HISTORICAL NOVELS   *Jane Aiken Hodge*   219

32 WRITE ME AN ADVENTURE NOVEL   *Bruce Cassiday*   225

33 WRITING PAPERBACK ORIGINALS   *Mona Williams*   233

34 WRITING FOR CHILDREN   *Irene Hunt*   240

CONTENTS

35 WRITING ACTION FICTION   *Desmond Bagley*   248

36 BUILDING FOUR-DIMENSIONAL
    PEOPLE IN SCIENCE FICTION   *John Brunner*   254

37 HOW TO KEEP THE READER ON
    THE EDGE OF THE CHAIR   *Joan Aiken*   262

38 WRITING A MYSTERY   *Patricia Moyes*   272

39 WHEN YOU WRITE A GOTHIC   *Elsie Lee*   278

40 IDEAS FOR MYSTERY NOVELS   *Stanley Ellin*   286

    Biographical Notes   292

PREFACE

The wide variety of approaches to novel writing presented here by forty successful novelists demonstrates that there is no *one* way to write a novel. In fact, almost every novelist in this book uses a different technique.

Some writers start with a character or setting; others with plot or a theme. Some follow an outline; others have no idea of how the book will end when they start to write; and still others have the end firmly in mind—even written down—before they begin, and practically write the book backward. The important point is that among these different writing techniques, there may be one that will be just right for you. No matter how different the *methods* of the novelists in this book, the *results*—their novels—are successful with readers and critics.

A. S. Burack

TECHNIQUES OF NOVEL WRITING

1

PLANNING AND WRITING A NOVEL

by David Westheimer

THERE is really only one sure way to write a novel.

You put one little word after the other.

If you do it regularly, and long enough, you will have your novel. Whether or not it is a good novel, or a publishable one—which are not necessarily interdependent—depends upon a number of things, but getting it written depends only upon persistence, putting one little word after the other until the thing is done.

If writing a novel is all that easy, why do so many of them remain unwritten?

I believe it is because the greatest deterrent to the would-be novelist is the sheer magnitude of the undertaking, the appalling prospect of the tens of thousands of words and the hundreds of pages which must be written to make the novel.

How to overcome that?

Shut your eyes to the mountain of unwritten words looming over you, the months of work lying ahead, and think only about the amount of work to be done today. It's the same sort of thinking which helps the alcoholic lick his problem when he cannot face a whole future without a drink but can accept a day without one. He fights his drinking habit one day at a time. You fight your novel one day at a time.

Although I had been fighting my own novel-writing habit this way for some years before, I discovered this parallel between the novelist and the alcoholic while doing research for a novelization of J. P. Miller's powerful screenplay, *Days of Wine and Roses.*

Now you know how to write a novel.

Put one little word after the other.

And how to prepare yourself psychologically for the ordeal.

Attack it one day at a time.

One little word after the other, one day at a time.

Self-trickery

If we novelists are often like alcoholics in our inability to accept the immensity of the task confronting us, we are also often like children in our need to trick ourselves into doing something unpleasant, such as writing every day.

In twenty years of writing regularly, many of those years while holding down a full-time job, I have used a method of self-trickery, discipline or routine—call it what you like—which has worked well for me. Since I am a conventional writer in work habits as well as execution, my method probably will serve just as well for most beginning novelists as it has for me. You brilliant writers, those of you who work more through emotional drive than sober, conventional craftsmanship, must chart your own way—you will know anyhow if you are a true original, or just someone who is unable to conform to schedules.

I began my first novel, *Summer on the Water,* in 1947. I had been writing short stories, without success, for several months, writing full-time and living on money I had saved in the military service in World War II. One of these unsuccessful short stories refused to remain a short story, and I realized with both joy and trepidation it was really a novel. The thought of all those words and all those months appalled me. I kept putting off actually getting down to work on the novel even though the blueprint was right there in the short story.

Then I remembered the first instruction in newspaper writing given me by Hubert Roussel, the brilliant and sometimes sardonic amusement editor of the *Houston Post* for whom I went to work in 1939. I had not studied journalism, had never worked for a newspaper, had never written a publicity story or review.

"Just put one little word after the other," he said—an understatement, it is true, but the only starting point all the same.

Fine. I had been doing that with short stories since my undergraduate days at Rice Institute in the Thirties. But this was a novel. I could do a short story in a week or less. Ten days at most. But a novel would take months. How many months at how many pages a day? How many pages a day could I expect to write?

I began with that.

I had been writing short stories long enough to know how many pages I could do comfortably—well, maybe not comfortably since I have never enjoyed writing, but do—day in, day out, whether I felt like writing or not. I could do, say, X pages a day. At X pages a day, how long would it take to write the novel? At this point, of course, it was necessary to face the novel as an entity, not as simply a daily chore. Naturally I did not know exactly how long *Summer on the Water* would be—and did not have that title for it, either—but I set an arbitrary figure.

I got a calendar and a notebook. In the notebook, I put down columns of future dates, one day to a line. I was ready to put the figure X by each date when I realized that if I pushed myself I could really do X + 2 pages a day. But what if I didn't push myself, or if I bogged down some days and could not do even X pages? I would fall behind schedule, get discouraged and perhaps not finish.

And this is the point at which I began the self-deception which was to see me through not only *Summer on the Water* but nine other novels, three unpublished, through the years. Beside each date I put the figure $X - 2$. I could do $X - 2$ pages even if every word was agony.

I put $X - 2$ beside every date except Saturdays, Sundays and holidays until, months in the future, the pages added up to a novel. At the date ending each work week, I set down two sub-totals—the number of pages for the week and the cumulative number of pages to that date.

On schedule, on target

Then I began writing the novel. One day at a time, keeping regular hours.

I tried to avoid even thinking about the novel except when I was actually at the typewriter, and then only of the portion which was to be written that day. There were sometimes nagging problems which had to be thought out in off hours, but they were usually individual problems, not those of overall concept.

And each day had not one, but three, production goals. There was $X - 2$ pages, which I had to write to stay on my schedule; X pages, which I knew from experience I could actually do, and $X + 2$ pages which I knew secretly I could do if I pushed myself. Most days I pushed myself, and some days I did more than $X + 2$ pages. At the end of each day I put down the actual number of pages written beside the scheduled number. I had a sort of competition with myself, trying to see how many pages above schedule I could do. Yet, on the days I did only $X - 2$ pages, I had no discouraging sense of failure, because I had stuck to my original schedule.

Childish, yes. $X - 2$ pages was actually less than I should have been able to do, and when I did only that number I was fooling myself with a false sense of accomplishment. And yet the sense of accomplishment was nonetheless there because I had done what I set out to do.

Each week I drew more ahead of schedule. Despite the fact the schedule was an arbitrary and artificial one, and I knew it was arbitrary and artificial, this did wonders for my morale. Except for those inevitable periods when the writing seemed to be going badly and I was certain the novel was dreadful (and even then I had no thoughts that I would not finish it anyhow), I worked with diligence and enthusiasm born of this delusion that I was moving faster than expected.

And now, after twenty-five years and more than a dozen novels, how did I go about writing my latest novel?

One little word after the other.

One day at a time.

A big calendar on which was penciled in every day but Saturday, Sunday, and holidays the figure 5. (I knew I could probably really do 7.) I finished it, as I did *Summer on the Water* twenty-five years ago, ahead of schedule. Was it really ahead of schedule? Who knows? Who cares?

The chances are you are working at a full-time job and cannot hope to do seven or even five pages a day. No matter. Schedule two pages a day, or one. At ten pages a week you can finish an average length novel in seven or eight months.

I wrote a novel called *Watching Out for Dulcie* while working at a full-time job. I scheduled two pages a day but usually did three. I got up an hour earlier than usual and wrote before going to work. You may want to work at night. I think it is more difficult to stick to a night-time schedule, however, unless you have fantastic dedication that resists the temptation of television, reading, movies, socializing.

Ready to start

Having overcome your reluctance to undertake a large-scale writing project, you now feel ready to start your novel. But even writers with a good story sense, the ability to develop credible characters, *and* with confidence and discipline often find themselves unable to produce a full-fledged novel.

What is missing is the flesh to clothe them. Whether from impatience to be done with the damned thing or from a feverish urge to tell the story boiling inside them, these writers rush to get the essential information down on paper and include nothing that does not contribute directly to the forward thrust. (Before going any further, I want to acknowledge that there is another type of writer, the old pro as well as the beginner, who chronically overwrites. But that is a different problem, and one more easily solved. Cutting and revising are child's play compared with getting things down on paper for the first time.)

Economy of style is an admirable quality, but not at the expense of the living, breathing flesh in which a novel should be clothed. And it is really not all that difficult to give your novel substance. You need only pause in your headlong rush to that magic phrase, "The End," to enlarge on incidental details and develop your minor characters.

Incidental details

Let us take, for example, a simple, conventional story idea, a cliché, really. Suppose you are writing about Mr. and Mrs. William Hardin, a young couple from Houston, Texas, drawn into a bizarre adventure while vacationing in New York. You develop the Hardins adequately; they are believable people. And your story moves along satisfactorily from one event to the next. But when you finish, you have a hundred pages or so which seem strangely lacking in texture, in sense of time and place, in color. In short, you should have put meat on the bones with incidental details and minor characters.

Here are a few of the many ways you may do that.

Suppose that on their first day in New York the Hardins are tired. After dinner they return to their hotel in a cab instead of doing the town. What happens when they get to their room will launch them on their adventure. Maybe what happens in the room is what gave you the idea for the novel in the first place, and you, the writer, are anxious to get there and get on with it. You write:

> The flight from Houston had been bumpy and the plane had been kept in the holding pattern at Kennedy for forty-five minutes. On the ground at last, Bill and Mary Hardin were too tired to see a Broadway show as they had planned and instead, after a quiet dinner, took a cab to their hotel. When they opened the door they were stunned to see . . .

What they are stunned to see is, of course, what you are getting at. But did you have to get there in such a hurry? We hardly know Bill and Mary Hardin yet. We may or may not be terribly interested in what they see this early in the game. And we know nothing about New York as they see it, or even about that hotel where they are staying. Or what time of the year it is. Or whether it is hot or cold. Or anything else except that the Hardins are tired, they had dinner and took a cab to the hotel.

Where did they have dinner? Describing that incidental detail has many purposes. Many readers who have never been to New York like to read about restaurants they've heard of, or even restaurants they have not. Others who know New York well might enjoy discovering in fiction something they have known in life.

What did the Hardins have for dinner? This is not only interesting for its own sake—Americans are preoccupied with food or else why all the successful cookbooks and unsuccessful diet schemes—but it also provides an opportunity to tell the reader more about Bill and Mary Hardin.

Are they well-to-do? If so, you show them dining in an expensive French restaurant or somewhere exotic—a Japanese restaurant, perhaps, where they are adept with chopsticks, or awkward, or demonstrate their independence by asking for knife and fork. If they choose an "in" restaurant or one with an exotic atmosphere, you have told the reader something about them.

Though not well-to-do, do they like to live as if they are? Do they worry about what the dinner will cost, perhaps calculate in their minds what they will have to go without later to pay for it? Do they drink or don't they? If so, is it something simple, say, Scotch on the rocks, or again, something more exotic? Mary might have a frozen daiquiri and Bill a margarita. Do they have wine with their dinner? If so, is it selected knowledgeably? If not, do they ask for coffee, iced tea or a Coca-Cola? Whatever the answer, it tells the reader something you want him to know about the Hardins.

They take a cab. Is it raining, and are cabs hard to come by? If so, is Bill aggressive about grabbing a cab from the grasp of others who are waiting, or is he victimized by New Yorkers better trained in competition? What about the cab driver? He's definitely a minor character. You will not see him again in the novel. This does not mean you have to dismiss him out of hand. Make him a person. Not a cute person or an eccentric; a real person. When you develop your minor characters, try not to make them "characters" in an effort to be clever or startling or even to make your readers notice them. Does the cab driver pick up on the Hardins' Texas accents? If so, what is his reaction? Does he needle them or does he happen to like Texans in general? Is he surly and taciturn or friendly and talkative? If he's talkative, does he talk about himself? Is he an over-careful driver or a reckless one? An important by-product of developing minor characters is that it gives you an opportunity to reveal more about your major characters. How do the Hardins react to this man? If the driver is a surly type, is Bill intimidated or does he squelch the man? What is Mary's response to her husband's reaction?

On the way back to the hotel, do the Hardins witness something that gives the reader some of the color of New York and/or something that tells us more about the Hardins because of their reaction? An altercation following a minor traffic accident, a policeman rousting a wino, a glimpse of Rockefeller Plaza, a militant Jewish organization with "Never Again" placards?

You've never been to Houston or New York and your novel is about growing up in Blooming Prairie, Minnesota. You still use incidental details and minor characters to put meat on its bones. If the novel is autobiographical (and ten to one it will be with such a theme), you know more about Blooming Prairie than anyone who did not grow up there. That knowledge provides your incidental details and minor characters, too. A lot of things you know about Blooming Prairie may seem commonplace and uninteresting to you, but they might be fascinating to strangers.

What about winter, for example? In many sections of the country, there is nothing special about winter. I myself was in my mid-twenties before I encountered hard winters where just getting dressed to go outside was a chore. Those who never had to wear long johns, wool shirts, two pairs of socks, overcoats, hats with earflaps, mufflers and gloves might be interested in knowing the trouble you had to go to just to go into town to buy a present for your best girl. And those who have gone through it may get a pleasant shock of recognition.

Did you go fishing in Blooming Prairie? Where, what did you fish for, and how? When I was a boy in Houston, I would fish for buffalo, a kind of large sucker, in Brays Bayou, using doughballs for bait. I had no idea other kids all over the country were not doing the same. When I grew up, I discovered that was not so, and most people thought fishing in a bayou with molded balls of bread for bait was colorful stuff. Chances are they would also think that the way you fished for whatever in Blooming Prairie is colorful stuff.

The point of all this is that wherever your novel is set and whoever the protagonists, you probably have the stuff of incidental details coming out of your ears. Use it.

(I seem to have overlapped another important precept of novel-writing: As a general rule, you should write about what you know best; what you know best is often the richest source of the incidental detail that gives breadth and texture to your novel.)

Minor characters

The development of your minor characters is simpler than you may think. You may develop them as you develop your major characters, only you do it more quickly and do not need to go so deep. You develop a character in exactly the same way you come to know an actual person—by the way he or she looks, acts, talks. Take that cab driver who drove the Hardins to their hotel. Let's improvise a paragraph or so and see who he is.

For no particular reason except to provide an identifying detail, you write, "The driver was a squat man with a small scar on the back of his neck, just above his faded blue shirt collar." Though you've mentioned this only in passing, it immediately opens up avenues for developing not only the cab driver but the Hardins as well. Is Mary Hardin repelled or intrigued by that scar, or does she not even notice it? If she doesn't notice, you have told the reader more about Mary Hardin than about the cab driver, which is fine if that's your aim. But suppose she does notice it because she is observant. And maybe she is also inquisitive and gregarious. There's some more character development already.

> "Excuse me," Mary said with a covert and faintly guilty look at her husband.
>
> It always embarrassed him for her to strike up conversations with perfect strangers.

"You talkin' to me?" the driver said without taking his eyes off the snarled traffic.

Before she could answer, he rolled down the window and shouted at a Mercedes Benz 300 trying to cut him off, "Jerk. You got money for a 'cedes, spend a couple bucks more on driving lessons."

He rolled the window back up.

"I hope you don't think I'm terrible," Mary said, "but I couldn't help notice that—that scar on your neck."

"Here we go again," Bill Hardin muttered, shrinking down in his seat.

"Hey, lady," the driver said, looking back over his shoulder. "Where you from? Don't tell me. Mississippi."

"Jesus," said Bill. "Mississippi!"

"Texas," Mary said. "About that scar . . ."

And so on. The foregoing is hardly brilliant, but it does show the possibilities.

There is another valuable by-product of being alert to the incidental detail and the minor character. Incidental details have a way of leading you along unexpected paths and becoming important details. Minor characters have a way of growing into major characters. And when this occurs, you have a full-fledged novel.

2

ELEMENTS OF SUCCESSFUL NOVEL WRITING

by Frank G. Slaughter

THE success of a novel, measured in book sales, the legal tender for authors, derives generally from three factors: the skill of the writer in transmuting unconscious material into written words; the interest-evoking qualities of the major characters; and the sequence of events comprising the story structure. Of these three factors, the first is largely intuitive and therefore not entirely learnable.

Story sense

The most important quality necessary in a storyteller (any writer who gains his livelihood from writing must be one) is undoubtedly that of story sense, the intuitive recognition of the quality of drama in a situation, whether entirely imagined, entirely real, or more often, some of both. Recognition of this dramatic situation—often called a "plot germ"—is not always a bolt from the blue, however. For example, the conception of my novel, *Doctors' Wives,* resulted from a feature story in *Newsweek,* describing a clinical psychiatric entity, "Doctors' Wives Disease," and reporting fifty cases from a private psychiatric clinic.

Cooking for several months on the back burner, the story suddenly erupted into a "sequential organization of actions and scenes" (the dictionary definition of a novel) upon my reading a newspaper account of a shooting, in which a husband discovered his wife and her lover *flagrante delicto*—and killed them both. Up to that point, the plotting had been entirely unconscious with no particular realization on my part, except for the occasional, vague unease that warns the experienced writer of a story-in-process. After that, writing the original draft of the novel took me barely three months, and the revision about the same length of time—fully a third less than I usually need.

I began the actual writing with an ideal, but wholly contrived, dramatic situation: five women—all doctors' wives, close friends and sufferers from the Doctors' Wives Disease, characterized by symptoms of boredom, lack of purpose, and marital estrangement—hear, under widely differing circumstances, the following radio broadcast:

> Tragedy struck this afternoon in Weston's fashionable Sherwood Ravine District. According to a report just phoned from an observer on the scene, a prominent Weston physician, Dr. Mortimer Dellman, shot to death a few minutes ago his attractive wife, Loretta. Details of the tragedy have not yet appeared on the news tickers, but a man with Mrs. Dellman at the time, said to be a prominent physician, was also seriously wounded.

The first mention of the tragedy occurs on page five of the novel. In the next few pages, each of the five wives hears the news and reacts in very much the same way. As for example, Della:

> "Who was it?" Cold sweat was breaking out on Della's forehead, though minutes before she had been hot and thirsty. It couldn't be Dave, of course.
> "Or could it?"

At this point, none of the five wives—or the reader—knows who the severely wounded doctor is. An explanation for the reaction of the wives, as well as a capsule characterization of the murdered Loretta Dellman, is given in the thoughts of Mike Traynor, a medical student Casanova, upon hearing the broadcast:

> "Christ! If this was last Wednesday, the guy being taken to the Emergency Room from Dellman's house could be me."

Less than thirty minutes into the story after the initial broadcast, the reader is now "hooked" and wants very much to know to which of the five wives the wounded husband belongs, whether or not he will live, and what effect the killing will have on five marriages. The author's job now is to milk the last drop of suspense from this tense initial situation without letting the reader's interest in plot or people wane. Here experience pays dividends.

On page five, the reader has learned only that *"Some doctor just shot his wife."* Seven pages later, during an instant mental replay of her just-completed successful campaign to become President of the State Medical Auxiliary, Amy Brennan hears the broadcast while driving home from the Auxiliary meeting— and almost wrecks her Cadillac. These seven pages establish the setting and also form the basis for the reader's concept of Amy as a dynamic, somewhat ruthless woman, intent upon advancing her own career as a "professional Doctor's Wife." They also reveal that her largely unconscious competition with her husband, Pete, is actually destroying her marriage. In the ensuing seventy-five pages, the essential character of each of the other four wives is delineated, as they rush to the hospital to see who is, or may soon be, a widow—all this is shown against a scene of continuing action.

Continuing action

The importance of having the action go on continuously cannot be emphasized too much. Once the writer captures the reader's attention, he must keep the story moving. To do this, the author keeps the suspense level on a rising curve, at the same time working in local color and description of the setting, and expanding the stature of the characters to give the final manuscript breadth and meaning.

To the would-be writer, words are pearls; to the craftsman, they are tools. The temptation to develop character and setting by stopping action and putting in background is always present in first-draft writing; unfortunately, doing so can ruin your story before it really starts—unless, of course, you cut it ruthlessly during revision.

The best characterization is achieved through action, which includes effective dialogue. This is based on the sound principle that a good fiction writer must "show" it, not "tell" it. In the early pages of *Doctors' Wives,* for example, I had Della, the club champion whose psychiatrist husband is practically a golfing widower, go to the driving range to work off her emotional tension. An old club retainer, watching her, observes:

> "You all right, Mrs. Rogan?" Leroy's soft-voiced question startled her. . . .
> "Why did you ask, Leroy?" She forced herself to be conciliatory.
> "You just topped your drive. Haven't seen you do that in ten years."
> "Take my clubs to the locker room, Leroy," she said in choked tones. "I've got to have a drink."

Della, remember, has not yet heard of the dramatic events in Sherwood Ravine moments before, but she is obviously already in a disturbed emotional state over something else, thus increasing the reader's desire to know why, as well as whether her husband is the man on the way to the hospital Emergency Room.

Still another brief characterization, applying to all the wives, occurs later, when three of them are watching a TV newscast about the murder, and Grace, whose marriage is foundering from general boredom, says to Della:

> "One thing's certain. . . . This will be the first night in a long time that the husbands—and wives—in Sherwood Ravine will all be sleeping in their own beds."

In the actual writing of *Doctors' Wives,* it was important for me to keep the identity of the unfortunate husband from the wives—and the reader—as long as possible. With the five wives converging upon the hospital and the imminent arrival at the Emergency Room of the patient (a member of the hospital staff who would therefore be recognized), the technical difficulty posed by the problem of keeping his identity hidden at first seemed insuperable. In such a situation, the factor of author omniscience comes into play—if he can make the plot device he decides to use believable. At this point, I introduced a new character—a woman doctor who had just arrived and was, therefore, completely unfamiliar with the medical school faculty. As the patient is wheeled into the Emergency Room, Dr. Marisa Feldman enters. She recognizes that the patient is almost dead, and she moves immediately to take emergency measures. The head nurse in the Emergency Room does exclaim, "My God, it's Dr. ———, but Dr. Feldman is using her stethoscope at that moment and does not hear those words. Note that this incident is told from Dr. Feldman's viewpoint only, so it is still not necessary to reveal the identity of the patient. Actually, by the time Dr. Feldman and the Emergency Room staff, working desperately with only seconds between life and death, are able to start his heart (page 81), we are a fourth into the book. During these eighty-one pages, constant suspense has been generated through continuing dramatic action, with all necessary details of setting and character simultaneously being introduced into the story.

Even after the wives reach the hospital, I reveal the identity of the shooting victim only by having the other four husbands arrive, and then I show each of their wives' reactions. With the erring husband finally identified, the first suspense climax has been reached.

Climax to climax

A well-constructed novel proceeds from lesser climax to greater climax on a rising scale that can actually be graphed. In fact, such a device is often a great help in revision, since it enables the writer to identify areas of relatively static story development that need correction, either by deletion or by the insertion of a new sub-climax to keep the action moving. The period just following a major story climax can be troublesome to the writer because of the tendency for the action to drop off. In this novel, fortunately, there was no such problem. As the identity of the wounded doctor is revealed, the reader also learns that the bullet is inside his heart and must be removed. The next rising curve of action continues as the critically wounded doctor is taken to the operating room and hurriedly made ready for emergency surgery.

Readers in general seem to like "doctor novels," particularly those involving surgery, my own specialty, so I make the operating scenes detailed, dramatic and, above all, intensely realistic. Preparation for the operation begins on page 82; it ends on page 147, sixty-five pages later, all played out against the rising suspense of the scene going on in the operating room, complete with heart-lung pump, flashing monitors and all the realistic trappings of surgery in fiction.

Against this tense backdrop of continuing action, the reactions of the major characters to the events of the afternoon are depicted, including the question (now moving into a center stage position in the story, since it will be the basis for a subsequent climax) of what is to happen to Dr. Mortimer Dellman, who fired the shot.

With the bullet safely out of Paul McGill's heart, the story has topped its second major climax, which Maggie sums up succinctly:

> "Mort Dellman might as well have shot all of us when he got Lorrie and Paul. That bullet blew our nice orderly little world apart—not that mine wasn't shot to hell already."

Beginning when Dr. Paul McGill, the shooting victim, reaches the Emergency Room, seven incidents—the bricks of story construction—cover the strictly medical procedure of resuscitation and subsequent removal of the bullet from his heart, on a steadily rising plane of action. Within that same period, fifteen additional incidents portray the effects of the entire plot action upon the major characters of the novel. The fifteen incidents are, in a sense, small dramas being played out against the action backdrop of the major drama, the point being that everything is moving, even as dialogue and minor action are being used to delineate character.

This action-within-action is the very essence of day-to-day dramatic writing. For me, it means sitting down every morning at nine with a yellow tablet, ballpoint and Dictaphone, into which I read the resulting scrawl at least every two hours. It means, on the average, six and seven days a week for four to five straight months of first-draft writing, with an equal amount of time to follow in cutting, shifting and rewriting. At every point, however, the essential ingredient is a story that starts to go somewhere and ends up by getting there.

3

LETTER TO AN UNPUBLISHED NOVELIST

by B. J. Chute

DEAR JIM,

Your letter has arrived, and I am truly sorry that your novel has just been returned to you with its fifth polite rejection from yet another publishing house. Black Monday, indeed!

My first impulse was to write you a sympathetic letter, full of encouragement and kind words. But, as I went on reading yours, I began to become uncomfortably conscious of a note of self-pity, so unlike you that I think I would be less than a friend if I let you indulge it. Self-pity is an easy emotional state for a writer to slide into. It is also a dangerous one.

Let me say, first of all, that I know how long and hard you have worked on your novel, patiently writing and rewriting it with a real respect for your craft and a real desire to communicate. Indeed, I do feel sympathy for you, and there is nothing that would please me more than to have those rejections turn into a nice check and a good contract. I wish you well, as I wish all serious writers well—be they professionals, amateurs, or in-betweens.

What I am about to say to you, however, has nothing to do

19

with the present quality of your work. It has to do with an attitude toward it, which I can only hope is temporary but behind which you seem to be taking shelter. There are two sentences in your letter which are really complaints, and, to be frank, I do not like them at all.

The first complaint reflects your understandable dismay that your novel, for which you have such high hopes, has now come home to roost for the fifth time. "I suppose," you say in your letter, "that all the publishers want to play it safe with big names, but it's tough on first novels."

I dissent strongly from this for two reasons. In the first place, I am not fully persuaded that your remark is anything more than another cliché about the publishing world. Someone is certainly publishing first novels, because I see the advertisements, the reviews, and often the novels themselves. It may well be true that, as printing costs go up, chance-taking on first novels goes down. (A first novel does well if it manages to reach the break-even point.) But, on the other hand, may I call it to your attention that it would be an even greater risk for a publisher *not* to publish first novels, since this policy would, eventually and with relentless logic, lead to no novels being published at all. This is a consummation which, I assure you, publishers devoutly do not wish.

My second reason for dissenting is that you have no business to be making this complaint so early in the game. You are basing your assumptions about publishers on rejections from only five of them. Come now, Jim! There are at least forty more highly respectable firms to which you can submit your novel; or, to put it crudely, you are only about one-ninth of the way through the possibilities. I am perfectly serious about this, and I consider it a perfectly sound professional approach. After all, the publisher who never gets to read your manuscript is certainly not going to offer you a contract on it.

Can success come too soon?

And now, before I leave Complaint Number One, I want to make one more point which may startle you and which you may not like. So don't think about it too hard at the moment, but put it away in your back pocket in case some day you need to take it out and look at it. It is this: *It is not always the best thing that can happen to a young writer to publish his first novel.* I know this is not a cheering thought, when you have invested so much time and hard work, but you would be amazed to learn how many established writers have one unpublished novel, or even two, tucked away somewhere. You are, as you are quick and frank to admit, still a very inexperienced writer. A full-length book is a considerable undertaking, and many first novels fail because the writer lacks the technique and experience the work requires. I am not saying this is true in your case; I am saying that it is possible, and that only time will tell. If a first novel is really good, and if its author is possessed of a fund of patience in marketing it, the chances are that it will be published. If it is not really good, the author will at least have learned a great deal about his craft. And perhaps, in the long run, it will be better if the manuscript becomes one of those that never see the light of print but whose creators nevertheless go on to fine careers.

This matter of the difficulty of finding a market is something that nearly all professional writers continue to face. It is really much easier to experience it early in a career than to have a succession of easy sales and then to find, as some bewildered writers do, that they are suddenly getting turned down. Nevertheless, early or late, it is natural enough for you to be sensitive about this sort of thing. Of course, you are sensitive. If you weren't, you wouldn't be a fiction writer. But don't waste your sensitivity on rejections. Save it for your written words, since it is by these alone that your career will stand or fall. If a novel is good, fifty no's from fifty editors will not affect its quality, and, if they scorn you now, there may well come a time when they will seek you out. Neither Rome nor reputation can be built in a day.

Write your *own* novels

This brings me to your second complaint, and it is the one that especially troubles me. "Maybe," you say, "what my novel needs is a lot of sex and violence and four-letter words—that's what gets into print nowadays."

I have heard this remark a good many times, and I have heard it from writers who ought to know better. It is, I think, a stupid remark, and—worse—it can be a damaging one. Your first complaint dealt only with the completed manuscript, but this one is a threat to the quality of the work itself.

Now, I do not intend, in this letter, to get involved in a discussion of liberty and license in literature. There is a current fashion for violence and obscenity. It is nothing new, but it is getting a lot of attention—so much, in fact, that some second-rate writers have come to regard it as a sort of device, too often relying on shock tactics to replace good writing.

I use the term *second-rate* deliberately, because this is something no first-rate writer will ever do. He will not twist his work to suit a theoretical public; he will not inject violence where violence does not belong. And, as to obscenity, the wise writer will remember that repetition diminishes shock, and the reader often becomes, first numbed and then bored. After all, if you want to characterize a garrulous woman, you do not drag your reader through every word she has to say. On the contrary, you work to put her on the page with such accuracy and brevity that the reader, his imagination engaged, says to himself, "That tiresome Mrs. So-and-so! I know exactly what she is like." You do not want him to say, "Five pages of dreary gabbling! I can get that from my next-door neighbor," and to toss your book aside.

When you wrote your novel, you started with a very clear concept of what you wanted to write. It was about certain people, certain emotions, certain places, certain situations. The form, the language, the style you chose were all directed toward a single end: to make the reader enter into the world that you were creating. This was your own way of looking at that world, and your own way of expressing it in words. Throughout the writing of it, you were truthful to no law but the requirements of the book itself.

Now, when it is finished and when it is as nearly what you want it to be as you can possibly make it, you turn suddenly unfaithful to your whole intention and say that it needs "sex, violence and four-letter words." You know perfectly well that it needs nothing of the kind. In fact, you know perfectly well that any such injection would do it real harm.

Do you write through other people's eyes, Jim, or do you write through your own? What have you to offer, as a writer, except your own view of the world, your own talent and style by which you express it, and your own integrity?

Integrity is not just a pretty word. Integrity is the cornerstone of a writing career, and you will be wise never to forget it. The idea that there is some magic ingredient which can be injected into a book in order to make it sell is as nonsensical as it would be if an architect, having designed a Colonial mansion, suddenly started to add chromium and steel because chromium and steel were the popular thing. Idiot you would call him and idiot he would be.

So write your *own* novels. Write them the way you want them written, using all the skill you have. Quit looking over your shoulder to see what other writers are doing, how much publicity they get, how much money they make. Creative writing is not a competitive art, and envy and self-pity are crippling. The artist relies on his tools, not on a crutch.

Remember, too, what Ben Jonson once said to a young man: "There is no statute law bids you be a poet against your will." You *chose* to be a writer. You never thought it was going to be easy; you always knew there would be mountains ahead.

But climb those mountains. Don't make them out of mole-hills.

4

THE INTUITIVE FICTION WRITER

by Janice Elliott

ANGUS WILSON once described fiction writing as "a kind of magic." So it is, and so, I believe, it is absurd for a novelist to attempt to communicate anything more than the most superficial techniques of his weird occupation. Journalism can, to some degree, be taught. An illusionist can tell you how to cut your wife in half, but a novelist can no more tell you how to write than a wizard can teach you to fly.

The only way to write, then, is to write, and if you're a novelist you'll write regardless, for better or worse, in sickness and in health, till death do you part from that heartbreaking, marvelous daily grind. I couldn't tell you how to do it, nor would I want to—not only because it would be an impertinence, but because too much technical self-analysis seems to me bad for the writer himself. If you were riding a bicycle blindfold across a tightrope, to stop and wonder how you did it would be the quickest way to fall off.

With that analogy I have given myself away as a writer who relies almost entirely on intuition. Magic is a nice word for it, but it feels more like groping; a confession which may be, if not of practical help, a comfort at least to others who work in

25

the same way. When interviewers ask me how I write, my first impulse is to run, my second to remember like Winnie-the-Pooh that it's time for a little something. I have never planned a novel; rather I have waited for it to overtake me, for my subconscious to signal that there may be a world waiting to be uncovered.

Audible and visual signals

The signal is curiously precise, usually audible or visual: in *Angels Falling*, a young woman (Frances, as it turned out) with reddish hair, wearing square-cut rings, in a comfortable room, beating her knuckles against a mirror. I could hear the sound of the jewels on the glass, and from this tiny, apparently inconsequential episode, grew a family, a series of interlocking tragedies, and finally a personal vision of England from the death of Victoria to the present day. The signal may haunt me for weeks or months or possibly years. I may even attempt to reject it, but if it is a true one, that sound or picture or fragment of speech will be the key to a wonderful land. Anyone who has ever shared this experience will know what Françoise Sagan meant when she said, in *Writers at Work,* "Instead of leaving for Chile with a band of gangsters, one stays in Paris and writes a novel. That seems to me the great adventure."

This intuitive technique (or rather, lack of technique) used to worry me, still frightens me a little, but I have come to trust it. In fact, I believe now that for any novelist who works as I do, by instinct, it would be positively wrong to attempt a more conventionally disciplined approach. We may have a more frantic time than the file-card novelist. In the early stages, those who suffer most are probably our husbands, wives, agents, friends, children, cats and dogs. But in time, I find, one does learn to relax a little. I still try to stick to my routine of two or three hours' fiction writing a day, either obeying a signal or listening for one; but once truly launched on a book, I no longer have the same crazy fear that if holidays or illness should keep me from the typewriter, the country will vanish and its people melt.

That, of course, is the fulcrum upon which this apparently haphazard creative process turns: character. The characters are the guides to the world you will, hopefully, reveal, and without them instinct is impotent. Some time after the war, I spent a few months as an unqualified and incompetent social worker in the East End of London, where social conditions and industrial unrest had prolonged beyond its natural term the effect of a hard war and a thankless victory. I was a mindless seventeen, but by some process of osmosis I absorbed and stored the memory of naked bomb sites, bitterness and the threat of anarchy which made it dangerous to walk alone in the streets at night. Violence is not so new, after all.

It was more than twenty years before the ghost of that time tapped me on the shoulder, but even then I could not write about it until in a tentative first chapter I found myself describing a dinner party on V-J Day. The signal was a woman raising a glass of water to toast the peace, but the one who interested me was her daughter, Olive, young and angry at the way the war had ended, desperately anxious for the new peace. "Follow that woman," said a policeman voice in my mind, and so *A State of Peace* had begun. Olive took me back to that bad peace and those years, and through her a forgotten world sprang to life. In fact, she and her friends took over, as so often happens, and I was embarked, before I knew it, on a sequel, *Private Life*.

So the intuitive approach does have its problems. People like Olive take over, uninvited characters barge in—as did Bob Wilson, Olive's lover in *A State of Peace*. Again, my method is to trust my instinct, not to throw these gate-crashers out. They may turn out to be valuable secondary figures; they might emerge, like Bob, as major protagonists. His break with Communism, which is suggested at the end of the first volume, became a principal theme of *Private Life*. If I had rejected him earlier for the sake of tidiness, there might never have been a sequel.

I would say, then, welcome these visitors; let them live. But I admit that keeping open house has its awkward side, especially if you are writing a saga or a sequence of novels. With *Angels Falling*, the longest novel I have ever written, spanning a vast period of history, for the first time I had to make notes. Historical headings were on one side, on the facing page two columns: one to record vague ideas as to the content of the next few chapters, the other a more precise synopsis of what actually happened. In this makeshift way I was able to keep some kind of authority over those wayward characters. I have stuck to the same method ever since, though I wonder sometimes whom I'm fooling. The historical notes are vital, of course, but as for the rest, I'm just as likely to find the clue to some intense moment of drama buried in the shopping list.

Hunches and images

Still, the more you work in this groping way, following hunches, the more important it is to stand back from time to time and see your work coldly. I should be very worried if by halfway through I had no idea of the scheme of the book, at least in my head. Often, at this point, images are as valuable as characters. They are the clues for subconscious plants: in *Angels Falling*, for instance, the images connected with the fall from innocence (though it took a perceptive American reviewer to make me see the significance of the serpent bracelet on the first page). With half a dozen chapters under my belt, I begin to study images for their meaning.

Then, just once, after *Angels Falling*, I stepped yet further back and gave my writing an even chillier look. Rightly or wrongly I decided that novel writing had become too comfortable for me, too fluent. The last novel had been a long but easy ride, and if I were to progress, to achieve the deep realism and honesty I hankered for, I would have to abandon temporarily the kind of setting which tempts one to get away with the beautiful picture, the elegant phrase.

Hence, *The Kindling,* set in the industrial north midlands where I was brought up. The characters were less articulate, the background far from pretty. I still don't know how good a book it was, but I did feel that at least I had written something uncompromisingly truthful. Since then I have returned to a broader landscape. My characters are again the kind of people who are capable of self-analysis, but I have struggled to preserve those standards of honesty which were unavoidable in *The Kindling*—an effort which made *A State of Peace* and its sequel the most painful, but in the long run the most satisfying books I have ever written. If there is a lesson here it may be that for anyone who writes in this obsessive, unstoppable way, it is valuable now and again to make life difficult for yourself.

Real people, real sentiment

Unexpectedly, I learned another lesson from *The Kindling*: not to be afraid of sentiment. However intricate and refined their perceptions may be, when it comes to the crunch, real men and women use the crudest, most sentimental terms. The emphasis is on *real*. Bad literary sentiment is a cardboard character calling farewell to his love as she speeds across the snow in her sleigh. Good, truthful sentiment is Zhivago whispering to Lara in the frosty evening: "Goodbye, my only love, my love forever lost." So marvelously has he been built up as a whole man of flesh and blood, the poignancy of that whisper is almost unbearable. Here it is even possible the intuitive writer may have the advantage over the rest—his instinct will tell him if his abandoned lover is real enough for this moment of crude, human truth.

I believe that for the instinctive writer the rewards outweigh the problems. Yet this technique does demand a discipline of its own. When it's good, the *deus ex machina* will be holding your hand, but he is a fickle visitor, and in between the daily grind is vital. A signal may come when you are least expecting it, out of sorts and thinking of growing cabbages. I work as a journalist as well as a novelist because I have found the signals come best under tension; one page written under pressure may be better than twenty conceived at leisure.

All I can urge then is faith and work. Trust your instinct and stick to the grind. "Writing a book," said George Orwell, "is a horrible, exhausting struggle, like a long bout of some painful illness. One would never undertake such a thing if one were not driven on by some demon whom one can neither resist nor understand." Except to say, listen to the demon, I can't tell you how to write a novel. If you can, you will.

5

FLASHBACKS AND FLASHFORWARDS

by Eugene Mirabelli, Jr.

SOMETIMES it is so hard to write one single chapter, so hard to get the clumsy thing straightened out, unsnarled, and underway so that it actually moves along and comes to rest someplace near where I had hoped it would; sometimes it is all so difficult that when at last a reader comes up and asks, "Why don't you write a nice, simple, straightforward story?" I don't know whether to say, "Next time I *will* write a nice, simple, straightforward story," or to punch him in the mouth. Actually, I am the mildest of men. I would never dream of punching anyone in the mouth, and the last time I met a person who had in fact read one of my books, I threw my arms around him, showed him to my wife to prove I did have readers, and invited him to dinner. But these people who ask for straightforward stories are a brutal lot. They want to impose the crudest sort of temporal order on every story —that is, they want no flashbacks, no roundabout digressions, certainly no flashforwards—no nothing but the simple *and then, and then, and then* from beginning to end. And I happen to be the sort who wants to write any which way that comes into my head.

Now, surely, we can all agree that there are stories which are best unfolded in strict chronological order. Stories which are driven forward by the inexorable force of event upon event—mystery stories, adventure tales, novels in which characters react and develop over long years, grand novels embracing historical epochs, vast geographies—the plots of such stories seem to fall naturally into a linear, temporal sequence. Edgar Allan Poe, Stephen Crane, Theodore Dreiser, Henry James, James Jones, J. D. Salinger, all write superbly while unfolding their stories in the simplest chronological order. If Hemingway had tried to rearrange the episodes which make up *The Green Hills of Africa,* the result would have been ludicrous, and if Tolstoy had done any tampering with the grand but simple chronology of *War and Peace,* he would have had a magnificent mess on his hands.

But I believe that if you examine any novel in which the story moves forward chronologically, you will discover that the linear, temporal sequence is not imposed on it at all, but is instead the natural order for that particular story. Let's take as an example *Office Politics* by Wilfrid Sheed. Now there are a number of more or less self-contained incidents which make up that novel, but if you take a pair of scissors to the book—the paperbound edition is less expensive—and cut out the episodes and rearrange them to your heart's content, you will not come up with a better order than the simple one Sheed used. If you do come up with a better sequence, by all means write to Sheed; it's the sort of thing an author likes to receive letters about. In other words, chronological order was not artificially imposed on that novel: the internal logic of the story determined its outward form.

On the other hand, the internal logic of another story may dictate an apparently jumbled time sequence. We do not always begin a story at the very beginning. Horace—that antique author of so much advice—tells us not to waste time on the approaches to a story, but to plunge into the middle of things. As he points out, Helen of Troy was born from the union of Leda and a swan, but when Homer launches his Trojan epic he does not start with the egg from which Helen was hatched. Few critics would call Milton a radical literary innovator, or accuse him of wrenching his time scheme to suit his fancy; yet, when *Paradise Lost* opens, we find Satan and his followers sitting on the floor of Hell, and it is not until we are well into the story that Milton detours through what we would now call a flashback to tell us how Satan got there.

Perhaps the most celebrated example of a radically altered time scheme occurs in William Faulkner's *The Sound and the Fury*. That novel is divided into four parts which are dated as follows: April 7, 1928; June 2, 1910; April 6, 1928; April 8, 1928. You will notice that the year 1910 is intruded into the sequence comprising events that occur in 1928, and that even the events of the year 1928 are not arranged in their chronological order, for April 6 is made to follow April 7. Moreover, the first part—April 7, 1928—is the turbulent stream of consciousness of an idiot for whom scenes past and present are hopelessly jumbled. *The Sound and the Fury* is one of the greatest novels of this century; it has, of course, been attacked as obscure, unnecessarily confusing, or simply too hard to read. But over the years the novel has triumphed over its detractors, and I know of no serious critic who has come forward with a better arrangement of the four parts than the one dreamed up by its author.

Determining time sequence

How, then, should you tell your own story? I believe it is best to tell it first the way it occurs to you. Usually this means letting your mind play back and forth over the events until they fall rather easily into some suitable order. Almost always you will discover that the episodes, scenes, dramatic moments, and so forth, arrange themselves into a simple chronological pattern. This is, after all, the way we live. Occasionally, you will find yourself with a story which comes to you directly made up of, say, flashbacks: for example, the scene is a wedding and certain members of the congregation think back over some segment of the history of the young woman about to be married. For though it is true that we live chronologically, it is also true that life presents us with occasions when we reflect upon the past. Anyone who has been in a church, watching and listening as the wedding service goes forward, knows how easily the mind wanders into the past and possible future of the couple being wed. In such an instance, a writer may discover that the flashback technique, far from being an artificial complication, is quite natural and proper.

Let us assume, however, that what usually happens has happened once again, and that you find yourself with a simple, linear story. Once you have the plot set out in your mind, you should consider whether or not it can be improved by altering the time sequence. For the writer who protests that reordering the time pattern of a story is unnatural, or sneaky, or perhaps even immoral, I can only shrug my shoulders and reply that in some sense every technique, every stylistic device, is to some degree unnatural and devious. Art is, after all, an imposition of order upon life—that is why we call it art and not life. Many a poor or middling story might be rescued by even the simplest of time shifts. For example, it may be possible to move the reader more swiftly toward the heart of the story by removing some necessary but rather dull preliminary skirmish from the opening pages and inserting it as a flashback a bit later.

A typical newspaper story about a crime begins with the fascinating dramatic lead first—the dead body, the ravaged apartment, the looted vault—and then goes back to describe the events immediately preceding the crime, and finally retreats even farther to sketch in the possible criminals, their motives, and so forth. Or it may be possible to put two contrasting scenes side by side for dramatic effect, even though they are separated widely in time. An ordinary courtroom divorce action may be made more vivid if it is right up against a wedding scene. Or perhaps you intend to use certain scenes late in the novel to parallel earlier events. In that case, the similarities of the episodes may be rendered more visible if they physically follow each other in the book, even though they are distantly separated in the internal time of the novel. After these digressions through the calendar have been made, you should judge as best you can whether the new sequence of events is more effective and, actually, more natural than the old one, or whether it is just more complicated, more artificial. If it *is* both dramatic and fitting, then keep it.

Pinpointing an event or incident

Finally, we must be kind to our readers and try to lead them as simply as possible through these flashbacks, flashforwards, and extravagant diversions. No one will continue to read a story if he is confused, or if he suspects that the writer is merely showing off to baffle him. You will recall that William Faulkner, in that most complicated of novels, *The Sound and the Fury,* uses the simplest device to help his readers—he dates the different parts. How a storyteller helps a reader distinguish one time zone from another depends to a degree on how precisely he wants to locate the time. If his story requires that the reader understand the exact date—not simply the decade, the era, but actually the year, month, and day—then, of course, he must find a way to bring in the date. Whenever things get this narrow and complicated, I recommend absolute simplicity: say right out what the date is.

But more often the storyteller wants to indicate not a particular date but a general time zone of some months, or some years. There are certain events in our history which are widely known and which have been used to characterize the time they occurred. The prohibition on the sale of hard liquor, the stock market crash, the attack on Pearl Harbor, and the Bay of Pigs invasion are historical markers so well known that they are often referred to simply as Prohibition, the Crash, Pearl Harbor, the Bay of Pigs, and a reference to events such as these helps the reader to get his bearings. When the reader of a novel set in the 1960's discovers that one of the characters is in a speakeasy, he knows that he is observing an event prior to the main action of the novel.

Most frequently, however, the storyteller wants only to indicate that the scene going on before the reader actually took place in an unspecified or personal past. If, for example, his story is about a woman contemplating divorce, the author may want to go back to a point early in the marriage when the heroine was deeply in love with her husband. In such a case, the past is private and is related principally to the character's personal chronology: all the storyteller wants to say is that the event he now shows us took place earlier in the marriage—the specific date is unimportant. When the precise time in the past is unimportant, the writer can use a wealth of subtle clues to inform the reader about a time shift. I doubt whether it should be necessary to introduce an elaborate gimmick into the novel, or into any part of it, in order to distinguish one area of time from another. If the scenes are truly in different parts of the calendar, some factor will naturally emerge in the writing which will indicate the time shift. It is the writer's task to isolate that factor and highlight it.

The episodes which make up the *now* of the novel may be in a broiling summer; the flashbacks may be winter scenes, and an alert writer can use the obvious difference in the weather to indicate the difference in time. There are other, more subtle, forms of weather which can be used to distinguish past from present; every era has its own climate, a climate not of nature but of society. Every epoch has its own sort of season. New York in the 1920's was a far gayer, more youthful place than New York in the 1930's—the economic weather had shifted from springtime to autumn, from exuberant boom to gray depression. A skillful writer should be able to use the marked differences in tone between the 1920's and 1930's to show the reader that the time has shifted.

Spontaneous juggling

As I pointed out at the start, I happen to be the sort who likes to write any which way that comes into his head. So if the idea of juggling flashbacks and altering time patterns rarely occurs spontaneously to you and never seems right—then forget about it. But if you want to try your hand at it, then by all means have some fun while doing it. No technique has ever delighted or entertained a reader unless it first amused and delighted the storyteller himself. One writer who obviously gets a great deal of pleasure from jumping back and forward through time is Julio Cortazar. Cortazar's novel, *Hopscotch,* is preceded by a Table of Instructions which tells us that the book "consists of many books, but two books above all." The first book, we learn, runs consecutively from Chapter 1 to Chapter 56; the second begins with Chapter 73 and then proceeds to Chapters 1, 2, 116, 3, 84, 4, 71, and on and on, in hopscotch fashion for many more chapters until the new story is completed.

My own work is by no means so complicated, and it derives not from the reading of any other writer, and certainly not from any abstract theory. I am a follower of my grandmother, a woman who had an incredible number of tales, not one of which she ever told in direct, linear, chronological fashion. She was not a sophisticated, self-conscious storyteller—her digressions, her reversals of time, her leaps forward in time, all were natural and spontaneous. She never told a story straight through from beginning to end, because it never occurred to her that way. She would begin by telling about some young girl who had nearly died in childbirth, then go on to sketch in the girl's father and describe how badly he got along with his son-in-law, and this would lead to a dramatic review of the large banquet which the father had provided for the wedding.

When I was working on *The Way In,* I tried to keep the form as natural as possible, and the result was—to some eyes—a rather complex time scheme. At one point in *The Way In,* there is a flashback to portray the founding of Cambridge, Massachusetts, an event which precedes the main action of the novel by more than three hundred years. And the wedding chapter which concludes my novel is preceded by a childbirth—for it is the birth of the child which interrupts the teller of that story. To my mind, the time pattern of *The Way In,* for all its wild digressions, is no more strange or complicated than if my grandmother had told it, and certainly it was an amusing book to write.

6

TELLER OF TALES

by Mary Stewart

RECENTLY I had to do two things which were very good for me.
The first was to reread three of my early novels for an Omnibus
Edition, and write a preface about them. This sent me back—
as I believe all novelists should be sent back in the middle stages
of their careers—to reread the three stories in close detail, as I
had not done for years. It was a salutary exercise and an
illuminating one. I had forgotten so much about them that I
was able to approach them for the first time from outside, come
to them almost as one of my readers would come—as a stranger.
At the same time, I was able to call on the extra knowledge that
their author has. Certain passages recalled to me very strongly
the reasons—half forgotten and never very obvious—*why* they
were written.

The second task was to write a brief autobiography; and in the
same way, while doing that and sending myself back to rebuild
my life in memory, I was reminded *how* and *when* I started to
write.

I'll take this first.

The when and the how

As far back as I can remember, storytelling has come to me
as naturally as leaves to a tree; this is the incalculable x that

you are born with or not born with. To say I was a born story-teller is not lack of modesty, it is fact; and it's not to my credit: I couldn't help it. Some people are good at sports, some can do mathematics; I can tell stories and bring fictional people and places to life. And I believe that those who have this gift never come to writing for any reason except that this seems to them the obvious thing to do with their time, and indeed their lives. I wrote my first stories when I was five or six years old. I won't pretend that I remember my thoughts or motives, but I do know that I wanted to open the door to my own wonderland. My first stories had my toys as heroes. I had only three, a horse, an elephant, and a cat, and I remember sitting on the attic floor with them round me, writing them into a story with illustrations. My stories were mostly fairy tales or tales of magic, animal stories or narrative poems . . . written carefully into exercise books and illustrated by the author. Throughout my childhood and youth I read avidly and reflected in childish writings what I had read. These stories were always tales of wonder and adventure, the poems written inside the severe discipline imposed by the child's sense of incantation and rhyme.

Then life crowded in, and work with it, and though I wrote a good deal of poetry while I was teaching at the University, it was two full decades later, after marriage and the tragedy of losing a first child, that I came again to story writing. The first thing I wrote was, I suppose, a sort of summary of all those childhood tales: it was a long tale for children called *The Enchanted Journey,* and into it went everything, all the bright images of youth. I suppose you might say it was not written so much for children (I have never been conscious of a reader looking over my shoulder) as for me and the child I had been. I certainly made no concessions to immaturity, any more than, say, R. L. Stevenson does in *Treasure Island.* My story had all the faults of a first story, but it had pace, danger, excitement, and an almost haunted feeling for place which seems now to be identifiably mine.

The Enchanted Journey did not come, suddenly, out of no-where. It had a model, Walter de la Mare's "Henry Brocken." I suppose it was typical that I came into the lists myself on the heels of a poet, to my mind one of the finest poets ever, and the best that England has produced this century. (I hasten to remind you that W. B. Yeats was Irish.) De la Mare's "Henry Brocken" had all that I had ever looked for then. Probably my story is no more for children than "Henry Brocken" is, but writing it satisfied something in me and got me into my stride. So I came to the writing of novels via poetry and literature and the myth or folktale of wonder, and the sense of history and fate that Walter de la Mare hangs along the branches of his verse like Spanish moss on the gray oak trees.

There is at the beginning of "Henry Brocken" an old English poem, probably Elizabethan, called "Tom o'Bedlam's Song." And the wandering madman who is speaking could speak for all tellers of imaginative tales. He certainly speaks for me:

> With a heart of furious fancies
> Whereof I am commander;
> With a burning spear
> And a horse of air
> To the wilderness I wander.
>
> With a Knight of ghosts and shadows
> I summoned am to Tourney:
> Ten leagues beyond
> The wide world's end—
> Methinks it is no journey.

Not only did "Henry Brocken" give me my way into storytelling, it gave me a form. My journey took me first to Provence with my novel *Madam, Will You Talk?* and this, my first adult book, took the form of the picaresque and episodic tale, the series of outdoor encounters linked but separate, which was the first novel form ever used, in Roman times by Petronius and

Longus, then in England with Nashe's *Unfortunate Traveller.*
Possibly the best-known modern example is John Buchan's *The
Thirty-Nine Steps.* The pattern of my linking plot, the unifying
line, was, too, the archetypal one of the chase; this is so old that
it is in the blood, like the count of three and the power of moonlight, so old that it is a dream pattern for almost everyone. In
my story, the pattern was updated with a Mercedes and a Bent-
ley, the quarry was a small boy, and the penalty for failure was,
as always, death.

The why

This, then, was the *when* and the *how* of my first efforts in
writing. The preface for the Omnibus Edition reminded me *why*
I had written what I did.

I have written ten full-length novels so far, and a long-short
novella called *The Wind off the Small Isles,* which is a kind of
coda to the others, and a bridge to my historical novel, *The
Crystal Cave.*

Looking at the ten main books as a body of work, a canon (if
I may for convenience dignify them with that word), I see them
as falling naturally into certain groupings.

The first five novels, up to *My Brother Michael,* are explora-
tory novels, sharing a theme and little else. They bear obvious
marks of a tyro experimenting with different forms. They vary
a good deal in structure, and make some use of sharp differences
in setting. *Madam, Will You Talk?,* the first, was a chase story
written, concerto-fashion, on two levels. As I said, it is ostensibly
a fast, episodic adventure tale embodying familiar thriller elements heightened by the setting and by deliberate use of coincidence. Above and dominating the thriller-plot run the love
story and the main theme together. They might be summarized
by the quotation at the head of Chapter Fourteen:

> Fate, I come, as dark, as sad
> As thy malice could desire.

The love story is that of a fate-driven love, self-contained, all-else-excluding, whose image is the enchanted bubble in which the lovers seem to move, while the violent world swirls around them, unable to touch them or destroy their faith in each other.

What I have called the main theme is the search for solid values in a shifting and corrupt world, and the affirmation that "the rules don't break themselves" and that "good does beget good."

Wildfire at Midnight was an attempt at something different, the classic closed-room detective story with restricted action, a biggish cast, and a closely circular plot. It taught me technically a great deal, but mainly that the detective story, with its emphasis on plot rather than people, is not for me. What mattered to me was not the mystery, but the choice the heroine faces between personal and larger loyalties.

With *Thunder on the Right,* I tried a technical change of approach, from first person to third. I had dropped naturally, without calculation, into the first person (perhaps another echo of "Henry Brocken"?) but now thought it right to experiment. Of course writing in the first person has certain drawbacks, especially in "danger" or "suspense" situations—certain elements of surprise are cut out, the viewpoint is limited, and direct action is also limited to scenes where the protagonist is present—but for me the advantages far outweigh the losses. The gain in vividness, personal involvement and identification is immense. I have always been interested in pinning sensation down into words, and first-person writing allows close exploration of physical reactions to the stimuli of fear, joy, pain, and so on. In my first book, especially, I was trying this out, analyzing in detail not only strong sensation, but sensation of every kind—being tired, being hungry and smelling food, going to sleep, coming out of an anesthetic—in fact, I suppose, what living itself *feels like,* not just how one thinks and acts.

In *Thunder on the Right,* with the third-person approach, I found I had more freedom of action and viewpoint, but in my next novel, *Nine Coaches Waiting,* I went back with a kind of relief to the first person, and have used it ever since.

Nine Coaches Waiting is yet again structurally different. This is the Cinderella story, openly acknowledging its great model, treating that model with some astringence, but keeping and humanizing the strong line of the traditional love story. The theme superimposed on the romantic thriller plot is the classic dilemma of choice between love and duty.

My Brother Michael was the result of my first travels to Greece and the start of my love affair with that marvelous country. Technically I was now surer of myself; what one loses in wild freshness one gains in technical assurance. By this time I had an idea that if I wanted a certain effect, I would get it, even if it *was* as often as not done naturally, and only analyzed afterwards on demand. And if storytelling itself, as I suggested earlier, comes as naturally as leaves to a tree, the stories, too, grow out of one another as branches spring in order from the growing trunk. *My Brother Michael* was the logical development of what I had been writing up till then; it rounded off something I had been quite deliberately trying to do through all my first five books.

Bizarre situations, real people

What these five books have in common—apart from the obvious superficial likenesses imposed by the cast of their author's mind—is a deliberate attempt by a new writer to discard certain conventions which seemed to her to remove the novel of action so far from real life that it became a charade or a puzzle in which no reader could involve himself sufficiently really to care. I tried to take conventionally bizarre situations (the car chase, the closed-room murder, the wicked uncle tale) and send real people into them, normal everyday people with normal everyday reactions to violence and fear; people not "heroic" in the conventional sense, but averagely intelligent men and women who could be shocked or outraged into defending, if necessary with great physical bravery, what they held to be right. (In this context it is perhaps worth noticing that the heroines of *Wildfire At Midnight* and *Nine Coaches Waiting*, faced with a choice between love and duty, reject the traditional choice of romantic fiction, and—as so many women do—choose duty.)

Along with this went a theme that I tried to develop up to and into *My Brother Michael*, a hatred of violence and a fear of the growing tendency to regard it as a solution to any problem. Because of this, it seemed to me (even in the early 1950's) time to discard the type of detective novel where pain and murder are taken for granted and used as a parlor game. In my first novels, too, I discarded and laughed at certain conventions of plot, including the romantic hero, unthinkingly at home with violence, who was still mainstream when I started writing; and his equally romantic alternative, the social misfit who was just coming into fashion. I was tired of "tough" books where the girl "heroine" is regarded purely as a sexual object, and where her qualities of mind and heart (if any) are treated as irrelevant. I tried unobtrusively where I could to show admiration for liberal ideas, common sense, and the civilized good manners that are armour for the naked nerve.

To present and not to preach

You might say that when I emerged from the romance-lands —Provence, the Hebrides, the Pyrenees, High Savoy—and traveled to Greece, I came at last hard up against the fierce logic which informs that brilliant, realistic people. I went to Delphi and asked a question, and was left to interpret the Delphic answer, "the smile behind the smoke." There comes a time when ferocity has to be met with ferocity, violence with violence. The bitter end of liberal logic is that if Athens remains true to herself, she falls to the barbarians of Sparta. I can find no answer to this. I suspect there is no answer, but a real writer's job is to present, not to preach. Michael's brother, in my book, resorts to violence and by it wins a respite for the good; he also learns another simple, age-old and cruel fact of life—that we are all members one of another; we are born involved, locked in the great chain of being. We need never send to know for whom the bell tolls; it tolls for us all.

After this, the branches grow rather differently from the tree. But I won't bore you by going blow by blow through the rest. *The Ivy Tree* made for me a complete change; this was totally different and was my nostalgia book for my home countryside and a very beautiful house I once knew, since pulled down. The story is summed up by a quotation in the text: *"Time hath his revolutions; there must be a period and an end to all earthly things, finis rerum, an end of names and dignities, and whatsoever is terrene . . ."* That's the story, but it also says that in spite of failure one can always rebuild, and better than before, provided one has kept faith with oneself. Then, after the light-hearted romp of *The Moon-Spinners,* came *This Rough Magic,* with its little cast of people who have failed, trying to escape the icy and terrifying world of their failure. They also learn about involvement. As Lucy Waring says: "It seems to me you can be awfully happy in this life if you stand aside and mind your own business, and let other people do as they like about damaging themselves and each other. You can go on kidding yourself that you're impartial and tolerant and all that, then all of a sudden you realize that you're dead, and you've never been alive at all. Being alive hurts." And she and her lover learn that the enchanted island to which they have escaped, full of sounds and sweet airs that give delight and hurt not, is every bit as rough and bloody as their own gray northern country, and the latter is the one which owns them and which they have to serve. One cannot opt out. And one can build a second time, success-fully, albeit a different structure and with different materials, but only if one has kept faith with oneself.

Perhaps, for those who have never read any of my books, I have made them sound altogether too ponderous and didactic. Nothing is further from what I tried to do as I wrote. The story comes first and is served first. The only legitimate way for a storyteller to speak is through the actions and opinions of her characters, and these are live and in many ways independent of me. These novels are light, fast-moving stories which are meant to give pleasure, and where the bees in the writer's bonnet are kept buzzing very softly indeed. I am first and foremost a teller of tales, but I am also a serious-minded woman who accepts the responsibilities of her job, and that job, if I am to be true to what is in me, is to say with every voice at my command: "We must love and imitate the beautiful and the good." It is a comment on our age that one hesitates to stand up and say this aloud. But looking back now on the way I was thinking over these fifteen years as I wrote, it seems to me that this above all else is what I have affirmed.

7

BUILDING READER IDENTIFICATION

by Alfred Coppel

As I look over my keyboard at the title I have just typed, I get the feeling that I have begun a piece for *Mechanix Illustrated* rather than something intended to help writers draw readers into their emotional nets.

Still, in a craft where there are few specifics, the business of involving real people in the lives of imaginary people is one of the few techniques that can actually be taught.

The novelist can only begin the work of creating a literary experience. It is the reader who must complete it. Much of the detail and color that flesh out a work of art must take place in the reader's mind, and the process cannot begin until the reader is made to share the fictional experience with the novelist's characters.

Remote control and transference

Unlike a film, a novel is not a visual experience. Much must be left to the reader's imagination and often, interestingly enough, the total experience is quite different from that conceived by the author. Probably one of the most disconcerting experiences a novice writer can have is the cocktail party feedback

48

from someone who has recently read his book and has visualized hero, heroine and setting in terms that are unrecognizable to the author. Still, rather than despair, the writer should realize that he has, to some extent at least, touched the reader's sense of *identity*. By remote control he has caused another human being to contribute something of himself to the reading experience.

The more effective the author wishes this remote control to be, the more definite must be the dominance of the fictional character over the reader's own personality. While the novel is being read, and hopefully for some time thereafter, the reader should be made to feel that he has special insights into the reality of the fictional person. This sense of knowing, this *transference*, should take place as quickly as possible after the reader has begun to read the novel. If it is strong enough, the reader will be touched, moved, and presently dominated by the novelist's creation.

I think most fictional characters are to some extent autobiographical. Note that I say *to some extent*. There is a good reason why so many confessional first novels end up in the drawer, unpublished. Self-examination and psychoanalysis are *not* fiction. Still, it is true that the writer skilled in his craft puts a great deal of himself into the people who populate his books. He does this extrapolatively, of course, saying in effect: This is what I would do, what I would feel, if I were in this given situation. Often this is difficult to do. Some writers, Hemingway and Scott Fitzgerald, for example, never managed to write convincingly about anyone but themselves. The point is that the author should give of himself—he should not drown the reader in confession.

Once that hurdle is past, the way is open to reader identification. How then to achieve it? I try to create, early in the story, a strong link between reader and character, a link that will bind the two together to create, *in toto*, that synthesis of fiction and perception that is the quintessential reading experience. If the writer is able to open his character's personality to the reader's scrutiny and give him a personal insight, the synthesis can commence at once and grow throughout the story.

Insights and perceptions

In my novel *Order of Battle,* for example, I needed to have the reader understand almost immediately the feel of war in the air. Meticulous descriptions of what a fighter airplane cockpit felt like, how it smelled, what one sees from it, what sounds one hears—all of these things were important. But even more important was the transference to the reader of the all-pervading atmosphere of fear disguised with bravado and seeming insensitivity that dominated life in a World War II fighter squadron. Thus I had my protagonist, Devereaux, awaken in the dark chill of a rainy morning during a stand-down. One of his squadron mates has died the day before in an accident. Devereaux is sensitive, proud, and afraid. This is what he sees as he lights the first cigarette of the day:

> In the brief light the room sprang into dark relief. The metal lockers were open and inside I could see half melted men made of helmets, goggles, flight jackets and overalls. The lockers were charred coffins. I inhaled the bitter smoke and chewed on my lower lip, regarding the fire images . . . Because that damned fool Marquis had lost an engine on takeoff and didn't do what he had been trained for hours to do. I remembered the tail column of oil smoke rising from the end of runway 29.

Perhaps very few of my readers were pilots in World War II, and perhaps even fewer have ever lived with a fear that cannot be put into words lest it paralyze them. But all have at some time felt despair or dread. Many of them must at some time have wakened to nameless terrors. This brief scene gives them a glimpse into the heart of a young man, a glimpse that none of his contemporaries in the novel is ever given. They know something about him that no one else knows, and they can begin to empathize.

These glimpses of the naked protagonist can be anything. In *A Certainty of Love,* the validity and poignancy of a love story depend on the reader's understanding of the loneliness and alienation of Robert Gilman, the protagonist. In this case it seemed best simply to describe the masculine disorder and barrenness of the room in which he lives. Here, I in effect told the reader, lives a man without a woman, a vulnerable man who is not even aware of his vulnerability. But *you* know. You understand something important about this man.

Darwin Teilhet, a friend and a writer of great sensitivity, once told me that a certain way to engage a reader's sympathy for a fictional character was to afflict the character with a flaw, sometimes even a physical flaw, citing as an extreme example Jake Barnes in *The Sun Also Rises.* The technique is valid, but in this time of cheap-shot sensationalism, it can be risky. Yet, if the writer gives the reader some private and personal insights into the personality of his protagonist, the result can be as satisfying and effective and less lurid than physical mutilation.

In both of my novels mentioned above, there is a single point of view and the story is told in the first person, which makes it easier for the reader to see the fictional reality as I would wish him to see it. But it need not necessarily be so. Often reader identification can be achieved by the relatively simple business of a character's reaction to a given situation. In my novel, *Between the Thunder and the Sun,* the main protagonist is the much-burdened pilot of the hijacked aircraft. But it is the dependence that his crew exhibits and the responses of the frightened passengers that serve to make the reader understand the weight the man carries, and the basic decency of his nature that marks him out as a character through whom the reader must experience the novel. Early in the book, the reader is given that deep glimpse into his self-doubts. The narrative is third person and there are multiple points of view, but the reader knows the protagonist best, better than *he* knows himself.

This insightful look given the reader doesn't have to be direct. In my most recent novel, *The Landlocked Man,* the first true glimpse of my protagonist's inner being is largely symbolic, presented in a way that begins the novel with a sense of foreboding that is essential both to the story and to the understanding of Martin, the narrator. In three short paragraphs, the reader is shown the character of the man: thoughtful, concerned for life, sensitive to his surroundings, and slightly ironic. Martin, at fifty, has fallen in love with a twenty-three-year-old girl and she with him. The central theme of the novel, the inevitability of tragedy, and the tyranny of time are suggested in Martin's view of a small natural tragedy.

He has been fishing a stream among the redwoods of the Pacific slope and encounters a pool containing a landlocked sea trout:

> I stand on the fallen elder and watch the almost motionless scene for several minutes. Then the trout moves, with slow and measured pace, gliding closer to the rock wall. The willow branches move gently in the current.
>
> It is bloody sad, I think, that probably nothing can save him. He should have stayed where he was, in the deep ocean, instead of listening to the urgings of fishy love.
>
> I step off the fallen tree onto the shore. When I look back to the pool, I see that the trout has drifted back to his station near the rill, near the lost road to the sea.

The reader knows what is suggested here, that Martin sees in the landlocked trout a symbol of what his life is becoming. He knows, as Martin does, that it is beyond fixing, that fate alone will decide the future and that he knows what fate will decree.

The point of the exercise, then, is to say that the only effective way for a writer to create reader identification is to share with the reader deep intimacies about his protagonist. Let the reader feel, sense and experience the character's inner life, and he must, to some extent, become the person about whom he is reading. And once this bond is forged, the reader will supply the detail, the total ambience, and the empathy that no mere writer, however talented, can create.

8

GETTING TO TIMBUKTU

by Cecilia Bartholomew

"I'D LIKE to be a writer, if I knew what to write about."

How many times have you heard someone say that, and laughed? How many times have you secretly felt that way your-self, with no desire to laugh? Perhaps never; perhaps for you, the only valid reason for wanting to write is that you have some-thing to write about. But if ever you have *searched* for a story, you will understand what "Getting to Timbuktu" means.

Story and Timbuktu. They go together for me like—well, like sun and sand. Sometimes a story seems as far away as Timbuktu. Sometimes it is as difficult to find the story as it is to get to Timbuktu.

I was going to Timbuktu; yes, actually. In a way it is a shock to find that Timbuktu is a real place. But I was going there, and I was counting on the trip to give me a story. What editor could resist the allure of that name? With the story sold, I could even take the trip as a deductible expense. But hold on! I must get to Timbuktu before I come back.

Getting from fact to fiction

At this time when almost everyone points out the trend from fiction to fact, I am stubborn enough to propose to get from fact to fiction. And like any serious explorer/adventurer I will chart my way, so that at the end there will remain a map showing the route I have taken to Timbuktu, for others to follow. Why do I believe there is a story in Timbuktu? Well, maybe it's a hunch; maybe it's a need. Maybe it's because nothing becomes real until it is put into words, and not just any words. A diary account isn't enough. To lay the trip to rest, I have to see its meaning; I have to find the story in it.

But beyond that general necessity, it is the symbolism inherent in the very name Timbuktu that makes me feel there has to be a story there. All fiction represents by metaphor. Timbuktu is a metaphor—for man's dream of reaching the unattainable, for finding the pot of gold at the end of the rainbow. I roll a blank piece of paper into the typewriter and start:

> It is a legend in the desert, a mirage in the mind. It is challenging, like a mountain peak, enticing as a siren, promising as Om, elusive as Erewhon, the Utopian Nowhere.

I sit for a time looking at what I've written. That's the symbolism, all right, no question about it. I can feel the skin on my arms prickle. But where do I go from there? Why don't I go on?

The truth is that no amount of symbolism can be a substitute for story.

Of course! To state explicitly is not the fictional way. I must give the facts, and let the reader find the symbolism.

What a history! From desert capital dazzling with riches, to a village today of 8000 inhabitants. That certainly is a story. But the paper in the typewriter remains blank. Those facts don't demonstrate the symbolism that I feel in the name, the symbolism that first convinced me that I would have a story. I'd be crazy not to use those facts, but . . . .

The truth is that no amount of historical background can be a substitute for story.

Do I have to give up? Not by a long shot. Look what Hemingway did with Kilimanjaro. Timbuktu is equal to any mountain. *The Sands of Timbuktu* is every bit as good a title as *The Snows of K – –*. I'll start with the setting:

> Timbuktu, once the jeweled oasis in the desert, the legendary capital of the vast Sahara ocean, now slumbers under the disdainful eyes of the camel, and of the tall Tuareg who cover their faces, womanlike.

It's a good setting for a story. I am trying to convince myself, but. . . .

The truth is that no amount of setting, even spectacular setting, can be a substitute for story.

If a story is not setting, background, or symbolism, what is it? It is a series of organized events, to quote a partial dictionary definition. In other words, it is a surface. Do I have a surface? Well, of course I do. My surface is the physical journey itself. The search. Everyone loves to read about a search. The strength of it, the simplicity of it! My fingers spring to life on the typewriter keys:

GETTING TO TIMBUKTU

I have a title, a wonderful title . . . I have a whole notebook of wonderful titles. The truth is—yes, indeed—*a title, no matter how good, cannot be a substitute for story.* But this title can give me the structure of the story. What is the story about? A search for Timbuktu. Whom is the story about?

Ah, that's what has been holding me up. You can't get very far into story before you come to character. For a search, there has to be a searcher. I don't have to look far. I am going to Timbuktu. I am the searcher. All writers write about themselves. The compleat writer is Narcissus who need never fear he will write himself out, because he himself is his Source. Now I am really ready to start.

Caravans of tourists cross paths at places called Bobo and Ouaga-dougou which are in a country named Upper Volta, for which no companion Lower Volta exists.

When I bang out that first sentence without a moment's hesitation, and when I read it back, I like it. Right away it gives the reader an idea what the story is about; it builds an expectancy from such a setting; and it includes some hard facts. But I cannot conceal from myself that something is bothering me.

Risk and quest

What troubles me is that my own trip to Timbuktu is too easy. Nothing is risked. There is no real quest. The trip has been arranged for me by a travel agent. Nine other tourists are making this trip with me, and we will be shepherded every step of the way by a practiced courier. I don't have a search at all; I have a tour.

At this point, I see my story retreating like the mirage that is Timbuktu itself. I get that panicky feeling. Maybe I ought to give it up. I don't have to be a writer. But I want to be a writer! Well, it doesn't have to be a story about Timbuktu. There are other stories. Like what? They are all as far away as Timbuktu; they are all as hard to get to, maybe impossible.

Why Timbuktu? I feel it in my bones. (Hang on to that feeling!) On the other hand, what do bones know about it? Maybe that is where stories start, in the marrow. It's not so farfetched. Life starts there. If I don't have a search, I have a tour. Can a tour give me a story? Let me see who will be my companions on my tour:

1. The Longs come first, first in the bus, first for meals, first to take pictures, first to buy souvenirs. *He* weighs upwards of 250 pounds and takes up a seat-and-a-half in the bus. He carries the most expensive movie camera in our group, with a telephoto lens as long as a rhino's horn. This is their fifth trip to Africa, but the

first to West Africa. They are already sorry that they didn't go straight to the animal country, or to South Africa.

2. *She* never sits beside him because there is only half a seat left, and she also weighs more than she should; and because she is allergic to tobacco, and he smokes cigarettes, even though they've been married for two-thirds of their lives, and she's always suffered from this allergy. She likes to talk philosophically about esoteric religions and she knows many poems by heart (poems like "Trees" and "Excelsior") and is skillful at weaving them into conversations. He calls her "Nuisance" and "Troublemaker," with winks all around to show, of course, that she is anything but. His first name is Julius, but he is known as Joe, not Jule, or Julie. Is that important?

3. Mrs. Jones, a widow, is traveling with the Longs. She doesn't know what city she is in, even what country; she leaves all that to Joe. But she knows everything there is to know about the hotels we stay in. "Don't tell me any more, I don't want to hear," she says, and slaps her thigh as if she is on a horse. She speaks with a strong southern accent.

4-5. A middle-aged couple from California who talk a great deal about the "beautiful black people," and are not getting themselves liked. They have grown to look like each other. They are both pale and dry of skin, gray of hair. They know all the statistics about the various countries, like population, gross national income, literacy percentages, etc.

6. Crystal is a white-haired lady, eighty years old. She is the only one in our group who doesn't take pictures; she doesn't even have a camera with her. But she is widely traveled. You can tell that because she is so good at the kind of repetitious kidding that marks the real traveler. In the bus she sits beside the driver, and she gets us across the rivers, and when we are on the other side, she brushes her hands together briskly and says, "There! Another river crossed."

7. Rose Fineal is an Osage Indian. Only partly. The rest is French. She doesn't look either French or Indian. She wears her straight dark hair pulled back in a large chignon; but then at Nairobi, she left the chignon in the beauty parlor and had her hair waved. I am not sure why she is on the tour (why I have put her there). I'll have to see how the others react to her. She wears two big diamonds on her left hand, but she is a Miss.

8. Mr. Oates is old and huge like an elephant, and deaf. He has come on the tour because at home he hasn't anyone to talk to. His French is doughboy (*"Parlez-vous français? Chevrolet coupé"*). He reads palms, for the ladies. He is pitiful, and he is a bigot. He is afraid of airplanes, and of a Jewish World Conspiracy. (Use the French language.)

9. Jackson (that's his first name) wears a real safari suit, with pants tucked into big boots, a jacket that is multi-pocketed, and a cigar in his mouth. (See Mrs. Long and smoking.) He doesn't know any French at all, but he knows everything else. He's a rich farmer, with more respect for machinery than people. What he sees in Africa makes him want to spit. He classifies himself as a conservative liberal.

The cast of characters strikes me as splendid. I've done a lot of good work. I'm eager to go on with the story:

We go from Monrovia, the capital of Liberia, to Bamako in Mali. Between Bamako and the desert queen Timbuktu, there is nothing. Here French is spoken.

Right away I am stopped again. It's that pronoun "we."

Point of view is something that always has to be reckoned with. Each point of view has its peculiar advantages and disadvantages. The problem is to choose the point of view that allows you to tell your story with the greatest impact. Sometimes you can find that out only by experimenting. First-person point of view will give a stamp of authenticity, of reality, to the story; but a plural point of view is awkward—it can't be maintained, it does not create reader identification. What that all boils down to is that it isn't accurate. "Here French is spoken . . . Here French is spoken." By whom? That's it. Stories are about individuals. I go on:

> *Parlez-vous français?* My French is coming back to me.

There! I've shifted into the singular. Not only that, I can *hear* the voice of the speaker. It sounds so real that it makes me jump. She has an atrocious French accent. She pronounces the word *"français"* as if it were the English name Frances. I get that spurt of excitement inside me that means I've got something. What I have is a protagonist/narrator who is not myself. If that is good, then what was all that jazz about the writer and Narcissus? Isn't it true? Yes, it is true, but until the writer can lift himself over from fact to fiction, he cannot become a real character in a story. Writing is full of contradictions like that. But now I have the problem of showing the speaker's execrable accent. I cross out my last sentence and substitute:

> My high school French is coming back to me.

I trust my high school French teacher will forgive me. But there's my heroine. She hasn't spoken any French since high school, partly because her husband—her late husband, I decide—a Canadian from Montreal, spoke beautiful French, but also because after the French Canadians began acting so pigheaded and demanded equal rights, and tax bills in two languages and all that, he took an oath that he would never speak another word of French again, if he never said another word in any language— and naturally neither would she. He is dead now, but that wasn't the fault of the Canadian French. It was—I believe I'll make it an accident.

There's the group, a round ten, a cross-section that can stand for the world. There is something of me in every single character, and I am capable of being each. But we can't leave, we can't go to Timbuktu without our courier. I think he is sexy, the courier. There should be some sex in the story. I attack the keys again:

> We are ten in our caravan, eleven with our courier, a tall young Dane named Poul, or perhaps he is Norwegian. Scandinavians are all the same to me. I think Poul has not been often to Africa. He is young, handsome, and wears beautiful tailored safari suits with shorts that reveal his thighs, which are covered with golden fuzz, and are hardly larger around than the muscular calves of his strong legs.

That sounds a bit much, but I can always tone it down. I need characterization as well as physical description. And I need to hear him speak, and see him in action.

> He makes a syncopated movement, a Conga-like twist with body and elbows and eyes out of that outrageous name Ouagadougou, the airport in Upper Volta where we have a stopover. Well, in a way it has a rhythm, and it is catching: "Ouaga," hesitation and shift to the right; "dougou," hesitation and shift to the left. Poul has already borrowed my suntan lotion, some aspirin, and a sleeping pill. I let him know that the Nembutal is precious to me, and I would not give it to anyone but him. "Ouagadougou" he replies, with his elbows and eyes. He has a flat rippling belly (he gets into swim shorts at every opportunity), a small head, and chapped lips.

Can a man with chapped lips promise romance? The question is enough of an interruption to stop me, and in the silence, other words are forming, words with a familiar ring: *The truth is that no amount of characterization is a substitute for story.*

It is time to take stock again. I have the "who," all those vivid characters. My title gives met the "what." (Getting to Timbuktu) What's missing? The story. Yes, of course. But what is the story? The surface. And what is the surface? Of course, the "how."

Before I know the "how," I have to know the "why." Getting to Timbuktu can mean many things; it can mean something different to each of the characters. I am off again:

Only the Californians—the old lady and I—really want to go to Timbuktu—the Californians because they have studied so much about it. Crystal has already written a sheaf of postcards to her friends at home, saying, "Here I am in Timbuktu," and naturally she needs to mail them there. The Longs and Mrs. Jones are going to Timbuktu only because it is on the itinerary. "Let's get there and get it over with," Joe says, and Nuisance rebukes him mildly. "Joe's been all over the world and he wants to go back everywhere."

"You're a Troublemaker, Nuisance," Joe replies. "Egypt is one country I don't want ever to go back to. I don't like Egyptians, no sir-ree, I sure don't."

"Joe doesn't mean that, he just talks that way. Anyway, Egyptians aren't Egypt," Mrs. Long says broadmindedly.

Mrs. Jones asks what there is at Timbuktu. The Californians start to tell her about the camel caravans carrying the salt. "Don't tell me about that," she cries at a high pitch, "all I want to know is about the hotel."

Mr. Oates will go anywhere so long as he is not alone, but he won't go on a DC-3. "They'll try to stick us with a DC-3," he says, "but if we stick together and refuse, they'll have to give us a better plane."

Jackson says, "I can take it or leave it, Timbuktu. I don't need to go to Timbuktu."

"What do you mean by that crack?" I ask.

"Was it a crack?"

"You've got a lot of nerve, making us all wait while you get a beer, and we're all dying of thirst, too."

"You've got a bit of nerve yourself."

"*Naturalment, mon vieux,*" I answer, sounding the "x" haughtily.
Jackson doesn't speak a word of French, so I have him there. "*Je
ne suis pas* Irish for nothing," I add.

The things she says—I have to laugh at her. She delights me.
I see her small and skinny, with little bird legs, sexy. And not
entirely truthful. She is not Irish. She was born in Winnipeg,
Canada. She gave up a good job, secretary to a government minister, to marry Walter. They never had any children, though they
were married almost eleven years. She has red-gold hair, fine, like
light. She is altogether transparent; you can see through her skin,
and through her blue eyes, but not through her mind. There
she is tough.

Why does she want to go to Timbuktu?

I do not feel that I am betraying Walter by speaking French in
Africa. I wouldn't in Canada, of course. Walter is the reason I
want to go to Timbuktu. I have been lost without Walter. Everything reminds me of him, even the tax bill, in French. "Get away,"
the doctor advised me. "Anywhere. Far away. Timbuktu."

It came to me that he was right. If I went somewhere where Walter
had never been, far away, as far away as Timbuktu—if I could get
to Timbuktu without Walter, that would prove, wouldn't it, that
I could be me again, not just Walter's wife. It wasn't that Walter
ever treated me badly—Walter was the kindest man in the world
(except where French Canadians were concerned), but he spoke such
good French. What am I saying? I was sure that I loved him. He
shouldn't have died. There was a girl in the car with him when
he crashed.

"Does the color of your hair come out of a bottle?" Jackson asks.

"I've never asked. Only my hairdresser knows."

"Your scalp is pink, you little liar."

"Don't you dare look at my scalp," I cry, and I tie a chiffon square
over my head. It belongs to my sister-in-law, Walter's sister. I bor-

rowed it one evening and I forgot to give it back to her. I decided I had had it so long, I might as well take it with me on the trip. It is pale pink.

They can go on like that for pages, half quarreling, half flirting, but . . . *The truth is that no amount of dialogue, however clever, can be a substitute for story.*

Doubts and questions

Go back to the surface. Go back to the title, Getting to Timbuktu. Implicit in "getting to" Timbuktu is doubt that we will. That's it! I must put in some doubt. Mr. Oates threatens to refuse to go on a DC-3, but Mrs. Jones is right when she says, "Be quiet, of course you'll go if we go." If we go? I have to raise a question in the reader's mind. I have to make him ask, Will she or won't she get to Timbuktu? There must be obstacles to overcome. Now where was I? We make stops at Ouagadougou and Bobo, and then go by way of Abidjan.

"By way of" is an African euphemism because of course Abidjan is not on the way to Bamako and Timbuktu. Abidjan (as everyone knows except Mrs. Jones) is the capital of Ivory Coast. (Mrs. Jones, however, knows all there is to know about the Hotel Ivoire in Abidjan.) And yet, with African logic, Abidjan is on the way to Timbuktu. It is in the Abidjan airport that the tourist grapevine begins to buzz: a plane has just come in from Timbuktu.

What will the news be? How was it in Timbuktu?

"It was an experience, I can tell you. I wouldn't want to go through it again, but I wouldn't have missed it."

"What hotel did you stay at?" Mrs. Jones demands.

"Are you kidding? We were lucky to be in a stable. That was so bad, the animals left."

Mr. Oates can't wait. "Was it a DC-3?"

"I can tell you that it was held together with glue and rubber bands."

"I won't go," Mr. Oates cries. "If we stick together—"

"Oh, be still," Mrs. Jones tells him. "There has to be a hotel."

"I was guaranteed luxury accommodations and gourmet meals," Rose Fineal says. "They promised. They dare not break a promise." For the first time, I see that she could be an Indian.

"You won't care about eating, unless you can look a dead goat in the eyeballs, with appetite. They knead their bread in the sand. God knows what they used for liquid—we never saw a drop of water, not to wash in, not to drink. Stock up. Look at my belt. It was snug when I went to Timbuktu."

"Hear that, Nuisance? You're going to have to diet."

Mrs. Long punches Joe, and the girl in her flashes into life.

"What is there in Timbuktu?" I ask.

"Nothing. Absolutely nothing."

"Changing your mind about going?" Jackson asks me.

"I am not, but maybe you can't take it."

"I'll go along just to see how you make out."

"*Erewhon*," I say to Mrs. Jones, ignoring him.

"Don't you speak to me in French," Mrs. Jones screams. "I'm American and proud of it."

The story is really on its way now, I can tell. From here on, I don't need a map. Once you get started right, you will roll on down the tracks straight into the station. Do we get to Timbuktu? Well, we try, and that's what is important, in a story. First we get to Bamako, on the edge of the desert, where we fight for the bottled water and the supplies, as if there were going to be a famine. There are cockroaches in our hotel rooms (the Californians have never seen a cockroach), and no soap. We are awakened at 4 A.M. to go to the airport. Why so early? Because that is Africa; and that is Timbuktu. Do we go on a DC-3? Does Mr. Oates give in or stay behind? Keep the action moving. At the same time show the characters in conflict. And one more thing: don't forget that a story appraises at the same time that it narrates. Beyond the events, it strives to make a believable comment. Connect, connect, always connect, as E. M. Forster preached. But what does happen? Well, you'll have to wait for that until (happily) the story may be published.

In the meantime, get busy on your own story. You don't have to go to Africa to find it. You just have to start out for Timbuktu.

9

HOW TO WRITE A NOVEL

by John Braine

No, I can't tell you how to write a best seller. Nobody can. But I can tell you how to write a novel that will be published.

My rules are all practical. They have to be. I've written for nearly every kind of newspaper and magazine, and I've done a lot of radio and TV (including a top-rated series). But the bulk of my income comes from my novels. Whether I'm good or bad is not for me to say; but I can honestly say that I'm a professional.

Because I've followed these rules I've earned a decent living for some fourteen years doing the one thing I want above all else to do. I'm not a rich man, but I am a free one.

Practical guide

Without any more preamble—because this isn't an article upon the aesthetics of the novel, but a strictly practical guide—I list my rules. They're not really mine: I stole them from other writers.

(1) *Finish the novel*. Find your theme by sitting down and thinking about it. Then write a chapter-by-chapter synopsis, noting the number of words to each chapter. Then write a narrative

of at least 80,000 words. Find out how much time you have, and make out a timetable. Note the number of words written. Don't revise, don't go back to check the color of a character's eyes or a name or any details whatever—just write as many words as you can as quickly as you can. Then within a surprisingly short time you'll have the first draft of a novel. Then you can do your research, then you can work out a full synopsis; now you'll have something to work upon.

(2) *Write from experience.* Sorry, I know you've heard this before. But your own experience, no matter how outwardly dull and drab your environment, is your only stock in trade. Remember this: no place, no era, no human being, is ever boring. And this, too: your own experience isn't merely what has happened to you personally, but what you've seen happen to other people.

(3) *Never be autobiographical.* This is a wasteful use of experience; you expend too much of it at a stage where you haven't the ability to utilize it properly. And if you take your narrative up to the time of writing, then what have you left to write about? And never, never write about writers—or painters or actors or musicians. This betrays a fundamental lack of invention.

(4) *Always describe the action of your novel as if it were taking place before you on a lighted stage.* Make the reader *see* what the characters look like, how they move and gesture, make him see the background—the wallpaper and furniture and ornaments or the hills and trees and the river—whatever it may be. But only you can select what you want to describe. It does not matter as long as you make the reader see it.

(5) *Your prose must always have the rhythms of ordinary speech.* If you can't read it aloud, it's lousy. This doesn't mean that you're limited to plain and simple prose, though that's not a bad idea. Look at the prose of Shakespeare and the sermons of Donne; of their very nature speakable, but abundantly rich and

complex. Americans are in a far better position than the English because of the greater variety and vigor of their vernacular.

(6) *Dialogue must always mirror character.* It goes without saying that it's no good if you can't speak it aloud. But if there were no narrative, you should be able to tell what sort of person is speaking from the dialogue alone.

(7) *The novel must tell a story.* Sorry again; and it pains me to say anything so obvious. But the public reads novels in order to be entertained—though a good novel does all sorts of other things besides entertain—and only a story with a beginning, a middle and an end will do this. Particularly with an end; the last paragraph should sum up the whole story. Look at the end of *The Great Gatsby* by Scott Fitzgerald, or, if I may be so conceited, my own *Room at the Top,* to see how it should be done.

(8) *Dramatize, dramatize.* Henry James said this, and I'm tempted simply to let it speak for itself. But if you know what he meant, then you don't need any advice on how to write a novel. What it means is that flat, monotonous statement isn't writing. There must be conflicts, contrasts, shocks, hooks to grapple the reader. Chapters must begin in different ways, descriptions must be more than mere lists, action must take the reader along with it. What at all costs must be avoided, what is death to credibility is the example Graham Greene gives: "He got up, went downstairs, and caught a taxi." It's a question of technique; and technique is acquired by observing how other writers do it. Use any technical device which you admire. That isn't plagiarism, and you needn't feel ashamed of it.

(9) *Novels musn't make propaganda.* This is not to say that the novelist mustn't have strong opinions about every subject under the sun, or that he may not involve himself in the causes he believes in. But as a novelist, he must concern himself with

human beings as they are and not as they ought to be. He mustn't take sides, he mustn't categorize people with whom he agrees as heroes and people with whom he disagrees as villains. For what matters to the novelist is how we see ourselves—which is rarely, if ever, as villains! Keep your opinions out of your novel. In fact, try to keep yourself out altogether.

(10) *Whenever necessary, break any of these rules.* This is the most important of all, and the most difficult to follow. You—and you alone—will know instinctively when and where to follow it. There isn't one of these rules of mine which some novelist hasn't triumphantly broken and which it wasn't absolutely right for him to have broken. I am far from being a supreme authority on the novel. Come to that, I've broken some of these rules myself from time to time. But if you do stick to them, your novel will be published. I can't promise any more than that.

Remember Rule One

P.S. Don't ever send your manuscript to established writers for their opinions. Above all, don't write to them saying that you've had a very interesting life and have lots of ideas, and suggest that you supply the material and they actually write the novel/autobiography. Instead, remember Rule One and *write.* There are all sorts of fancy psychological explanations for what makes people writers. My simple explanation is that a writer is a person who writes.

10

THE UNIQUE/UNIVERSAL IN FICTION

by Joyce Carol Oates

As A teacher of creative writing, as well as a writer, I am very deeply concerned with the phenomenon of "creativity"—it is one of the most mysterious of all human endeavors, and must ultimately be considered in the light of long-range evolutionary patterns in man. The process of creating art cannot be understood, cannot be explained in rational or scientific terms. Assistants of Einstein's at Princeton were often astonished at the apparent ease with which Einstein "thought" through problems that seemed opaque to them—he would pace slowly around his office, curling a lock of hair around a finger, his face quite abstract, showing no effort of concentration. Then after a few minutes he would smile happily—and the problem was solved. Though his assistants were, of course, grateful for his superior imagination, they were rather frustrated because they could not begin to *comprehend* the thought-processes that Einstein experienced; nor could he explain them. So in the end it is better not to attempt explanations, but to rejoice in this spontaneous and only partly-willed miracle of the imagination.

What writers can share with one another, however, is their knowledge of how the process can be stimulated and formalized into art. For, without the conscious and intelligent *formalization* of one's deepest, instinctive fantasies, no communication at all is possible. I think that post-Romantic, existentialist attitudes toward art—that it should be "spontaneous," that it should reflect a vital but unintellectual reality—are quite erroneous, and present a dangerous temptation to writers who are not certain of themselves. Whenever a writer or philosopher or poet stresses the Unconscious, one should remember that it is not his "Unconscious" that is speaking, but his conscious mind. If Sartre's apparent judgment of man is that he is a "useless passion," one should ask whether Sartre himself seems to believe this—whether, in the light of his long, distinguished, dedicated career, his own writing can be considered "useless." We must never take writers at their own estimation of themselves or of us; probably we are all more complex and more noble, if we bother to examine ourselves.

Private experience and emotion

Fiction and poetry celebrate the "unique"—what the writer has experienced or thought, personally; without this personal, private experience, the story or poem will be simply manufactured. One really cannot "manufacture" emotions. But there is no reason to make them up, since everyone has emotions—daydreams—unique and unrepeatable experiences—the important thing is, Do people correctly value themselves? If they are writing, *why* are they writing? Anyone who is writing "to make money" is deluding himself; he is writing for other, deeper reasons, reasons he cannot explain. But as long as he believes that he is writing "for money" or "for prestige," he will write in a falsifying way, manufacturing emotions in conformity with emotions he sees in others; and yet his own life is filled with enough drama to constitute any number of novels. . . . When one writes about his true subject, in contrast to the usual "false" subject, he really has no difficulty with writing. But he must understand how his "unique" life is related to a vast "universal" life: the connection between the two is what he must write about.

I would be unable to write about anything that did not seem to be both unique and universal—an event I have lived through myself, or experienced intensely through my imagination, and an event that has some meaning, some larger appeal, which may go far beyond the temporal limitations of the subject. If art has any general evolutionary function, it must be to enhance the race, to work somehow toward an essential unity and harmony —survival and growth—and perhaps an integration of the human world with the natural world. The genesis for my novel, *Wonderland*, was a newspaper item I read years ago; it took a very long time for this to work its way through my imagination, and to emerge into consciousness, and the entire process is unknown to me. But the important thing, for me, is that the novel's basis is a real event; that it happened in the world "out there" and not in my head; that it must be sent back out into the world, and given a definite time and place, and related to current history.

Until this is settled I am unable to write and would not care to write—my own fantasies, however intriguing, simply don't seem substantial enough for me to formalize into art. I can sometimes "marry" them to objective events, since we all experience a number of the same things, and this allows me to write quite swiftly and happily; one of the large consolations for experiencing anything unpleasant is the knowledge that one can communicate it, especially one's triumph over it, to other people. Critics who chide me for dwelling on unpleasant and even bloody subjects miss the point: art shows us how to get through and transcend pain, and a close reading of any tragic work (*Macbeth* comes immediately to mind) will allow the intelligent reader to see how and why the tragedy took place, and how he, personally, need not make these mistakes. The more violent the murders in *Macbeth,* the more relief one can feel at *not* having to perform them. Great art is cathartic; it is always moral.

Therefore, one should contemplate his own experiences and see how they illuminate the experiences of others; how they transcend the finite; how they may be of value to other people. Unless there is a real "value," the resulting art will be manufactured and one-dimensional. I firmly believe that mankind is so instinctively, unconsciously involved with the survival and growth of the species that when an individual attempts to live *selfishly,* he will either fail or will fall into despair. Only when men are connected to larger, universal goals are they really happy—and one result of their happiness is a rush of creative activity. Any writer who has difficulty in writing is probably not onto his true subject, but wasting time with false, petty goals; as soon as you connect with your true subject you will write.

Challenge and response

My purpose in writing this essay is to point out, I hope not dogmatically, that the average person is deeper, more talented, and more intelligent than he probably believes. He is transformable—even overnight. Exhaustion and fatigue are mainly psychological; if man is faced with a new challenge, he can summon up amazing reservoirs of energy. Unfortunately, our complex civilization reduces "challenges" for us or makes them seem apparently insoluble. It is the task of the writer to think his way through all the temporal, private, petty, headline-tormented confusion of his life, and connect with deeper rhythms, either through a conscious exploration of art, history, music, literature, or through personal discipline and meditation. Man is the only creature in possible control of his own destiny, and the most imaginative people will imagine their futures and the future of their society, not through being passive or influenced by current fashionable trends, but through a conscious exertion of the mind.

If anyone who reads this is doubtful, he should ask himself *why* he is doubtful; very likely he hasn't much idea of his own mind, and thinks himself far more limited than he really is.

On a more practical level—since writers are involved in the real world, for better or worse—I can offer only a few general advisory words, which may be too personal for broader application. My "ideas" come to me partly out of the world (I scan newspapers often) and partly out of my own life. They seem to sink into unconsciousness, sometimes for a long period of time, and are drawn out again by some stray reminder in my daily life (in the case of *Wonderland,* I came across a number of similar news items—dealing with the murder-suicide tragedy, eerily common in our country, in which a father kills his entire family and then himself). Then a long process of "dreaming-through" takes place, in which I think about the entire novel—living through various scenes, hearing or inventing dialogue, walking around with my characters in my head for months; only when the process is completed can I begin to write, and I can't hurry the process. I can assign to myself occasional tasks—how to manage a certain scene, how to dramatize the relationship of one character to another—before going to sleep at night, and sometimes by morning I have figured out the problem—sometimes—this might work about half the time. But I never despair or become impatient; it is simply a matter of waiting until the entire book is thought out. Of course, writing a short story is far easier. Henry James dictated his long, excellent story "The Beast in the Jungle" in *three mornings*—which suggests to me that he dreamt through his writing in great detail, before formalizing it.

After this strange, uncanny, intuitive stage of a novel is more or less completed in my mind, I write the first draft. I usually write very quickly, chapter by chapter, though I try to alternate work on a novel with shorter pieces—stories, articles, or reviews —in order to keep some objectivity. I always know exactly how the novel will end, even the wording of the final paragraph.

I always know exactly the crucial scenes, the dialogue, even the way my characters look, though I may not describe them in that much detail. But as I write this first draft, I often discover new, small things about my characters, and allow any workable rearrangements in. This year, spent in London, I wrote a rather long novel titled *Do with Me What You Will*, which is a complex narrative dealing with the Law—the legal profession in America—but concentrating on two individuals who happen to be lovers, and who are married and "thinking back" over the circumstances of their having met and fallen in love; it involved many exasperating problems, but as long as I waited patiently the narrative always straightened out, and the characters asserted themselves in accordance with their own integrity.

The real reward

After the first draft is finished, I put it aside temporarily and work on other things. Then, when I feel the time is come for me really to formalize it, I begin the second and final draft—and this part of the process is, strangely enough, the most enjoyable of all. I cut each chapter drastically, seeing as objectively as possible what can be eliminated or shortened (my manuscripts would be very long, sometimes twice as long, if I didn't cut so severely), trying to read the work as if from another part of myself, or from the point of view of another person. Though the original, spontaneous part of writing can be very exciting, the real reward for me at least, is this third and most conscious, most "intellectual" organization of material. Man is a problem-solving animal, and the organizing of vast subjects must give pleasure, evidently; nothing seems to me to involve more intellectual effort than the organizing of a big novel, and I cannot imagine anything more rewarding.

In all this, I try to keep in mind the delicate relationship between what is unique, perhaps even eccentric, and what is universal—what will, hopefully, transcend the finite nature of newspaper headlines. Only in this relationship is there a true subject, worthy of long hours of work. I believe that all art is moral and that it must communicate either directly or through metaphor; I also believe that many people are true artists who imagine themselves only consumers, or at best only careful imitators of what seems marketable and timely.

11

HOW PEOPLE SOUND

by Marjorie Lee

I BEGIN this piece in longhand while relaxing in an armchair in a painter's studio. The painter is a friend of mine, a portraitist, who asked me to sit for her today. As usual (is it a writer's tic or simply a personal flaw?), I arrived twenty minutes late. And I am recalling, at this instant, the dialogue which took place as I reached the top of the stairs, breathless, to find her standing at the door.

> ME: Hi Susan I'm late I'm sorry! I was held up at home and the traffic was—
>
> SUSAN: Yeah, well. The parakeet was out and flying around like crazy, so it doesn't matter, we'll just—
>
> ME: The 'phone kept ringing, I couldn't get off. It was Ellie Fisher, and you know. . . . .
>
> SUSAN: Boy, does she talk, it's like the bubolic plague, I mean bubonic. I got a whole new tube of lampblack. It's gonna be dark, Renaissance I'm doing you. . . .
>
> ME: How do you want me?
>
> SUSAN: Head. Write. Twiddle your thumbs, just don't make faces and shut up. You talk, I can't get your mouth right.

I'm recalling this now; I'm remembering it. But not for its message, because of message there is little; and not for its eloquence, because of eloquence there is none. I am remembering it for its sound: the sound of two women exchanging words, easily, casually, without thought to grammar or syntax; two women making an everyday sound of dialogue.

The memorization, or the process, really, of reconstructing human sound, is a rather specialized one. The inner receiving set has undergone several changes, improvements of a sort, so that, like a souped-up car, it is no longer quite what it was originally. The motor has been tuned for a maximum sensitivity, and the more conventional parts have been replaced by a number of doodads which come off a bit more flashily.

For young and/or new writers of dialogue, the dumping of old rules and admonitions is difficult. For example: *"Never end a sentence with a preposition."* At elementary school, I had Miss Kane for English. You had her, too. We all did. She was a good woman, dedicated to her job. When I wrote a "composition" in which one person asked another, "What are you thinking of?" —she flunked the paper. Yes, she was good. And dedicated. But the number of children in that class who would never, for the rest of their lives, write a decent piece of dialogue was something else again. Too bad. I've often wondered: *Of what had she been thinking . . . ?*

People, those people who surround us every day, who live with us, however well informed, however well educated, are rarely grammatical. The fact is that most people have a good deal of trouble expressing themselves in the first place. They pause. They falter. And by the time they are finished with what might have been a simple statement, it would take three magicians and a code-breaker to parse the sentence.

Dialogue for characterization

In fiction as in real life, characters should differ. It makes no sense whatever to put a hippie's swinging lingo into the mouth of a village priest orating from the Sunday lectern. Dialogue is far and away the most important key to personality. And the writer of fiction must work forever in the role of eavesdropper. At a party a woman once said of me, "She doesn't come for fun, she's taking notes is all." I don't doubt that I was. How else could I remember the funny and somewhat endearing *"is all"* tacked onto the end of that articulation?

It would seem now that the point is simply to listen. But it isn't. The point is to hear. Schoolrooms, theatres, cocktail parties all over the world are filled with people listening. Very few are hearing a thing. The reason is that while you listen you can be doing any number of other things at the same time: lighting a cigarette, pushing back a cuticle, remembering a laundry list, or, mentally, having an entire conversation with someone who isn't even there. But when you are actually hearing, you are doing nothing else. It takes just about all you have to hear. And not just words and names, which are hard enough. But the sound of the words; the quality; the sounds below and above and around the sounds: the color and the texture, the living fabric of human noise. Because we do make an awful lot of noise. We don't merely speak. In our words, there are thunder, and stillness; shrieks of anxiety (however well hidden), and the door-creakings of weariness; claps of applause, and the hisses and boos of disapproval; often laughter, felt if not expressed; and these days, unfortunately, far more often, tears. Love, too—which is perhaps most difficult to hear.

The love story is the hardest of all to write dialogue for. "I love you! I love you!" will fill the bill at some quite specific point of climax in drama *or* comedy, but it will fall on the reader's inner ear with the plop of a dead fish when used to represent the *sound* of love. Other words will be needed for that—words which say it *without* saying it as in the following from Gertrude Stein's "Melanctha" (*Three Lives*):

> "Yes I certainly do see that very clear Dr. Campbell," said Melanctha, "I see that's certainly what it is always made me not know right about you and that's certainly what is that makes you

really mean what you was always saying. You certainly are just too scared Dr. Campbell to really feel things way down in you. All you are always wanting Dr. Campbell, is just to talk about being good, and to play with people just to have a good time, and yet always to certainly keep yourself out of trouble. It don't seem to me Dr. Campbell that I admire that way to do things very much. It certainly ain't really to me being very good. It certainly ain't any more to me Dr. Campbell, but that you certainly are awful scared about really feeling things way down in you, and that's certainly the only way Dr. Campbell I can see that you can mean, by what it is that you are always saying to me."

In the above passage, a number of things are being made to happen. Read it again, not only visually, but trying to hear:

a) *Love* happens: without the use of the word "love" or any direct synonym for it. Love, and caring-for, come through in the deep, earnest repetition of the word "certainly"— and in the emotional hang-up on the name "Dr. Campbell."

b) *Rhythm* happens: the slow, nearly lullabyed ebb and flow of a mind speaking aloud as it thinks quietly to itself. Melanctha isn't a member of The American Psychoanalytic Association. She doesn't mouth formulations, i.e.: "Dr. Campbell, your neurosis is one of repression resulting in an inhibition used as a defense mechanism against the working-through of The Unconscious." Melanctha's rhythm carries with it not something patly known, but something still living in the being-knownness of its own discovery.

c) *Dialect* happens: and in a way that Gertrude Stein made it happen first—without the use of comic mispronunciations or odd-ball spellings. Melanctha is a young Negress. Yet it isn't at all necessary to saddle her with the vulgarity of something like this (see sentence #2): "Ah sees thass suttenleh whut 'tis . . ." Stein's use of dialect in dialogue relies on essence rather than on caricature. Thought by many to be an incomprehensible trickster, she has done more for dialogue than will ever be fairly judged. She is, in fact, our Picasso of words. As Picasso has not only looked but seen, so has Stein not only listened but heard. And what she has written is not merely an experiment with sound; it's the result and finished product of that experiment. Her hearing of Negro speech went beneath the usual top layers. She was able, then, to allow it its true, Biblical dignity. How is this done in the sense of technique? Through a system of musical timing and subtle choice of word-placements in the sentence.

In Stein (not in Stowe!) we have a dialoguist who reached an epitome of sophistication. Hemingway learned at her knee, and did well. And on some scores, although certainly not all, John O'Hara has outpapa-ed Papa. Of all our modern writers, he is (consistently) the best sound-reproducer. And again—not through slapstick distortion, but through a choice of straight words and word-placements. He has heard, unerringly, the sound made by each and every one of his characters. King-reporter (no, not *journalist*) of the Christian American Middle Class (*Appointment in Samarra, A Rage to Live, From the Terrace,* etc.), he widens the range of his inner ear to beam in on the Pennsylvania Dutch (*The Farmer's Hotel*) and, among others, the young hopefuls and aging hopelesses of Hollywood ("Naticka Jackson" and "The Way to Majorca," both short stories included in *Waiting for Winter*). His males, from the stodgiest to the most loose-tongued, are authentic; and, for me, there is a very special response to the way that he, a man, is able to record the sound of women.

The following is an excerpt from "The Way to Majorca." It is begun, here, with the words of renamed, type-cast, trapped-at-twenty-seven Sally Standish, in a conversation held with Meredith Manners, a very worried Hollywood screenwriter:

"But what I should have done was be more independent. When I was a few years younger I should have told the studio to give me different parts."

"They would have told you to go to hell."

"Probably. But then I should have told *them* to go to hell. And *then* I could have."

"No. They had you sewed up in a contract that you couldn't break."

"But what if I refused to work?"

"Is that what you're thinking of doing now?"

"What I'm thinking of doing now is retire."

"You must have saved your money."

"No, unfortunately, I didn't. But I could retire for maybe a couple of years. I'd have to sell this place, and some jewelry, and live on that for a couple of years."

The excerpt illustrates several subtle touches:

a) A woman's habit, all the while knowing better, of trying to solve a problem with what "should" have been done, wasn't, and is now too late to be done.

b) The male approach: reality.

c) Stress builds up: two underlinings in Sally's voice: *them* and *then*—hence, an addition of effort to fight reality.

d) Further stress, through stubborn rationalization: "But what if I refused to work?"

e) Still more stress, to a point, now, where grammar and syntax go down the drain:

    (i) "is retire." No time left for the correctness of "is *to* retire" or "I'm thinking of retiring."

    (ii) The repeat, within two consecutive sentences, of "a couple of years."

Repetition and selection

We're taught that a good writer avoids repetition, uses synonymous words and phrases rather than the same ones over again.

That's valid for exposition or description. It's most *in*valid for dialogue. People are constantly making a mess of their utterances with word-for-word repetitions. But those messes are beautiful, because the sound of them is human.

It is important to clarify the difference between real-life conversation and written dialogue because there is definitely a difference. It lies in selection. Neither the limited time and space of the short story (or the specific novel scene) nor the natural span of the reader's attention will allow for a total reproduction of most real-life conversations. Often it takes an hour or more of talked-out give-and-get before we actually make our feelings clear, let alone draw our conclusions. And think of our pauses. It's quite possible for people to fill up the tough spots of communication with no sound at all. In this field, the art of cinematography has us beat: the screenwriter is able to *show* the silent face. We, however, are only able to "show," in any direct sense, through exposition or "description of." We are unable to put that much into poor dialogue. So we're forced to choose. From an entire mass of human communication we must sift and cull for those words which will deliver an essence of the whole, and which will best carry out the nature of sound. This is more difficult—and surely no less an art.

Were I to teach a class now, I would ask for five pages of pure dialogue without the aid of a single passage of exposition. You would have a week to listen: to strangers at bars or in restaurants, planes, trains and buses; to friends in your own living room; to children, fighting or playing; *to yourself.* It might take you several days of listening before you began to hear. Having heard, you would then choose. Finally, you would write the pages.

Try it.

"What're you afraid of?" she asked.

12

AN INTERVIEW WITH
EVAN HUNTER—ED McBAIN

by Evan Hunter

The following three-way "interview" is the result of
a series of questions sent to Evan Hunter, who also
writes under the name of Ed McBain.—*Ed.*

EDITOR: *What is the process whereby you as a novelist translate*
experience and fact into an imagined, invented work like a novel?

HUNTER: I'm not sure I can define a process that is essentially
unconscious. For example, what started out to be an exploration
of a very special and enduring adolescent friendship (based on
an idyllic summer one of my sons spent with a band and a dance
troupe in Israel) turned out to be *Last Summer* instead, a comment on our adult society as revealed through the behavior of
three hardly admirable teen-agers. I can't honestly say at which
point the novel began to turn. I know that somewhere in the
early pages, I began to foreshadow something horrible to come,
and then went back to rewrite those pages and to intensify the
sense of foreboding. By the time I was thirty or so pages into the
book, certainly, I was consciously directing my thoughts toward
the new thematic approach.

McBAIN: The city in the 87th Precinct series is a distortion of
the city in which I was born and raised: New York. The police

procedure was learned from cops, and it is as unvaried and as disciplined as the pattern of a bull fight. Invention and imagination enter the books in the guise of the various people the cops meet along the way. I always give them center stage when they appear, relegating the cops to supporting roles at that time. I don't know whether or not those characters are based on any real people. I lived in a slum for the first twelve years of my life, and I would imagine I saw at least some of those faces on the streets.

EDITOR: *What are the kinds of people and places and situations that trigger your mind and set you thinking in terms of a fictional form for what stirs your imagination?*

HUNTER: It doesn't usually work that way for me. I think the genesis of most of my novels has always been thematic, and only then do I begin thinking in terms of the setting or characters I will need to make my point. There are obvious exceptions, of course. *The Blackboard Jungle* was based largely on my own brief experience as a substitute teacher, an example of the writer enlarging upon reality to cast himself as the hero fighting a battle against overwhelming odds. (*I* quit teaching; Richard Dadier stays on.) But certainly the characters, the setting, and the incidents were all firmly rooted in my memory before I sat down to write the book.

McBAIN: The one time a setting triggered a novel for me (and this was not an 87th Precinct mystery, but a straight suspense novel) was when my wife and I were driving through New England and suddenly went through a town which, at three in the afternoon, seemed uncommonly still, almost uninhabited. I suggested that perhaps someone had taken over the town for one reason or another, and we began building on that nucleus, speculating wildly on the reasons for the town's silence. The result, many months later, was *The Sentries,* wherein a group of fanatics intent on starting World War III invade a town on the Florida

Keys, hijack a Coast Guard cutter, and sail it toward Cuba, hoping it will be fired upon and sunk.

EDITOR: *Are there certain kinds of reading that stimulate your storytelling? Newspapers as well as books? Events?*

HUNTER: I'm sure there are, but I can't think of a single instance where any *specific* reading inspired me to sit down and write. (I'm reminded of the old Henry Morgan skit in which Beethoven sits barren at the piano, while his wife putters around cleaning, and he suddenly turns to her and says, "Vot's dot you're humming, sweethott?") I don't believe in inspiration as such. That's for movies about writers. I think that the weight of living eventually forces a reaction out of a writer, and he puts that onto paper as best he can. I do, though, believe in a muse, however romantic that may sound. There are times when I've written ten pages non-stop and then reread them in wonder, hardly knowing where they came from.

McBAIN: I never read mysteries. I read whatever non-fiction material I can find about policemen, but I never use real-life cases as the bases for my novels. I don't like to saddle my imagination with someone else's actual crime, especially since *he* probably got caught after its commission. I think I would make an excellent murderer; for me, the hardest part about writing a mystery is figuring out how to catch the killer.

EDITOR: *Knowing the seemingly inexhaustible interest of readers today in sex, sensation and sordidness, do you consciously think in terms of style and the inclusion of some "shocking" sections—or just how does an experienced fiction writer determine how "frank" his book will be? Do you think of the audience, age level, etc., when you are planning or writing your novels?*

HUNTER: To begin with, I am not easily shocked, nor do I believe today's reading audience can be easily shocked. I did use sex for its shock value at the end of *Last Summer,* but only because I had very carefully led the reader into believing one of the girls would eventually be drowned. When she is led *away* from the ocean, the reader thinks she is now safe; her rape is symbolic, and she is as effectively destroyed as if the others had held her head under water. The scene becomes shocking. But I do not consider sex scenes "shocking" per se, and I usually use sex primarily to explore character, it being my belief that no two people behave the same way in bed (or *out* of it, for that matter) as any other two people. I think the new freedom in using frankly sexual words for describing the sex act is good and honest. I don't know of anyone who uses medical terminology in bed (except doctors, maybe) and I don't see why a writer should have to describe "lovemaking" in language alien to the actual sound of bedroom talk. I would no more expect a ten-year-old to understand the sex scenes in one of my novels than I would expect him to understand what it is to be unemployed and the father of six hungry children. I write for adults.

McBain: The violence in the 87th Precinct mysteries is used not to excite but to define. Policemen, after all, are not usually engaged in trying to dope out who's been cheating in a game of jacks. They deal with violence every working day of their lives, and the crimes they encounter are often sordid enough to cause extreme nausea. I describe these crimes in detail because I would be writing fake books about cops if I didn't. Similarly, and probably to the dismay of hard-core, private-eye-type mystery readers, the sex in these novels is largely clinical (as in *laboratory* clinical) and will more often concern itself with the suspected presence of sperm in the vaginal vault than with a flash of thigh above the ribbed top of a nylon stocking.

EDITOR: *Do you believe that Erle Stanley Gardner, Ellery Queen, Ross Macdonald, Rex Stout or John Creasey could write a serious novel?*

HUNTER: No.

McBAIN: Yes.

EDITOR: *Do you believe that John Updike, Saul Bellow, J. D. Salinger, Bernard Malamud, or William Styron could write a mystery?*

HUNTER: Yes.

McBAIN: No.

EDITOR: *Do you work out the complete plan of a novel, outline, delineated characters, etc., before you begin to write it?*

HUNTER: Whether I will first outline a plot and subplots, or first outline my major and minor characters, will depend on the projected novel. My plot outlines are the loosest sort of things. I don't want to become trapped by an initial idea and sacrifice something fresher later on because the entire novel has been outlined in such detail that any changes become unthinkable. Instead, I'll outline only two or three chapters ahead, using such terse descriptions as "Boy argues with father, tells him to go to hell," and then allow the characters to determine for themselves the full content of the chapter as well as their behavior in subsequent chapters. My characters are outlined in much more precise detail. I will often write pages of description as a warmup, outlining physical characteristics, genealogies, education, reading tastes, occupations, hobbies, important past events, etc. But this, too, is subject to change. I will not pin myself down to an exact outline, because that would take all the surprise out of writing and make it a chore rather than a joy. One reason I dislike writing films is that far too many producers and/or directors insist on "talking" a detailed outline with the writer—what's the character's motivation here, how does he manage to get out of this situation, is his mother a drunk, etc. Half the time, I don't know the answers to specific questions about character and plot until I come to them, and I prefer it that way.

McBAIN: I don't have to outline the major characters in my mysteries because they're series characters whose personalities have been established over the course of twenty-one books. Nor do I ever outline the characters they come into contact with.

They just sit down and start talking, and somehow their characters emerge. I don't worry too much about motivation in the conventional mystery sense, it being my belief that a solidly realized character doesn't need "motivation" for anything he does, especially if what he does happens to be murder. When plotting, I usually start with a corpse. I then ask myself how the corpse got to be that way, and I try to find out—just as the cops would. I plot loosely, usually a chapter or two ahead, going back to make sure that everything fits—all the clues are in the right places, all the bodies accounted for—only *after* I've finished the first draft of the book. An 87th Precinct mystery runs some two hundred pages in manuscript and takes me a month to write. I can't plot too tightly or I'd lose the forward momentum necessary to meet my self-imposed schedule of ten to twelve pages a day. I believe strongly, by the way, in the long arm of coincidence because I know how much it contributes to the solving of *real* police cases. I'll use it unashamedly whenever I choose because I don't believe in mystery-writing rules—for example, I allowed the murderer to escape at the end of *He Who Hesitates*. A mystery should be exciting, believable, and entertaining. If you're lucky besides, it might just say a little something about crime and punishment.

EDITOR: *What steps would you advise a beginning novelist to take to help him improve his chances of success in getting his fiction published?*

HUNTER: I would tell him to write what he feels. This doesn't necessarily mean "Write what he knows," because he can always find out what he doesn't know. (People all over the world are dying to explain in detail exactly how they cut diamonds or fly airplanes or lead cavalry troops into battle. All anyone has to do is ask them.) I would also advise him to write whether he feels like it or not. If it's raining, and he's miserable and has outlined a happy party scene for that day, forget it and go on instead to the scene in which the hero's wife says she's running off with the butcher. The hardest part about writing is getting *something* down on paper. After that, it's all rewriting, which is infinitely easier.

MCBAIN: I would warn him not to talk about what he's working on, or to show partial manuscripts to his friends or loved ones for opinions. A writer doesn't really want criticism, he only wants praise—someone to say his work is marvelous. If he knows it's marvelous, he doesn't need approval in the writing stage. If he knows it *isn't* marvelous, then he'd better start rewriting at once, before anyone has a chance to deflate his ego. A writer's ego is his most important tool.

EDITOR: *Are there any special qualities that you consider essential for a writer of fiction today?*

HUNTER and MCBAIN: A heart and a head.

13

THE LURE OF "I," THE TYRANNY OF "HE"

by R. F. Delderfield

In the course of almost half a century of professional writing, I must have been asked almost every conceivable question about yarn-spinning. Sometimes, standing on a public platform, a willing if slightly wary target for an audience, I have been asked to comment on slants of the craft concerning which I have never had a private, much less a public, thought. And yet, curiously enough, I cannot recall anyone's ever asking me the question that must exercise the wits of any man or woman who seeks to make a living by writing fiction: the terrible choice before the words "Chapter One" are put on paper, of whether to use the first or third person in the unraveling of a story. It occurs to me that this is a topic worth examining here, for my benefit as much as for readers of this book.

I see it as a chilling choice between the lure of "I" and the tyranny of "he," a veritable Scylla and Charybdis of fiction writing. For when these two forms of narrative are considered in isolation, each of them is seen to possess enormous advantages and handicaps. Yet the choice, given the material at one's disposal, is vital. A wrong decision at the outset can turn a potential best seller into a disaster; alternatively, if the choice of viewpoint is right, you often have an opportunity to make something worthwhile out of almost nothing.

First-person or fly-on-the-wall narrative?

Let us briefly examine the merits and demerits of both points of view.

A first-person narrative has certain built-in bonuses. Among them are directness, potential speed, clarity of thought, immediacy of action, veracity, and the kind of simplicity that lures the reader into imagining that fiction writing must be a very easy way to earn a living. One has only to think of a few first-person classics to detect this. How much less immediate, for instance, would have been Robinson Crusoe's discovery of the footprint in the sand if Defoe had been describing it secondhand? How much less effective would have been, say, Huckleberry Finn's moral debates with himself, had Mark Twain (and not his hero) described the torments of indecision to which poor Huck subjected himself in the matter of whether or not it was right to help Jim escape from bondage? And how much less exciting would have been the impact of the attack on the stockade on Treasure Island had not Jim Hawkins been describing the battle as an eyewitness?

One could go on posing these questions all the way down to the bottom of literature's wild and ordered gardens. Robert Louis Stevenson's punch in *Kidnapped* was twice as powerful in the roundhouse on Captain Hoseason's brig than it would have been had the story come to us, so to speak, thirdhand. But, to venture into quite another field of writing, would detective Philip Marlowe have been such an interesting and complex character had Raymond Chandler denied him the chance to tell us precisely what *he* (rather than what Chandler) thought about the ethics of his profession?

All these stories establish powerful claims for first-person narrative. All have an immediacy they could not possibly have had if their authors had chosen the alternative approach. It would therefore seem that for writing action fiction, the first person is almost obligatory—but to accept this would be to fall into a trap that many young writers spring in their early years at the job. Why?

Let us look, for a moment, at the built-in advantages of third-person narrative. One that immediately recommends itself is breadth. No first-person narrative can hope to attain the breadth of, say, *War and Peace, Crime and Punishment, Westward Ho!,* or, on a more domestic level, *Little Women* and *Gone with the Wind.* For a writer using the third person can play fly-on-the-wall in a way that dwarfs the efforts of a direct narrator, can get inside characters and situations to a depth that is but rarely achieved in the first-person narration, where one is sometimes driven half-mad by obligatory phrases like "in my opinion" or "I think he thought" or "it seemed to me."

All of which is by way of a preamble. No two writers set down their words on identical lines. There are bound to be obvious differences of approach, sensibility, and fitness of phrase. Characters outwardly alike in most respects will have subtle distinctions that are inherent in the author's psyche. One hero will catch a ball with his left hand rather than his right, or tie his shoelaces in a different fashion from the other; one heroine will respond to gallantry in a different way from another. The balance of dialogue and descriptive prose will vary. One can only recount how and why the choice between first- and third-person narrative was dictated to *oneself.*

The looser collar

Looking back on some thirty published novels which I wrote between the ages of eighteen and sixty, I have asked myself the reasons that governed my decision toward first- or third-person narration. It seems to me that theme and background are the two factors that predetermine the selection.

When I first began writing, I was influenced, as are all young writers, by the current stream of popular fiction at my disposal. I remember that Conan Doyle's historical romances contributed a large slice of my literary diet at this time, notably the exploits and adventures described in his books, *Brigadier Gerard* and *Micah Clarke,* two of Doyle's best. When, therefore, I wrote the derivative *Adventures of Cornet Cavendish* (mercifully unpublished!), I naturally gravitated to the first-person narrative, and went on using it until I became absorbed in plays. By then, of course, I was on more solid diet, caught up with writers like Dostoyevsky, George Eliot, the Brontës, Cervantes, Victor Hugo, and many others, all of whom favored the third person. It was here that I began to realize the severe strictures of the first person, even when used by such masters as Defoe, Stevenson, and Twain. One could never penetrate the minds of subsidiary characters (Man Friday, Ben Gunn, and Jim), and one could only view Crusoe's island, Treasure Island, and the Mississippi through the eyes of the central character. I think Hugo, more than any other writer, led me through the gate into open country, showing me what enormous vistas there were to be explored the far side of the hedge, so that when I began *The Avenue,* first of the sagas I was to write, I was never tempted by the immediacy of "I," but settled comfortably to the looser collar of "he" and "she."

Writing in the third person, I was able to get an intimate look at all the houses in the Avenue and project the dreams of the dreaming suburb firsthand. I could also be impersonal in describing the atmosphere of the suburb and its surrounding countryside and found that the freedom of the exercise more than compensated for the extra work.

I used the same mode of storytelling for my Sorrel Valley saga—*A Horseman Riding By* and *The Green Gauntlet*—even though most of the story is projected through the eyes of one man, Paul Craddock. Perhaps he never seemed one man to me, for the story embraced his life at Shallowford from the time he was twenty-three until he died aged eighty-six.

When I came to write the four-volume saga, *God Is an Englishman* and its sequels, I felt that third-person storytelling was obligatory, for here my canvas was the whole British Isles, and the development of the transport firm, Swann-on-Wheels, was recounted not only through the eyes of Adam Swann, its founder, but through his wife Henrietta and some sixteen of his different managers. The form of telling played a great part in keeping the story moving through hundreds of printed pages. I was able to invent dramatic incidents taking place hundreds of miles apart and put the local spotlight on them in a way that could never have been achieved had the story been told by Adam Swann alone.

And yet, every now and again, I am lured back to first-person narrative, as in "Come Home, Charlie, and Face Them," the story of a Welsh bank clerk's fall from grace; in "There Was a Fair Maid Dwelling," a teen-age romance; and "Cheap Day Return," the story of a small-town photographer involved with two women.

It was refreshing to tell these tales firsthand. Each was set in a background where I had grown up, and many of the characters were composite re-creations of people I had known in my youth. They constituted a kind of literary therapy after the labors of the sagas.

My overall preferences? For a long book, involving frequent changes of scene and many important subsidiary characters, third-person storytelling is a must. For shorter stories, involved with one scene and three or four major characters, first-person telling is faster, less laborious and far more rewarding—to the author in the telling, that is. *For it is a curious fact that nine-tenths of my financial rewards and all my best sellers have been derived from third-person narratives. Perhaps this proves that, on the whole, readers prefer them.*

14

MAKE IT HAPPEN

by Rosemary Gatenby

WHAT is the chief difference between a salable book manuscript and an unsalable one? It is seldom a matter of fine prose style—a plus that belongs to the top-quality writers. I think what counts most is making connection with the reader—making connection and then taking him along, keeping his interest to the bottom of the last page.

I am not recommending that quality should ever be compromised for the sake of slick readability. Neither good style nor important theme content is incompatible with good storytelling, as is easily demonstrated, for example, in the novels of Evelyn Waugh, Graham Greene, or Iris Murdoch. No matter how well a book is written, how perceptive it is, how full of meaning it is for the writer, if the reader abandons it partway through, it might as well not have been written.

When I say "the reader," I suppose I really mean the reader in the publishing house, who, in considering your manuscript, is first and foremost keeping in mind all the readers "out there." I don't think writers can or should think of any future readership while writing. Yet "art for its own sake" is only a piece of cant in which the artist can take refuge—unless the art is also commercially successful, and then art for art's sake is a luxury he is well able to afford. There is always this nagging fear: perhaps you're deluding yourself? Do you really *have* any talent? The cure for this, in the case of novel writers, is the sight of one's book, bound, in hardcover, with a stunning jacket. So with that in mind. . . .

The other side of the looking-glass

What started me mulling over some of the differences between salable and unsalable fiction was a recent project of mine—sorting through a closetful of old, unpublished work. Inevitably, I found myself comparing what I used to do with what I do now, somehow trying to grab hold of and identify those all-important elements that make a manuscript publishable.

I'd had a thorough grounding in the mechanics. With this knowledge and *some* talent I assumed that I could automatically produce salable fiction. Wrong. Like the alchemists of medieval times, I was trying to make gold of dross; for I had nothing to write about. I'd already used up all the material I could think of—handed it in, segments at a time, in the form of class assignments: stories about my mother, my sister, the neighbors; a novel on the true-life tragedy of the widow who lived across the street, which ended with her thwarted lover dying of cholera in India and her husband dying of a broken heart. (She still had her piano, though—upbeat ending.) At 22 I was more or less written out, but still trying, scraping the bottom of the barrel for story material.

Much of my early trouble with characters and with subject matter can be traced back to that old teacherly advice, "Write what you know," and its corollary—that literary gold is to be found in your own backyard. Experience has taught me that the real difficulty with these professorial maxims is one of interpretation. *"Use* what you know, but *write* anything you think you're capable of." Imagination and/or research prove perfectly adequate for the creation of fictional scenes, events, emotions, reactions one has not oneself lived through. Gold in the backyard? Not mine. But a backyard *like* my backyard. Characters *like* the people I know. . . . It is this word *like* that makes the difference. Because I cannot make fiction of real stories or people. Maybe you can, but everything I write about must be on the other side of something very like Alice's looking-glass. Therein lies the magic.

By the time my first book was published, I was writing—and I still am—entirely fictional characters, who, however, sometimes do bear a *physical* resemblance to someone I have seen or have known slightly—the more slightly, the better. Personalities are 100% imaginary, as is what happens to them in my books.

Another false dictum I picked up at some point was that novels could be divided into two groups: *plot* books, in which you began with a plot, and *character* books, in which you began with your character(s). In the first place, book-length fiction is not that easy to categorize; and in the second, for me at least, neither plot nor character is the starting point. For years I didn't try writing a novel because no plot occurred to me, and I couldn't think of a character on whom to base a book (having exhausted my only possibilities with the girl with the piano and the lover with cholera).

Finding a situation

The truth—which I eventually discovered—is that one starts with a situation. Even if a book stems first of all from a character, *that* is a situation: the situation is that this character is a possessive mother, or a compulsive liar. If a book begins with a particular background, that, too, is a situation: Your characters are in some relationship to the background—they are in accord with it or in conflict with it, and that is a situation. If theme is what your book springs from, you still cannot begin to put it on paper until you have your situation.

My first published book, *Evil Is As Evil Does,* began with my trying to think of a plausible but unhackneyed motive for murder among ordinary people. What occurred to me was bigamy, suggested by my husband's once having known a bigamist in the army. Opportunity for bigamy? I discarded a convenient plane crash as having been too often used; thought instead of the commuter-train wreck that had occurred several years previously, when we had been living on Long Island. And for my book, a girl—opportunistic. When she survives the train wreck she is suddenly presented with a once-in-a-lifetime chance to walk out of her disappointing marriage and start a new life. This book almost wrote itself. In it I was able to use the particular world I live in—that of the New York commuter. A real train wreck, then; a possible situation; and a familiar milieu.

My second published book, *Aim to Kill,* began quite suddenly as I was reading a newspaper review of *The Boston Strangler,* by Gerold Frank. My attention was caught by mention of a writer who had volunteered to help the police in their investigations and who had seemed to know too much about the murders. He did not turn out to be the Strangler, but along with dozens of others under police scrutiny, he was for some time under suspicion.

Within half an hour I had outlined my book, which would be about a newspaper reporter who decides to write a non-fiction novel à la Truman Capote's *In Cold Blood,* based on a local series of apparently random killings with a telescope-sighted rifle —and in so doing becomes a suspect.

This book, then, was suggested by a real situation, out of which the plot developed easily and logically—around the reporter and his investigations, the police captain who opposes his book project and comes to suspect him, and the widow in whom they both become romantically interested. The murderer and his continuing crimes, of course, become more and more closely bound up in the action.

Before writing *Aim to Kill,* I had to research the background, reading book after book on journalism and taking a conducted tour of *The New York Times.* Also, I consulted books on police organization and on hunting rifles and telescopic sights, and then checked my facts with the local police department! Certainly not a case of "writing what I knew," but of writing what I found out.

Sequence—cause and effect

Some of my early difficulties came from putting the cart before the horse. For me, it didn't work to begin with a character; it didn't work to begin with a plot. But once I had the sequence right, I was unstuck.

First a situation, which is the start of a book. Then a cast. And situation can be taken from real life, but I must let it work itself out logically, with my best powers of invention, instead of sticking to what may actually have happened. The ultimate resolution of a good story situation is inherent in its very beginning, but such are the laws of chance, that seldom in life do events work out in true cause and effect fashion. And a satisfying ending is certainly the major aim of a novel.

From my starting situation must come conflict and suspense which build up to a climax; in it the characters must be closely interrelated, not necessarily by blood, but by circumstance, motivation, opposition, for they must interact upon each other. More than once I've had to change my cast to get closer relationships, because characters kept leaving the scene of action.

It is essential to me to visualize my characters clearly. Sometimes the right person springs to life just as I need her—or him —fat or thin, sly or awkward; sometimes with teeth a prominent feature; once even with a slight facial tic I had no idea he was going to turn out to have. But sometimes no particular mental image appears on cue to suggest the new character. Then I have to concentrate on the problem like a producer casting a play; and eventually I come up with someone. He may have the face of a stranger—or he may look a little like my bank teller, who seems to me the right physical type. But looks, character, personality will all merge together into someone tailor-made for the book. Once in the story, then, the characters become more and more themselves as a result of what they do and what is done to them.

In reading over my early work, I found that the greatest single fault in it was the amount of simple narration. I was telling *about* something happening instead of *making* it happen.

Today's reader, conditioned by movies, television, picture magazines, etc., expects to be placed on the scene of a book with as much immediacy as he is in the visual arts. Or, perhaps, more immediacy, because fiction can go inside characters as no other art form or entertainment can. Reading fiction is unbeatable vicarious experience. The way to get the sharpness of actual experience into your book is to go deeply into each scene yourself; make yourself live through the moment with your characters, imagining their feelings, seeing the action in your mind's eye, and putting down the thoughts, the lines of dialogue, the gestures, the small specific touches that will make the scene visual and felt by the reader. Smell, touch, taste—these are often more effective, more evocative, than sight and hearing, which become jaded with use. Major scenes must, of course, be linked together and augmented by connective narration. But the dramatized portions of the story should be fully realized, made vivid—and not by purple writing, but by imaginative participation in what goes on.

Objectivity and human experience

Of equal importance with this use of imagination is *objectivity* —the ability to evaluate your work impartially. Each day before

I start writing, I go over what I wrote the day before, making needed changes. Particularly I test for verisimilitude and for correct timing—the latter being a question of how a scene "plays." Sometimes I stop the action and study it. It is in thus going over every moment of it that I try to make my book real.

The kind of identifying with my characters that I find necessary is much easier for me if they are imaginary rather than based on someone I know. Nor does "identifying" mean that my characters are ever *me*. Some authors put more of themselves into their books than do others. But in most cases, to say that a novelist is writing about himself in his book is an oversimplification of the creative process; he is writing about someone perhaps *like* himself, but with many differences. Or he may be writing about someone entirely different, yet someone whose emotions and reactions he is able to imagine. What he relies on is the universality of human experience. He has his own experience to draw on, to refer to, and that of everyone else who has ever written a book about people. Literature is proof that men think and feel in like manner. And to get really to the point, a novelist is drawing on the reader's experience; for it is to the reader that the book must mean something in terms of his own life.

Snag the reader's interest early. Since I write suspense novels, I like to get my story off the ground at once—though my slam-bang starts are probably a little extreme. But in any case, the reader should at the outset be given the *promise* of something happening that will keep him turning the pages—the feeling of something impending, or the implication that something has already happened that is going to have far-reaching consequences, or simply the setting of a scene in such a way that the reader knows ominous forces await someone who is going to walk on-stage any minute now.

There are lots of ways. Be as subtle as you like. But put something on the first page that will induce your reader to turn to the second page, and arrange it so that before he has gone far, he will scrunch down farther into his chair, settling himself more comfortably for a long read.

15

BALANCING PLOT AND CHARACTER

by Elizabeth Cadell

PEOPLE have often asked me how I manage to make the people I write about real.

The answer is simple: my people *are* real. They have been present in my mind for weeks as real people, talking to one another, drawing vitality and life from one another and becoming almost more interesting than the flesh-and-blood people around me. I know that a new book is being created, but so far there are only characters. There is not even the vaguest plot.

I sometimes envy writers whose plots spring ready-made to mind. They, however, have to fit characters to their story; I have to put my characters aside and work out a framework in which they can be presented to the reader. For characters must *act;* it is not enough for them to *be.* It takes me a long time to shape my framework. My next problem is to induce my people to go into it.

Plots and people

This is perhaps the first major problem that faces new writers: this balance between plot and people. Characters develop, speak, grow ever more interesting; the writer races on, lost in the interesting world he is creating, but where is the plot? Or, conversely, when the narrative has flown on, page after page, brimful of action, where are the characters? Dead. Lost. Lifeless. They have been engulfed by the action.

One of the ways of achieving balance between plot and character is to draw away for a time and try to get the book in perspective. I myself make no notes; if I do, they vanish like the shopping list until no longer needed. But I do exercise patience and self-control, putting nothing whatsoever on paper until I am so certain of what I am going to write that descriptions and dialogue appear as easily as though the typewriter were doing the whole thing.

There are three major ways of presenting characters: (a) by describing them (b) by letting them talk and (c) by letting them act. In a light novel, the second of these methods is very much the best; descriptions, however interesting, tend to hold up characterization, and it is far better to let the reader build up his own picture. Three pages of dialogue will do more than six pages of labored description. Make the characters *talk,* and make them talk as they would talk in real life. If they are not real in the writer's mind, they cannot become real to the reader.

Young writers sometimes tell me that their conversations won't *flow.* This worries me, because my trouble is how to stop my characters' conversations. The reason is the one I have already given: from the live people in the mind will come lively speech. But new writers have to be reminded that one of the ways in which to write is to *listen.* Listen to people talking—on buses, on trains, in shops. As you listen, note well who says what—and try to *remember.* Once you begin to fit remarks to the type of person who makes them, you are at the beginning of true characterization. As you write, you will see before you, quite clearly, the person who is speaking; you will merely record his words. If you are making up words for him, his conversation will read not as real conversation, but as stiff, stilted stuff.

I stress dialogue because it is such a good medium for revealing a character to the reader. Just as after overhearing a conversation between strangers it is possible to get a fairly good idea of what the speakers are like, so in a book the reader will build up, line by line, his own picture of the people he is reading about.

Detailed description of the characters, in a light novel, is very often unnecessary. Coloring, build—these of course it is necessary to give, but further information comes better from other characters rather than from the writer.

The light novel

A serious difficulty for the light novel writer comes from the fact that the people in a book, like the people in real life, very often tend to have difficult or contradictory natures. It would be fitting, in a long or analytical work, to ravel and then unravel long, winding strands. In the light, modern novel, however, unity and continuity are essential, and it is, therefore, necessary to simplify—perhaps to oversimplify—difficulties arising from the conflict between the stronger characters in the book. This is not as easy as it sounds; a light touch is a delicate touch. (The dictionary defines delicate as nicely discriminating or perceptive, tender, and requiring nice handling.)

Another aspect of the light novel presents difficulties to the young writer: how to handle comedy. More than half the letters I receive contain the plaintive query: "Why is it that when I try to write amusingly, I don't succeed?"

The answer lies perhaps in that word: *try*. All and any writing requires long and sustained effort, but in art, the effort mustn't *show*. In writing an amusing situation, it is essential to let the reader discover his own pleasure. Do not jog him. Write down the incident without any attempt to nudge readers into smiling; if it's funny, they'll see the joke. Avoid expressions that give life to a verbal description; most of these sound exaggerated when put on paper.

Do characters run away with the plot?

Yes and no. My own problem is to prevent one or more of the characters from running away with me. I *like* my characters; unfortunately, I get to like them too much, and I find, to my dismay, that they're pushing the other characters aside, if not out of the story altogether. This happens every time I create a character who talks amusingly. I like to hear them, and so I go on making them talk more—and more. The result is that I have to tear up several days' work and apply myself afresh to the ever-present problem of balance.

For the writer, one of the most interesting aspects of novel writing is the interplay between characters. Some people get on; some don't. As a great part of a light novel is dialogue, the writer is free to play his characters, main or minor, against one another in conversation. If the writer has done his job well, the reader will end by taking sides. The letters which please me most are the ones which demand indignantly how I could make this or that character in a book behave so outrageously. I can only answer that all the other characters thought the behavior outrageous, too!

Sub-plots are fun. They don't have to be developed with the same detail, the same exactness as the central theme; they run through the book giving variety to the reader and, in some cases, rest to the writer. Unlike the main plot, they can be left, so to speak, in the air; the reader can be left wondering whether they really did marry, whether they ever made it up, or whether this or that really happened. This uncertainty can be irritating when applied to the principal characters and plots, but in the case of sub-plots and minor characters, it is all right to leave the reader with one or two little problems he can work out for himself.

Pruning the irrelevant

The last problem I would touch upon in the hope of helping the young writer is the one of *selection*. Write—and then cut.

And cut again. It is heartbreaking work, but it is essential, for if the story is to flow, everything that tends to hold up the action must be removed. Conversations must not go on too long. Incidents must not be over-played. Descriptions, whether of scenes or of persons, must not wander pointlessly.

It may be imagined that the writer, seeing nonessentials in the first draft of the book, would cut them out without a qualm. This is not so. Several things operate to make him hesitate: the writing, he may feel, is too good to be lost to the reader; the incident is so amusing, or so interesting, that nobody could have too much of it; the girl is so charming that nobody could have too much of her. Only the firm, undeviating adherence to the best of all rules, balance, will give the writer the necessary resolution to prune and lop off everything irrelevant. It is a sacrifice, but it is a sacrifice worth making.

A final point: More than half my correspondents ask whether it is difficult to get published. Had I, they ask, any "pull"? I had none whatsoever. I wrote a book purely for fun. I put it in a drawer and went on with the job of earning money to bring up two children. Later, I looked at the book again and liked it. I sent it to a literary agent and said: Can I or can't I write? There was no answer for a time. Then, four months later, came the news that a publisher was willing, nay, anxious, to take the book. That was the beginning.

16

THE FACTS OF FICTION

by Monica Dickens

NOTHING in a novel can be completely invented. Everything must have been seen or heard or felt or read. All I'm going to do is try to show you how the facts of an author's life become the fiction of his books. You can create a quite imaginary character, but he must have a nose and eyes and legs, like an actual person. Even in science fiction, if your invented character is a Martian, with one eye, antennae for ears, and wings on his feet, his non-reality has to be explained in real terms: eye, antennae, wings—since those are the only terms in which the author and the reader can communicate.

Reality and invention

There is no fiction. All fiction is fact, molded, manipulated and enriched by the author's imagination. All authors write about what they know; some of them don't know very much, and keep writing the same book over and over again, as you've probably noticed. Others, like William Faulkner, John Marquand, John O'Hara, Louis Auchincloss, know quite a lot, but deliberately choose to narrow their writing fields to what they know best.

Everyone thinks he would like to be a writer. It seems such an easy life—working in your own home on your own time; getting thousands of dollars for paperback and movie rights; jaunting all over the United States babbling your opinions to captive audiences.

People say things like: "I've always thought I could write a book. My friends all say I write such good letters." Or: "I've often thought I might scribble a bit in my spare time."

And you can't answer that letter writing and scribbling in your spare time have nothing to do with the sheer slogging agony of writing even a bad book. You agree: "Go ahead."

"But what should I write about?" they cry, not pleased by this encouragement, but alarmed to find themselves thus pinned down.

"Write about what you know."

The old cliché, "Everyone has one book in him", is true. (All clichés are true; that's what makes them so irritating.) Even if you live a restricted life in the back of nowhere, that's no handicap. Look at Jane Austen. Look at Louisa May Alcott. Both led sheltered and narrow lives. It was their vision of it that counted. Look at the Brontë sisters, imprisoned in their bleak moorland parsonage. *Jane Eyre* and *Wuthering Heights* came from the small feminine world of their experience plus the turbulent inner world of their imagination. Heathcliff is their brother Branwell, but he and Mr. Rochester are also the demon lovers of every woman's subconscious dreams.

Another question people often ask a writer is, "Did that scene in your book happen to you?" or, "Who was this or that character supposed to be?" Somerset Maugham answered this in his autobiography, *The Summing Up*:

> In one way and another, I have used in my writings whatever has happened to me in the course of my life. Sometimes an experience I have had has served as a theme, and I have invented incidents to illustrate it. More often I have taken actual people and used them as the foundation for characters of my own invention. Fact

and fiction are so intermingled in my work that, now, looking back on it, I can hardly distinguish one from the other.

John le Carré, author of *The Spy Who Came in from the Cold*, that brilliant book which started the whole tedious avalanche of less brilliant spy books, answers this way:

> Of course one must select physical and moral attributes from people one has met or seen. But writers should have the humility to realize we know almost nothing about each other. It's only our imagination that gives them life on the page.

That's why you can't describe people exactly as they are. Because you don't know. Also, people in books must be understandable. People in real life are more inconsistent. No one is always stupid or always clever, all bad or all good. The perfect wife and mother secretly lusts after the laundryman. The sadistic mass murderer loves children, and gets up out of a warm bed to let the cat in.

Daphne du Maurier echoes Maugham:

> A novel is made up of bits of experience, bits of emotion. Even imagination can come from some forgotten source—things heard or seen or felt as a child. It comes welling from within, impossible to say how it comes, or why. It just comes.

That's true of every novel. One moment, you've no idea what you're going to write next. The next, you're committed. Long before Daphne du Maurier bought the house in Cornwall (which became the setting for her great novel *Rebecca*), she used to wander about its garden, trespassing, and wondering about the owner, whose beautiful wife had died, and who was now, like Max in the book, married to a shy, much younger girl. Daphne du Maurier went to Egypt, and there, homesick for Cornwall, fused those remembered images all at once into the plot of *Rebecca*.

Another fine writer, Paul Gallico, recalls that he made one

visit to Assisi and was strongly moved by its atmosphere, which does make you feel that you might meet St. Francis around any corner. Months later, waiting for the lights to change at the corner of 46th Street and Madison Avenue, he suddenly thought of the boys and donkeys in the market place at Assisi, and between the red light and the green, the whole story of *The Small Miracle* came pouring into his head.

Propaganda and satire

Whatever his story, whoever his characters, each writer writes about what he knows. To illustrate this seemingly obvious but really rather complex truth, let's look at the various ways in which facts become fiction. First, there is the novel of pure propaganda. *Uncle Tom's Cabin,* of course, is an obvious example, as is a lot of Charles Dickens: *Little Dorrit,* propaganda against the prison system; *Nicholas Nickleby,* against the schools; *Oliver Twist,* against the Poor Law; *Bleak House,* against the tortoise processes of the Courts.

Second, we have the novel of satire, which isn't as dedicated as propaganda, but isn't objective reporting either. Almost any novelist with any humor has elements of satire in his comments on the world he sees. Sinclair Lewis had this brilliant gift for observing the details of the American scene in the 20's and 30's. *Main Street, Babbitt, Arrowsmith, Elmer Gantry* present a satirical record of Midwest America. Modern satire is lighter, sharper, funnier, in the hands of people like Tom Wolfe, and in things like "Dr. Strangelove", and also more destructive. All the devilishly clever young men in slick magazines and on television poke fun at established things, and having torn something down, they have nothing to erect in its place.

Then we have the novel in which history is turned into fiction. Sometimes one person or incident in history is the novel's theme, as in Somerset Maugham's *The Moon and Sixpence,* where his real-life model was Gauguin. Rebecca West's latest book, *The*

Birds Fall Down, is based on a story she heard fifteen years ago, about a double agent and a fateful conversation in a train, which may have changed the whole course of the Russian Revolution.

All novels inevitably use the history of the times in which they are set, because the characters can't operate in a vacuum, but with books like *War and Peace* and *Dr. Zhivago* and *The Red Badge of Courage,* the facts of history and the fiction of the story are inseparable. Every war brings out novels from people who perhaps would have never written a book if they hadn't been driven by the need to communicate the most intense experience of their lives. And with the war more or less out of their system, some never write anything as good again. Take, for instance, Irwin Shaw, James Jones, Norman Mailer. I don't think one of them has lived up to the promise of *The Young Lions, From Here to Eternity, The Naked and the Dead.*

Truer than life

It is an odd truth about all creative writing that if you describe things exactly as they are, they are often much less convincing than if you show them as you imagine them to be. This is why, although we're always being told that the novel is dead, people will always go on reading fiction. At its best, it seems more real than real life, and the novelist can have greater influence than the journalist.

Authors write not only about what they know but also about things that make a great impression on them. Charles Dickens is a good example of writers whose books are made directly from their own experience. The greatest influence in Dickens' life was his miserable childhood. When he was twelve, his father was shut up in the debtors' prison, and Charles was put out to work, "like a little labouring hind," as he describes it, in the warehouse of a blacking factory. Not only did he relive this traumatic experience through young David Copperfield's miseries in the warehouse of Murdstone and Grimsby, but the whole of his wretched childhood was burned so deeply into him that he never stopped writing about pathetic children. Little Nell, Pip, Oliver Twist, Paul Dombey—the list of Dickens' waifs is endless.

Many things in Dickens' books are easy to identify in his own life. To take only a few examples: His perpetually insolvent father was the original of Mr. Micawber. His mother, whom he despised because he felt she had let him down, was shown as Mrs. Nickleby. The first great love of his young life, a capricious girl called Maria Beadnell, was the model for David Copperfield's child-wife Dora. And twenty-five years later, when he again met Maria, now fat and middle-aged, he vented his disillusionment by creating the absurd Flora Finching in *Little Dorrit*.

Experience between covers

My own start as a writer came directly from events in my own life—so much so, that if a couple of things hadn't happened to me, I wouldn't have written one book, much less eighteen.

The first thing was that my mother tried to make me a debutante. I was hugely fat at the time and hated going to debutante balls, because nobody danced with me. I rebelled against the Season. I would have a job. What as? I was trained for nothing. I'd been expelled from high school for refusing to wear the uniform, expelled from finishing school in Paris for refusing to be finished, and expelled from a dramatic school for not being able to act. The easiest thing seemed to be cooking. You could learn as you went along. So I wrote myself some references and signed them with impressive names: "Lady Ogilvie wishes to recommend her cook, honest, sober, good plain cook, etc.", and went to an agency and said: "I'm a cook. What have you got?"

They had a lady who wanted someone to cook a six-course dinner for twelve people. I bought an apron and a cookbook. I was in business. You can imagine what happened. It was an elaborate dinner—and everything went wrong. I got there much too late, and everything that wasn't burned was half raw. I don't know what the guests thought, but the hostess told me what she thought when she handed me my 7/6 fee—about a dollar then —for the evening's disaster.

I didn't care. After the dinner, the other servants and I had a great party in the kitchen. I realized we were having much more fun than the guests upstairs, or, for that matter, than I had ever had at any party when I was a guest. I'd discovered what I wanted to be. I wanted to be a servant.

I went back to the agency and said: "I'm a cook-general now. Housemaid, parlormaid, kitchenmaid—whatever you have."

They had plenty. In two years, I had about twenty jobs. I found out you can stand anything as long as you know it's not forever. If I couldn't stand my employers, I'd leave something warming for them in the oven and go and work for someone else. I'd be doing it still, if the second thing hadn't happened: the maid next door took me to the local fireman's ball. There I met a young man who said: "What do you do?" When I told him, he said he worked in a publisher's office, and suggested I go see his boss. Did the boss need a good cook? No. The boss told me that if I would write a book about my experiences in other people's kitchens, they would publish it.

So I bought a notebook and pencil (didn't even know you had to type) and wrote the book in three weeks. (Now it takes me six months to a year to do a book.) I called it *One Pair of Hands,* after the despairing cry of all overworked maids: "I've only got one pair of 'ands, madam."

Since then, almost all my books have been about things that I've done in real life: hospital nursing, working in an aircraft factory during the war, reporter on a local newspaper, marriage into the Washington Navy, etc. And this is one of the best parts about being a writer: Nothing in life is ever wasted, because you can use it in a book. Sadness, boredom, disappointment. Even heartbreak. How can you write of these things unless you know them? As a critic once said of Scott Fitzgerald: "Even the breaking of his own heart was a sound to be listened to and enjoyed, like all the rest."

Writers' dream life

There is this "dreamself," this half unconscious element in writing. Readers read books for escape, but authors write them for escape, too. Into them they put what might have been, the way life could have gone, the person they secretly wanted to be.

The perfect example of this is Ian Fleming, who at forty-three began to write those fantasies of super-escape, the James Bond novels. To understand Bond, you have to understand Fleming. At school, he was overshadowed by his brilliant brother Peter. In self-defense, Ian made himself into a kind of eccentric dandy and forced himself to be a brilliant athlete. At this age, he already showed the paradox of self-indulgence and masochism which came out much later in Bond. And his vast and varied experience with girls was also given to Bond, together with Fleming's own sadistic take 'em and leave 'em attitude, which grew from antagonism toward a dominating mother.

In the war, he worked for Naval Intelligence. He learned judo and karate and all the James Bond tricks in a school for sabotage. Some of the half-crazy, half-possible tricks he suggested to the Navy—like parachuting into Berlin to kill Hitler—are also recognizable in the books, where the exploits are fantastic, but always there's a glimmer of possibility.

After the war, he lived in Jamaica and married. One day, his wife wanted to keep him quiet while she was painting, so she said: "Go away and write a book." He went into his study, and in ten weeks he came out with *Casino Royale* and the extraordinary James Bond. Bond is Fleming, but in reverse. He is the uncomplicated man of action, "that blunt instrument", his creator called him, while Fleming was a complicated neurotic dreamer, dreading old age, wanting always to be something he wasn't, wanting to be younger, healthier, handsomer. Bond is the dreamself. When he looks at himself in the mirror, the face he sees is the face of the younger Ian Fleming.

If you feel like writing a book—and everybody does at some time or other—but you don't know what on earth you should write about, just write about what you know.

17

A TIME TO LIVE, A TIME TO WRITE

by Sylvia Wilkinson

WHEN I finally saw my first novel between covers, what struck me most was the finality of the printed page . . . it was too late to mark out those adjectives and too late to have the pollen falling off the trees in the right season in Chapter 4. The familiar, unruly stack of papers I knew well had become a neat little package that took me thirteen years to write and would take anyone about two hours to read, two hours I've been unable to devote to it yet. I looked at the novel then as if I'd found it under a rock or on the sidewalk; now, over a year later, I am trying to recollect how it all came about. Thus follows an attempt to reconstruct the process of writing a novel. Actually I relate only the major points . . . omitting spreading the manuscript on the floor and cutting and taping the parts together, or searching the mailboxes across the countryside looking for a name for a character, or reading four books on the habits of spiders. The list of particulars is endless, so I will try to deal with the particulars that I believe are generalities, aiming toward the person who is trying to channel in some manner his urge to write a novel.

The journal—subjective history

My first suggestion is the journal. Start it as young or old as you are now; don't hide it so well you can't find it when you tire of it, and go back and reread what you wrote. Often when I sit at the typewriter struggling with a paragraph, a sentence or even a word, I feel a complete loss of perspective. I suddenly don't know where my writing is going but, most frightening, where it has been; and all I have is a lame passage in front of me that can't get out of its own way. Then I turn to the journal, all the scattered writings accumulated over the years since the seventh grade when I wrote: "The ship was caught in a blizzard, the captain ran around like a lizard." You will discover that the journal is a great place to "get it out of your system," all the undisciplined outbursts that can't go into novels, papers, or even letters to a friend. In the journal, anything goes; you don't have to be afraid of what you say, of criticism, of humiliation—not unless you happen to be a masochist. And, most important, in the journal you will discover *seeds*—things that impressed you but that you were unable to understand at the time, or a funny story someone told you, all part of your subjective history that can start your imagination going.

I choose a page from my journal for illustration:

all snowflakes are different, so are fingerprints

the female spider destroys the male, is larger, only one who spins web, hunger stronger than love

Uncle X got his finger caught in the candle holder on the back of the pew in church and had to send Papa home for a screwdriver to get it off

if the summer is too dry the trees turn brown without colors first

What would have made for a bad encyclopedia entry ended up generating two chapters in my second novel. Often as not you will find that the little seed that started the idea in your novel will disappear entirely, but in the process of disappearing, it set your imagination off down a path it might never have traveled without a familiar guide, some remnant from your own personality. Randall Jarrell once asked our class if we had a great many of our best thoughts and inspirations just before we fell asleep at night. When we all agreed that yes, it was true, he then told us to leap from bed and write them down in a journal, for they might disappear into a dream and be lost forever. How many times we remember the color and intensity of a dream but are never able to verbalize it or even reconstruct its image when we awake fresh, our minds flabby and untroubled.

Imagination and memory

A great part of writing for me is learning how to stimulate the *imagination,* to generate the energy that is there but toned down and muted while I wash dishes or ride a bike. I for one don't want the intensity of the *act of writing* possessing me twenty-four hours a day and would prefer to choose a time for writing instead of attempting to float around a teeming mass of perception. I consider it a part of the writer's self-discipline to achieve a time to live and a time to write, and I have a rather colorless and unromantic vision of the writer with sweat on his brow instead of a heavenly light in his eyes.

While the journal serves as a source of written imagination, the true power of the imagination is hidden in the unwritten— for me, in memory. Memory is the path through the senses or a thought, a fascinating form of backtracking. I never smell vinegar without thinking of dyeing Easter eggs and putting on those little decals that always smeared. And there was the sound of my grandmother scuffing her bare feet on the floor when she was warming up to tell me a story, or my mother letting me taste a wad of biscuit dough, or the color of my outgrown taffeta dress darting through the tobacco rows on one of the little tenant girls. These are the bits and snatches, the door-openers to prose, but a novel doesn't come from stitching these pieces together. Hopefully, the sense impression will start the prose tumbling along, and not be an incident but an instigator. The temptation to splice together moments is always there, with my first novel unavoidable, since the novel had come to me in bits over such an extensive period, leaving my only hope for organization my consistency as a human being.

Actually, all a young writer can hope for is a consistent *growth* with constant questioning of his own attitudes and values, and the strength and good judgment to turn loose from what he has outgrown. After all, at twelve most of us thought "Trees" was a pretty good poem. Although I was able to discard a lot of the horses and Indians from my junior high original, I still ended up with quite a few horses and Indians. But it is certainly to be considered the contrary of tragic when a young writer bursts the seams of his original idea and sees his great philosophical novel is just another dead horse.

The second phase of memory writing is more dangerous, I think, but like most dangerous ventures, more rewarding. When you first start exercising your memory for the specific purpose of fiction, you will probably find an overwhelming tendency for your thoughts to turn only to the shocking and sad incidents, for they are the ones printed the deepest in your memory. Seeing the face of your grandfather in his coffin; running from the bull in the pasture and hearing his breath behind you; or losing your pet dog will at first come to you, all valuable memories but all in the same high key. You will have to struggle harder for the quieter realizations, searching out the turning points in your thinking that came more gradually. But with practice and experience, when your mind starts to work as a prose writer's mind must work, you will select and choose, control and pace those memories of feelings until you will see them take on a completeness in fiction they never had in life.

Place and people

Next for me is the importance of *place*. I must know the seasons, the flowers and bugs or lack of such, the color of the earth; and I must know what *people* have done to the place. My place happens to be rural North Carolina, yours may be New York City or Arizona; but whatever the place, your awareness of it accounts for far more than a tapestry to pin characters to. Go to a favorite or familiar setting . . . go three times and each time record your reaction to this place. . . . The place is the same, the reaction is different, and you have made a discovery. *Place* has told you a great deal about *character.*

This may oversimplify the writer's response to place, but it can be safely said that knowing place will determine direction, and in the course of finding direction, you will get to know your character. For example, think how much you learn about your grandmother when you take her from her familiar chair in her living room to a chair in your living room. She contrasts, and by seeing what something *isn't,* you see what it *is.* In *A Killing Frost,* I took Miss Liz from her farm to the ocean; as soon as I got her there she wanted to go home—she was afraid—and in so doing I had learned something about Miss Liz. Also I chose to write the book in the dying season, when the old woman felt herself going the same path as the world outside; it would have been another book entirely if the season had been spring and Miss Liz's farm world had chosen to mock her instead of join her.

The character and his book

Lastly, there is *character,* which for me encompasses everything I have said about writing a novel. I create the character and then the book belongs to him. Through dialogue, responses to place, memories, physical description, actions, I feel the writer can come to know a character in much the way you can come to know a person, whether meeting him, reading about him, or writing about him. After a few chapters, with your guidance he takes on a life of his own, and from there on out, the writer's job is to be true to him, even if it means writing against the grain of the original idea. A living, illusive character is certainly worth more than a dead idea.

This is why I find beginning a book so difficult, for certain aspects will remain constant and I will have to be willing to live with them until I complete the book: the age or sex of my character, his relationship with the other characters, the season of the year, the location of his home—just simple, basic facts, yet decisions that commit me to follow a certain course of creativity for the months or years to follow. After the characters start to grow, I become their servant, not their master, and am obligated to give them the depth and breadth that they deserve and that they promise as fictional characters. Becoming the servant of a character doesn't make the writing easier; it makes it harder. As the character becomes complex so do his motivations and decisions, and so does your novel.

Personal views

I have covered what I consider the major aspects of writing a novel, and if I go on any farther, I will undoubtedly raise only problems and procedures that relate to me in particular, not the writer in general. For instance, I begin and end each work with a character; he brings his story along. The writer who starts with a story and then looks for a character to tell it will not find my method useful. Beginning and ending for me are painful; the middle, however, is a joy, for I feel the freedom of exploration. If my story starts to sag, I start inventing tricks to keep myself working. . . . I take out four sheets of paper and say to myself, no sleep until the pages are full. Or if my story goes flat, I think of the most exciting and thrilling incident I can, it happens to my character, the story starts moving again, and likely as not, the incident gets removed in revision. I have always welcomed revision time instead of despising it, because that is when I discover the writing that "happened" without a total consciousness. Then I have something fresh to work with that must be paced, intensified, or played down, expanded or cut—in other words, put into the shape it deserves. It's a good feeling to find something worth revising, and it somehow makes the whole struggle worthwhile.

In the category of personal pitfalls, my biggest is impatience. I'm as bad as the man who picks up the mystery and reads the last two pages: I want to know what is going to happen and I end my books too soon, making revision a doubly hard chore. Yet a writer never knows about himself until he does write that novel. He can expect some things to be frightening but also can expect some pleasant discoveries to take place at the typewriter, the existence of which he would not have known had he not attempted to write that novel. And in fiction a feeling becomes a sort of possession once it has been successfully verbalized. In closing, one last bit of advice: when you have asked as many as five questions about the novel you are planning to write, it's time to go on and do it. You're the only person who can teach you to write.

18

"I LOVED THE WAY YOU DESCRIBED
AUNT MARY . . ."

by Evelyn Hawes

OFTEN at a dinner, a cocktail party or at times even on the street, someone approaches a writer and says, "I loved the way you described Aunt Mary." Perhaps the name used is Uncle Walter, or Bill Higbee, "old Cousin Ruth," or even the ubiquitous "friend." That statement is guaranteed to send an author screaming into the woods. It may be the writer doesn't know Aunt Mary, or has met her along with several hundred others only once at a church social or civic function. If so, he is lucky. It is unfortunate if he *does* know Aunt Mary. She could be unhappy with what she believes is the writer's interpretation of her character. In fact, the family may stop speaking to him or consider suing in order to apply the unguent that only money can provide. The writer had no intention of projecting a complete picture of an actual person. It isn't done that way.

Possible and believable

The writer of fiction is not a newspaper reporter; he is not a detective seeking the facts of a case. The novelist neither attempts nor wants to describe a real scene or individual exactly;

126

he tries to avoid such exactness because he is well aware that his setting and cast of characters have never existed and never will exist anywhere but in his own mind. Of course, fictional people must have qualities common to mankind; the location of a story must be not only possible but believable. There is no problem here: human nature remains constant, and so do the forces of nature. There was a time when, studying Greek literature in depth, I was discouraged to find that people had not changed since the days of Homer, when even the gods were all too human. Now I find this fascinating. Technological progress is only frosting. Underneath there's the same old cake. Jack London's Klondike remains much as it was, even if one may fly over it in a jet, and there is always the possibility of coming to grips with nature that runs amuck.

A writer is an observer. He collects information (stories, scenes, what have you) in a ragbag mind. When he needs material, he goes through the ragbag, examines the bits and pieces, and puts them together. The result is a matter of his selection, and the way the subject is handled depends upon the author himself. The reader also responds according to his own personality and belief. A writer's tools are imagination and recall and words, which lead to communication, one hopes. A statistician works with figures and graphs and his common sense and intelligence. Each to his own.

When a reader sees his Aunt Mary in your work, it means that he has identified, for a little while, with you. That is highly desirable. Reading Shakespeare at any age is an awakening. One is apt to murmur, "How true, how *true*." True *then*: true *now*. But Shakespeare's works are not true to the facts, even though they were often based upon historical incidents. With a turn of phrase he can project reality—a reality that neither Shakespeare nor the reader (viewer) ever knew. The castle of Kronberg at Elsinore, setting of *The Tragedy of Hamlet, Prince of Denmark,* was never seen by Shakespeare, nor, certainly, was the long-dead Hamlet. But they live. We know the castle, we know the man. Shakespeare's *Antony and Cleopatra,* derived from "The Life of Marcus Antonius" in Sir Thomas North's translation of Plutarch's *Lives,* described a foreign clime, a foreign scene . . . and men and women. Shakespeare's Cleopatra is like no other. She lives, and she belongs to Shakespeare and the reader.

Edgar Rice Burroughs had not been in Africa when he wrote *Tarzan of the Apes.* Whether or not the book is true to Africa is not the point. Many generations of Americans not only believed in it, but risked neck and limb in backyard trees emulating the hero.

Impact is filtered through the writer. The action he describes is not as it *is,* but as he imagines it is or it might be. The fable of the six blind men who examined an elephant is pertinent here. One blind man fell against its side and thought it was a wall; a second, feeling the tusk, thought it a spear; the third, touching its trunk, thought it a snake; the fourth felt its leg and decided it was a tree; the fifth who happened to touch the elephant's ear insisted it was a fan; and the last, who grabbed its tail, swore it was a rope.

The word of the familiar

No one, certainly no writer, knows absolutely what is in another's mind. (Somerset Maugham suggested that if we did, we'd all become hermits.)

Then how do we know Aunt Mary? How do we describe her? We *do* go to the world of the familiar.

Was the father in my first novel, *The Happy Land,* my own father? Some would answer, yes. But my father was many things to many people. There were complaints that he was rather more positive with his daughters in the novel than he was in life. There were complaints by old friends that the entire family was made to seem too noble. No doubt. And yes, Father in the

novel was harder than he was in our home, and quite possibly
he was more "noble" in the novel. So, then, the character wasn't
really my father, was he? No, not really.

Did I ever meet a man like Mr. Ludmack, the villain in *The
Happy Land*? The answer is that I have known a number of
people with *some* of the qualities of Mr. Ludmack. I described
him in this way:

> I no longer hate Mr. Jasper A. Ludmack. I got over hating him
> the year I worked for my father. I watched him and I saw how it
> was with him. He was a bystander in life. He wanted to be great
> and good and brilliant and he could never be any of those things.
> Sometimes he tries to be great and good. He doesn't know how; he
> is limited. I am very, very sorry for him.

Do you recognize Mr. Ludmack? Is he the image of your Uncle
Victor? Let us establish this right now: I do not know your
Uncle Victor.

Are the conversations in fiction exact? Be reasonable. How
could they be? *I* can't remember what I said last year to a certain person about a certain problem. But I hope readers think
those conversations occurred, that they are true to life, even
if such an assumption alarms me.

If I write about a girl who is retarded, is it anyone I ever
knew and loved? No. I have known and loved many "excep-
tional" girls and boys. My character will be all of them, some
of them, and above all, an individual.

As far as setting is concerned, in *The Happy Land* a small
town is described in this fashion:

> The houses were built on the lower slopes of Big Iron mountain,
> and the valley was spread out before them. Main Street was at the
> edge of the valley; it was paved and so were the six blocks forming
> a T which led to the depot. All the streets in town were wide, but
> Main was the widest. It used to take so long for me to cross. My
> legs were shorter then.
> In the residential section there was a lot of dust in the streets in

summer. We had a water wagon, but something was always wrong with it. Fast-growing poplars had lined the board sidewalks, causing sewer trouble, until the elms and maples grew big. Then the poplars were cut down, and cement sidewalks were put in at the same time. Poplars were poor trees to climb; they grew straight up, with no spread.

The description fits the small town where I was raised except for some important differences. It also fits a great many small towns of the same vintage. Perhaps you recognize it. I found such towns in Idaho, Kentucky, Michigan—all across the country.

A snowstorm is a snowstorm, whether it's in Buffalo or Boston, with some differences. A mountain is a mountain, yet no two are alike. Where does the familiar come in, and how does the writer use it? He takes the specific, veers to the general (a number of mountains he has seen), goes back to *his* specific, and includes the geographical location and terrain necessary for verisimilitude, plot, and character development—the latter being the most vital factor in fiction. Often, in the writing, the character takes over from the author and becomes a force that actually does seem to move mountains. One knows instinctively what that character would or would not do, and he becomes unique.

Certainly the familiar is the mainstream of the writer's consciousness, but he is not bound by it, and must not be. The familiar is patterned to fit the plot; it is changed; it is enlarged; it may be so beautiful or so coarsened that another observer would not recognize the subject. Unless one is writing science-fiction or an "original" fantasy such as J. R. R. Tolkien's *The Hobbit,* the familiar is just that. Familiar—not true.

A writer *ought* to be delighted to hear, "I loved the way you described Aunt Mary." It means Aunt Mary is real. But, you see, the author wants *his* Aunt Mary to live. And if he is a good writer, Aunt Mary *does* live.

19

NOVEL WRITER'S WORLD

by Margaret Forster

SOMEWHERE in my life there is a book-lined study in the center of a quiet house. I see myself walking into it, around ten in the morning, refreshed and ready to work. I sit down at the large leather-topped desk, take my manuscript from the bottom drawer. Perhaps I will work straight through until four in the afternoon; perhaps I shall break about noon and walk round the garden, thinking about the novel in progress as the feathered songsters of the air warble around me. The day is my own. I need only emerge from that study when and as I wish.

I suppose that at the age of seventy when my hands are too arthritic to hold a pen and I can hardly see the paper, this little dream may materialize, and then, who knows, a Novel That Matters might finally break through. As it is, I go on producing Novels That Do Not Matter in conditions that should cheer all those slaves who are sure they could write a novel if only they had the time, the peace and the opportunity.

For a start, there is no study, office or any other kind of den to retreat to. I work at the kitchen table. Before I start work, I have to clear away the dishes and wash them (can't work with dirty dishes around, none of that sort of thing, thank you).

I keep my tatty bits of paper in a folder wrapped in a sheet of newspaper and stuck up on a shelf between the flour and the sugar, like a bundle of fish and chips. It's the only place high enough to be safe. I put the ink bottle on the tray of the baby's high chair and make a great show of spreading out my pen, paper and paper clips. Then I start, after carefully concealing the clock, the significance of which will emerge later.

That is it. Every night as I lift that pen a shattering scream pierces the literary air. My eighteen-month-old son is off on his evening shift—not quite as arduous as the night shift, which requires him to sound off every half hour, but pretty tough work all the same. The entire two hours I spend writing are punctuated by this magnificently efficient full stop. I've learned how to see to him and not be totally put off, but the interruptions of my three-year-old daughter are harder to weather. I see the head coming round the door and think, oh, Lord, maybe if I do go on writing she will go away. She never does. It's better to stop at once and start the psychological warfare. I swear that none of my novels has ever been written in anything but fifteen-minute snatches.

With all this to fight against, I tell myself I must be strong. God, I must be strong. I've never sat down not exhausted after that usual daily round of a housewife's which has been so well documented. I wrote *Georgy Girl* while I was seven months pregnant and feeling lousy. *The Travels of Maudie Tipstaff* was written when I was six months pregnant and feeling even worse —and my husband was in bed with jaundice for six weeks. So no feeble excuses from you, sir, about how you do a full day's work and when you get back from the office you're so tired. You can write anywhere, whatever the conditions. With all these men writers withdrawing into sunny seclusion in the Bahamas for six months to write their great opus, this seems to me worth stating.

A person in mind

You must by now think I'm on dope of some kind, or at least mistress of a fiendish system to take me through. I don't have any system. I have no plan, no outline, and no notes. I don't know, when I start, what I am going to write. I never think about it when I'm not writing. What I do have is a person in my mind who has set me off thinking about some aspect of his or her life. It is always a person I know only slightly, and always someone I see duplicated around me. I take the person and the thing that connects her with everyone else—with Georgy it was girls who want marriage but not necessarily a man, except as the means to the end; with Maudie it was parents being excluded from their children's lives, though neither side wants it to happen. I just think very hard about that person, literally imagine I am that person—and the rest follows. The fun is in seeing exactly what will come—or rather, who, because the minor characters invent themselves fast and furiously.

I write very quickly. I work for two hours, three nights a week, four months a year. I never sit and look at the paper, but get cracking immediately, averaging 2,000 words an evening. I never, ever, read what I have written—always finishing at the bottom of a page and beginning the next night at the top of a new one. This has hilarious consequences: Mary becomes Janet and ends up as Jane; six o'clock strikes loudly hard on seven; and the sunset invariably follows bang after a dawn chorus. (That's what they call pace.) I can't remember why I made this rule, but it was a stroke of genius. The loss in little details is well worth the gain of a fresh entity each night, and makes for continuity, rather than the lack of it, because it means I have to keep the main thread very firmly in hand all the time. I am sure, too, that it has other blessings. If I read what I'd written, I'd never write another word, I'd be so depressed.

The actual mechanics of what I write are saddening. My standards are of the lowest. I am very easily bored. I pass on quickly from one scene to another because I think, oh, God, I'm so fed up, let's get on. Laboriously, I write a few pages of description to give it tone; then I decide I'd better break the page up, and I rush into dialogue. I push in the odd simile and metaphor every time I'm really pausing before going on to some real stuff. Never at any time am I so involved that I don't know where I am, or anything like that. I sit and fidget and stare around and think about everything dispassionately as I write.

I try hard to write simply, to make my sentences short and terse. My first-ever novel was 450 pages long and was so pseudo-Dickens, Balzac, etc., that I tripped over the purple passages as they fell out. When I'd torn that up, I thought, *Right, lesson learned: be stark; you aren't capable of anything else.* Oxford had tried to teach me that. When I went up, I wrote fabulous hyperbole: "King John, whose very name conjures up dark shadows, was one of the most dastardly Kings ever to rule that medieval sink of iniquity called England." It had grieved me very much to have that pruned to, "King John was reputed to be a bad King. He ruled England at a difficult time." But it wasn't until I'd covered the ground that I really saw my limitations and realized that all I could manage were words of one syllable and sentences without additional clauses. For me, this is a necessary thing. When I do get going and the brakes slip, it isn't too drastic if the bulk of the novel is restrained.

To someone as lazy as I am, with no plot worked out, technique becomes everything. I've never consciously thought about anything as high sounding as technique, but I'm aware these days that I must have learned a lot in the process of writing six novels. With my first, I had revealed all by page ten—or rather, as I had no "all" to reveal, I'd made this obvious by page ten. Now, I've noticed, I've got cunning. I approach characters obliquely, deliberately laying trails that I hug to myself and long to follow up when I get to a slack bit. The slack bits themselves have become fascinating. I sit there, knowing I am padding something out, and then, through the sheer grind of marking time, to my pleasure something good comes out. I find dialogue is beginner's joy. It is a bit too easy, simply a matter of seeing the people in front of you and listening to them. But narrative is harder. Then, the reporting and observation count for nothing, and you are solely concerned with being the person.

A novelist's motives

You will gather, from all this, that I write for myself, pure and simple. If, in the process, I get what I write published, that is very nice, because a book is a satisfyingly real memento of my enjoyment. But I don't want to know if anyone has read it, or what people think. Writing is private—not personal, but private. I'm indifferent to what people say about my books, simply because the writing is an experience now over, closed. I can't bear writers who want to talk about what they are writing, or who seem to write for attention and encouragement. I don't think any writer with motives like that should write.

When I finish a novel, I do read it (bully for her!) before I send it to be typed. I usually bawl my head off and feel dreadfully depressed. Realizing time after time that I am a third-grade writer is awful. I read it and think how good it could have been, but I don't make excuses any more. That study, those notes, that peace wouldn't make the slightest bit of difference. It's a question of stature, of depth. All I can do is entertain. I have neither the ability nor the power to give people an experience. But on the other hand, this has its compensations. Writing is no struggle for me, because I'm not striving. For great writers it is anguish as they battle away. I regard it as a pleasant way of amusing myself. I'll always be sad that that is all it is. (Pause for weeping.)

What is inexcusable is that I don't at least try to work on my stuff. Every novel remains shoddy and superficial. Always, this is just going to be a first draft. Always, that's it.

The urge to write is nonetheless very real—only slightly less than the urge to read. It was through reading I came to writing. I've always read voraciously, and after reading a really great book, I'd feel elated and thrilled and burning with the desire to write one just as good. I still have this feeling of excitement about writing, even though what I turn out is mundane in comparison with the stuff that continues to inspire me. Often, I'm so tired, I think I really can't write tonight. If I don't, I feel gloomy and cheated. If I force myself to overcome the fatigue, it's fantastic how it refreshes me. It seems to give me energy rather than having me give energy to it. Proves something.

20

EVERY NOVEL IS LIKE ANOTHER PLANET

by Hannah Lees

THERE are as many ways of writing a novel as there are novelists. I always have in the back of my mind something François Mauriac once said: "Every novelist ought to invent his own technique, that is the fact of it. Every novel worthy of the name is like another planet, whether large or small, which has its own laws just as it has its own flora and fauna." To me this says it all. No one can tell anyone else how to go about writing a novel beyond saying: You take a pile of paper (I prefer yellow) and sit down at a desk with a pen or pencil or typewriter (I type). Then, as another novelist said, "You start putting black on white (or yellow)." You can't, that is, start writing a novel until you have some words to look at.

Maybe you'll start making notes on your characters. Maybe you'll start describing a situation or place or happening. For a story does have to have characters and situations, and things do have to happen. Even if your novel is made up entirely of the complex irrational feelings of a schizophrenic, it is still the story of how a schizophrenic feels. You can start anywhere, but you do have to start somewhere.

One way to start, my way in fact, is with characters. A novel, however beautifully and poetically written, is only as interesting as the person or people who come to live in it, and they do have to come to life. A character has characteristics. (I am now faced with the decision of whether to say *he* or *she* or *they*—the greatest weakness of the English language, and since this is the day of women's lib, I feel disinclined to say *he* all the time, and *they* doesn't work. I'm going to try the experiment of saying *she* all the way through.) She has a personality. She does or says things. And it is because of what she says or does that things happen. Or things can happen to *her*. Either way that is your plot. But then when things happen, she has to react, and you, the novelist, have to decide what the reaction will be. Elizabeth Bowen, in her "Notes on the Novel," says that the way she evolves her plots is to think of every possible way a character can react, and then discard them one by one until all that's left is the one way that particular character could react to that particular situation.

Before you get to that, of course, you have to know a great deal about your character: age, sex, color of hair and eyes, features *and* personality and character. Some of this can develop as you go along. Characters change as you get into your fictional situations—the very change is often the main storyline of the novel—but you have to start with some assumptions, and as the characters change, you have to make sure they can reasonably change in that particular way.

I start a novel with a few characters, not too many. You can bring in as many as you can comfortably cope with later on, but start simple. I taught a brief course on the novel at a writers conference last summer and had about fifteen budding novelists submit plots and first chapters. The variety was incredible. "Every novelist has to invent his own technique. . . ." and they did, and many of the plots were quite interestingly conceived, but all except a few had much too much happening much too fast, too many people and situations jumping at you far too soon.

I don't say start slow. The more dramatically you start, the better, of course, but keep the plot simple to begin with.

Write yourself a letter

Start with one character who interests you and who will probably be a combination of people you know or would like to know. Write yourself a letter about that character: what she (or he) does, thinks, feels, looks like, works at, enjoys playing with. Then your character has to have a husband, wife, friend, lover or enemy, maybe children. So you have to write yourself letters about them and their relationship to your main character, and pretty soon you have the beginning of a plot. You'd better think a good deal about what has happened to her (him—it doesn't seem to be working to say *she* all the time) before we meet her (him). It isn't absolutely necessary to write all that down, but it helps. You can't write many pages before you have to know whether your character has been to college or not, what kind of childhood, where from, what kind of life up to now. You don't have to tell the reader all this at once; in fact you mustn't, but the picture is going to have to emerge gradually, so you do have to know.

It isn't necessary to know the end of your novel when you start, but it helps if you know before you are too far along. Not that it will necessarily be the ending you end up with, but in a general way, it can give you something to work toward. You have to get from here to there, and, as you think about it, possible episodes, conversations, confrontations, conflicts will leap to your mind. So write yourself notes about them. Before I really start writing page 1, I am apt to have a whole sheaf of notes about characters and about things I have decided may happen to them, about potentially interesting situations, relationships, even snatches of conversation. I am bound to discard a lot of them as I go along and find other more interesting situations or relationships, but they give me something to start on.

The important thing is to start and to keep reminding yourself that this isn't necessarily the way it is going to be later on.
Many writers are blocked—I have been—by the feeling that
someone is looking over their shoulders saying, "What tripe!"
Well, you're often going to feel, "What tripe!" as you write, and
you're going to squirm. But you'll also have moments of feeling,
"What genius!" which keep you going, and the only way to get
to something that is finally valid is by trial and error. You
mustn't be afraid you'll be stuck with what you first write. You
can always throw most of it into the wastebasket and keep the
little nugget of gold. But you mustn't keep on throwing everything into the wastebasket or you'll never start. Actually, I confess to throwing very little into the wastebasket in the beginning,
even when I make a fresh start. I'm always afraid I'll throw away
something I may want later on.

Let yourself go

Don't be afraid of overwriting to begin with. You can always
cut and prune later. Just let yourself go. If you feel you are
really floundering, you are probably trying to tell too much too
soon, or don't really know enough yet about where you're going.
But the important thing is to get something down on paper to
look at. I don't mean an outline. Some people can work only
with an outline. I can't, but I can write a scene roughly and then
skip to another scene and another scene and another, and fill the
intervals in later on.

Part of what I meant when I said, don't be afraid of overwriting, was, don't be afraid in the beginning to say right out
what's happening and what people are feeling. In your second
draft, you can think of ways of letting the reader know through
conversation or significant small actions. In the end you can't
just say, "John was angry." Or, of course you can, but it's a lot
better to show him being angry. Your readers are intelligent, so
don't insult their intelligence by telling them too much. Leave

them with a certain amount to figure out from what has already happened. Half the fun of reading a novel is feeling, "But, of course, now I understand, because. . . ." But the "because" may be back fifteen pages or never actually stated at all. You just know by then what the scene or character is all about. In the beginning, however, you may have to spell it out to yourself, though every now and then there is the marvelous experience of having a situation you've created suddenly imply something tremendous you hadn't thought of at all beforehand.

After I've finished my first rough draft or partway through the second draft, I take a big sheet of shelf paper and divide it up into squares or oblongs and put the characters down one side, and time and place—day by day, week by week, or year by year, depending on the kind of novel—across the top. Then I start trying to fill in what each character is doing at any given time, and when the various ones coincide. That way I don't have Hortense going to bed with someone in January '65 and having a baby in June '64. Not, incidentally, that going to bed always leads to pregnancy. In too many novels, a woman has one love experience and immediately gets pregnant. It ain't necessarily so. But even if she doesn't, it is normal for her to worry about it unless she is on the pill.

Bringing characters to life

Your characters have to come to life, or you won't have a novel. They all have to think and feel and talk and act, and each one has to do it in quite a different way or you won't have characters. The only way is to get inside their skins and look out through their eyes and try to talk with their tongues. It isn't as hard as it sounds, if you have your characters at all well thought out. What's your creative imagination for? You just have to keep asking yourself (as Elizabeth Bowen said): Would he do that? Would she say that? It doesn't matter how unexpected or even bizarre the action or speech is; actually the more unexpected and bizarre, the better, as long as it is a possible reaction for that particular character. As, for example, perfectly well brought-up teen-agers or college students today may quite casually say four-letter words, but their parents wouldn't, unless you have already established them as the kind of people who may be that vulgar or that liberated.

Don't be afraid to write what you've seen or heard, known, or experienced. Your family and friends are going to think you've put them in your book anyway. They want to think so. They're bound to read themselves into it. So go ahead and use their experiences or characteristics. Obviously, you can't put your husband or wife or lover or friend down verbatim. But you can put what they have said or done into some different character. You almost have to. A novel is the sum total of what you've learned about life.

When I was in my early twenties, I wrote about forty pages of an autobiographical novel, all about my own very personal (I thought) adolescent struggles and pain and yearnings. It never got beyond that, but I showed it to my sister. She read it with rapt, and very flattering attention, then looked at me awestruck. "How did you know all that about *me?*" she asked. And we couldn't possibly be more different people.

You have to decide fairly early on, from what viewpoint you are going to tell your story. You can shift to seeing and telling it through various different characters' eyes and mouths, but each time you can tell only what that character would see or hear or know or understand. It is better not to involve too many viewpoints, though you can, of course, tell your story from the author's omniscient height, viewing each character or situation as it comes along. The most superb example I know of a special viewpoint is in Faulkner's *The Sound and the Fury*. Most of the novel is viewed through the eyes of a mental defective, and while never telling anything this very limited human would not register, it tells a highly complex story of love and hate and despair. This is very difficult, highly skilled writing. I don't suggest it as a technique for just anyone, but it is as good an example as I know of what is meant by viewpoint.

Does a book have to have an attitude? I think it has more impact if it has. I don't mean a message, but a personal philosophy, and it almost has to be your philosophy, because you're writing it. Your novel should be a new experience to readers. They should feel, when putting it down, that they know something about life, however small, that they didn't know before in quite that way. Because isn't that why writers write novels, unless they're frankly writing to formula to make money? And I can't tell you how to do that, because I don't know. If I did, I'd now be rich and famous. A great many years ago I wrote three mystery novels that people liked a good deal. I had a fine time writing them and made a certain amount of money, and I realized then that I should be able to go on writing mystery stories and making money and maybe get famous for it. But I had the misfortune of wanting to write a book that *said something*, that gave my own special view of life. And I did. It didn't make nearly as much money as the mystery stories, though it sold fairly well, but it was an entirely different experience. I tried to go back to writing mystery stories, but I couldn't. People are still asking me when I am going to write them another mystery to put them to sleep, and I answer, "Never, because I don't want to put you to sleep."

I guess, deep inside, I just didn't want to turn out story after story and get rich and famous. I tried to, but just couldn't, and as a result I had a fiction block for more years than I care to tell. Recently I wrote a book that told some of what I had learned about life in all that time. It didn't sell well at all, but most of those who did read it liked it so much, it was worth all the time and pain it cost. I guess in my unconscious I just didn't want to be rich and famous. (I've always felt it would be kind of awkward in all sorts of ways.) I just wanted to say something, however long it took me to get around to it.

But no matter what makes you want to write a novel, whether to "say something" (You can be an awful bore trying to do this, unless you can do it lightly; Shaw once said, "My method is to take the utmost trouble to find the right thing to say, and then to say it with the utmost levity.") or to entertain or make money, I think most of what I've said applies to the process. I've been trying to think, as I've gone along, whether it all applies to the contemporary far-out novels that are being produced. But, however diffuse or subjective or inside out or upside down, a novel has to be about people, or even if it's about insects or Martians, it has to say something about people, so maybe what I've said here does apply after all. At all events, take courage, brace yourself, and put down the first word. Every novel—is like another planet. Your planet.

21

THE CORNERSTONE OF THE NOVEL

by Anton Myrer

A GREAT deal has been written about the importance of accurate, credible setting and locale in fiction, of the need for painstaking research and observation, detailed journal entries, and so on. This is indispensable advice for the novice—and many is the veteran who has learned these lessons through grim experience; but less attention has been paid, it seems to me, to the vastly more crucial problem of credibility of character.

Moments of crisis

It has been said that character is the cornerstone of fiction. When we think of the great American novels of the past century and our own, it is their heroes and heroines who leap to mind —and our mind's eye instantly conjures up the scenes in which they face their moments of crisis: Natty Bumppo standing in the prisoner's dock, rebuking the implacable Judge Temple; old Ahab raging as his whaleboat is shaken playfully to and fro in the jaws of Moby Dick; Gatsby and Buchanan tensely facing each other in that sweltering room at the Plaza, with the hilarity of the wedding party floating up from the ballroom below. These are the people and the moments that make these novels live for

us. They continue to move us because there are no inconsist-
encies in their characterizations to suspend our credulity in them,
and because the conflicts which involve them are powerful and
inevitable.

Every writer has his own way of coming to the core of a novel,
the germinating idea which sets in motion the creation of that
particular world. For me, each novel seems to spring from a
sharply envisaged confrontation between two people from different backgrounds and with violently opposed aims or views—
and then everything builds in arduous accretion from that focal
point: forward and backward. This is admittedly a highly un-
orthodox attack, but the resultant problem is typical enough:
How to endow one's characters—particularly if they come from
diverse social backgrounds—with an actuality the reader will
accept without question.

Observe, study, listen

To the developing writer I would say first of all: Observe.
Observe, and study, and listen with the greatest of care. Train
yourself the way a baseline coach trains himself to watch cease-
lessly every detail, every movement of the opposing infield and
outfield, the pitcher, his own hitter. Observe a person's hands, his
facial expressions, his bodily movements, as though he were the
last man you might ever lay eyes on. We are (automation's en-
croachments notwithstanding) all of us individuals, each with his
own idiosyncrasies and attitudes—and it is the rendering of these
sharp particularities which helps establish the reader's credulity,
the lifeblood of fiction. A friend of mine has gained tremendous
control over his emotions (he is a prominent foreign service officer), but two fine white crescents appear just outside his nostrils
when he becomes angry or distraught; a young girl I know draws
down the corners of her mouth and narrows her eyes when she
is surprised. These are unique actions, and they have already
found their way, in very different contexts, into my work.

Secondly, always be on the lookout for the unexpected—the

often elusive detail that may make a person memorable. To give a brief example: Some years ago I stopped for gas in a small town in the Midwest. The attendant, a rather handsome, sullen boy, was not paying attention to the automatic shutoff on the pump he was holding, and when it cut in, it splashed gasoline over the side of the car and my shoes. His apology was curt and perfunctory. Angrily I followed him into the station and while he was filling out the credit slip, I looked around idly, trying to think of something sufficiently cutting to say to him. There was the usual welter of gas station paraphernalia: parts manuals, girlie calendars, oil rags, a greasy jacket, discarded windshield wipers, old batteries, socket wrenches—and a copy of the collected poems of Edwin Arlington Robinson, lying open on a shelf behind the air compressor, with paper chits and matchbooks stuck in various places.

That stopped me. I forgot all about saying something sufficiently cutting; and while driving on west I kept asking myself: What kind of gas station attendant would pore over the poems of Edwin Arlington Robinson? A very unhappy attendant, probably—a boy of blasted hopes and wild desires, a boy who hated grease and the foul undersides of cars and who longed with all his heart and soul to sit in a café terrace on Montparnasse and write poems; a boy who had undoubtedly got into trouble with customers long before this. . . . Whether my suppositions were wrong or not (they probably were) is immaterial: supposition— often of the wildest kind—is the great springboard of fiction. The important thing for me was that the process of sympathetic conjecture, of identification, had begun. It was the germ that was much later to emerge in my novel *The Intruder,* in the character of Joe Castaldo, a cab driver who dreams of a world of sensibility and meaning he can never hope to attain.

Sympathetic conjecture

This gives rise to the third and most important element in the construction of character: empathy. Without it the odds against involving the reader are formidable. According to Webster, empathy is "the capacity for participating in or a vicarious experiencing of another's feelings, volitions or ideas and sometimes another's movements to the point of executing bodily movements resembling his." This is the crux—and the ultimate challenge—of fiction: How deeply, how richly, can you enter into the body and soul of your character? Give to the hero you choose —or who chooses you—the most painstaking study, for your novel may stand or fall on his unshakable reality. Try to "discover" everything you can about this person: the factual things —precisely what he looks like, where he lives, where he went to school, his home life as a child, his parents' social standing in the community, and so on. Jotting down thumbnail biographies can be very helpful.

Above all, *try to see the world through his eyes.* What are his fears, his hopes, his memories; what are his opinions about love, justice, courage, a man's chances in the world he knows? Was he in the war, has his best friend betrayed him, has an older brother been killed in a highway accident—and if so, what have any or all of these things done to him? You may like to develop your character as you progress in the novel, you may prefer to start with a fixed and unalterable dossier on him. Either way, what is demanded is the submergence of the author's personality in favor of the character's—a kind of temporary suspension of one's own identity.

It is often helpful if your character possesses some quality which is also yours. Jay Gatsby is the magnificent character he is largely because, although the backgrounds of character and author were substantially different, Fitzgerald was able to imbue Gatsby with his own sense of "outsiderness." This was something Fitzgerald felt acutely all his life, but in Gatsby he raised it to a higher power—with Gatsby it becomes an obsession that rules his life and actions utterly. When Daisy spurns him he is finished; he has nothing to live for. The terms are distended for the needs of the novel.

One of the dominant traits of my own nature is a deep-rooted sense of justice, springing from my New England background. The thematic demands of *The Intruder* led me to decide on this quality for Gardner Lawring—but in Lawring I tried to increase it to an overweening passion, an obsession which ultimately causes him to take the law into his own hands and seek vengeance on the man he believes has destroyed the fabric of his marriage and his life.

Occasionally the needs of a book may force the writer to work from whole cloth—that is, to create a character with qualities utterly different from or even opposed to his own. Nearly any veteran novelist would agree that this is one of the most difficult feats to bring off. An old friend of mine once told me, during one of those rare moments of self-revelation, that he was deeply troubled by the fact that he lacked the capacity to *feel*, to respond emotionally to an incident or a person. Years later this seemed right to me for the dominant characteristic of one of the protagonists in a novel of mine, *The Big War*—the withdrawn, introspective Newcombe, who regains his capacity for emotional commitment through the love of a girl he meets just before he is sent overseas. All well and good; but I myself have a highly emotional, highly committed nature. It was the most difficult characterization I ever attempted—and Newcombe is not a successful portrait.

Of course there are hundreds of ways to build characters. The writer may give to several characters in the same work differing aspects of his own nature, as Dostoyevsky is said to have done with the three Karamazov brothers. (This attack is predicated on the most ruthless and accurate self-analysis; in fact, it goes without saying that incessant observation and understanding of one's own nature is a primary requisite for a writer.)

Fusing the elements

The novelist may also fuse elements of several different actual people (including himself) into one character. In an early draft of *The Big War,* it became abundantly apparent to me that my hero, Kantaylis, was too wooden, too monolithic in his sturdy resilience and goodness of heart. All at once I realized I had "frozen" on the memory of my model, a man I had been fond of who had been killed. Without being aware of it, I had fallen victim to the simplest of creative fallacies: my sentimental attachment to a dead friend had blinded me to the fictive lacks of my character in terms of the novel. I melted Kantaylis down then and recast him completely, drawing on elements from two other men I had known, so that his great moral sense became at the same time an oversevere inflexibility of attitude, and ultimately led to his death. In succumbing to this flaw, he became more human, and more properly fulfilled the thematic intentions of the novel.

Tolstoy's law

Another extremely important (and often overlooked) device is the matter of emotional preparation, of letting the reader come to know your character, become sympathetically involved with him, *before* he is plunged into a situation of crisis. I like to call this method—quite arbitrarily—Tolstoy's Law, because he did it so masterfully and because he rarely violated it. The death in battle of little Petya in *War and Peace* is merely pathetic, of itself. What renders it unbearably poignant to us is that we have had ample opportunity to see him playing with Natasha and Sonia in the Rostov home, sleigh-riding and singing at the piano, serving as a cavalry subaltern and wondering romantically about battle; at the moment of his death, we have become almost as fond of him as Tolstoy was—and so we can accept perfectly Denisov's animal howl of anguish when he turns away from the boy's body and clutches the fence.

Needless to say, there are many other ingredients that work for the construction of believable characters in fiction—a quick sense of mime, a keen ear for dialogue and the rhythms of speech, a wide-ranging speculative ability, the careful study of the great psychological masters old and new. In the last analysis, however, the decision lies with the imagination of the writer: his power to give us characters larger than himself, people who become to us—as they must to him—more vivid and entrancing for the brief, vicarious reign of the novel than our friends or acquaintances in the "real" world outside.

Soon after the publication of *The Big War,* a young writer said to me unhappily, ". . . but I never was *in* a war! Nothing like that ever happened to me. . . ." To which I could only reply: Read Stephen Crane's *The Red Badge of Courage,* which is still the most eloquent war story ever written by an American—and it was written before Crane had ever seen a battle. Melville knew whaling as no other novelist before or since—but his portrait of the demonic Captain Ahab is an imaginative descent into the deeps of the human soul that no amount of sheer "experience" could prepare any writer for.

Therefore, I said to the young writer, as an older novelist once exhorted me: be bold; dare everything. Observe, and listen, and take copious notes, and be perpetually watchful for the unexpected revelation of character that can transform the casual encounter . . . but above all, trust the intensity of your emotion. We may not all of us become Balzacs, asking after our characters on our deathbeds as if they were old friends; but if we care terribly enough about the people we have elected to carry our vicarious worlds, the chances are that many a reader will be caught by that same magic.

Special Fields

22

"I COULDN'T PUT IT DOWN"

by Phyllis A. Whitney

WHEN readers—young or adult—write me to say, "I just couldn't put it down," nothing could please me more. They can't know how hard I've worked to keep them turning my pages, and how many balls I've juggled in the air to hold interest high.

The high interest we call suspense is no chance matter. Neither does it belong exclusively to the mystery or so-called "suspense novel." Perhaps the degree is greater in the mystery, but it is necessary in all fiction. I am not dealing here with the modern "non-story," which is far from reader-oriented. The present-day success of suspense fiction, with its appeal to millions of readers, seems to indicate that most readers still want to be entertained and interested.

Active purpose

Tension keeps the reader turning the pages, and to have tension you must build suspense. Both grow from many things, but four ingredients are paramount: Problem, Purpose, Conflict, Goal.

All four are necessary. Three are fairly obvious, and anyone who means to write a short story or a novel is aware of the fact that there must be a problem, there must be conflict (or difficulties), and there must be a goal which the main character wants to reach. "Purpose" is hardly ever discussed, even by other names, yet it is one of the prime ingredients if you want to keep interest high *in every scene.*

A working definition of "purpose" as I use it here will be: *an attempt* to resolve. A problem and a goal may exist, but until the main character has an active purpose, until he attempts to take action and resolve some problem, there will be little interest, and conflict can come only in the form of outside attack. Even in a short story there are individual scene problems which lead eventually into solving the main problem. Your main character must take some action concerning these scene problems. He must have a purpose.

Every piece of fiction should start with a state of crisis, out of which future action grows. This crisis must depend on the main character for action; it can't be someone else's problem. Once it is made clear, from then on in every scene there must be problem, purpose, and goal. There must always be difficulties in your hero's path, and these usually (not always) contain conflict; this includes conflict that can occur within the character.

The developing of an active purpose for your main character is not as easy as it seems. Unless I take care I frequently find that all sorts of problems, both my heroine's and those of other characters, are just sitting around in a story doing nothing. Or else some other character is working at *his* problem while she watches as if she had none of her own—in which case she is drifting, just letting things happen to her. When this is true, there is no purpose, no "attempt to resolve" on the part of the main character, and interest is likely to lag.

Purpose is something you must consider deliberately to make sure it exists in *every scene.* It always leads to action and makes the reader want to know what will happen next. Of course there should be uncertainty about *what* will happen. The more often it is unexpected, unforeseen, the stronger the story interest. When we know what's coming, we are bored. When your main character is attempting to resolve some problem, has a purpose, we cannot know what will happen, and we are carried along to find out.

To use an example from one of my own romantic suspense novels, *Listen for the Whisperer*, in the beginning of the story the heroine's father has recently died and left her a letter stating his last wishes. She is to go to Norway to seek out her mother, an actress who abandoned her to her father in infancy and of whom she has no recollection.

Leigh's immediate problem is whether or not to carry out her father's wishes and go to Norway to find her mother. If she just sits and thinks about this, the story will be dull. To help her resolve this problem, she *takes action* by going to a theater which is showing an old film starring her actress mother, Laura Worth. Leigh's attempt to resolve this indecision is her purpose. The motion picture so disturbs her that she rushes from the theater before it ends. The next scene takes place in her father's study at home. Her purpose is still to come to a decision, and she takes action by going through old clippings, looking at a picture of her mother, at her father's books, etc. She is thinking, yes, but she is also *doing* something. The conflict is within herself. She wants to go, and she doesn't want to go. At the end of the scene and the chapter, her initial purpose is satisfied, the immediate problem is settled: she will go to Norway. We know now that her goal is to meet her mother. Curiosity as to what will happen carries us into the next chapter. Of such small things may suspense be built.

Variations

This is not always the case. A piece of fiction may open with a dramatic scene in which problem, purpose, conflict, and goal are immediately apparent and are worked out in exciting action.

This way, however, may not always suit your material in hand. A story that is difficult to get into can be helped by having the main character think in terms of purpose, of taking some sort of action, however quiet. The main character *makes* things happen through his own action, and there are chain reactions to whatever he does.

There are three things which may happen to purpose and problem.

1. Purpose is fulfilled; the problem is solved.
2. Purpose is defeated; the problem is not solved.
3. The problem is carried over to the next scene, and a new purpose evolves.

In the case of the first, we must *immediately* find a new problem about which the main character means to *do* something; that is, he finds a new purpose. Otherwise, interest drops with the solving of the previous problem. In the second case, the main character is blocked, and interest continues as we wonder what he will do next. In the third case, the problem increases, produces unexpected complications, and the main character continues to work on it, attempting to resolve the problem in new ways.

When Leigh reaches Bergen, Norway, her new problem is how to meet her mother. If she does nothing about it, she has no purpose. In the novel, her first purpose in Norway—the thing she takes action about—is to phone her mother's house. She is not allowed to speak to the actress, so we have a defeat of Leigh's purpose and the problem is not solved. The problem remains the same, but her purpose in solving it must take a new course. Later in the day, the man her mother is now married to comes to Leigh's hotel to talk to her. Her purpose in the exchange is to persuade him to let her see her mother. He forbids this. Defeat. But Leigh is still trying. Main characters do not give up, and her purpose again takes a new course.

She now seeks a friend of her father's, a man whom she has

been instructed to see if she needs help. He agrees to meet her. The problem changes form and a new purpose develops. Can she persuade him to help her? He agrees, and they make a plan. Her immediate purpose is fulfilled, and the next attack upon the problem of meeting her mother must be made. Nothing is standing still. One thing grows from another and there is no doubt that the heroine has a purpose in each scene.

It is not always necessary for the reader to know at once what that purpose is. Occasionally, for the sake of suspense, we may postpone making the main character's purpose clear to the reader. We may write, "I knew exactly what I must do, and I hurried downstairs to find him." It is enough that the main character knows what he is doing, and we follow along to find out what his purpose is. The same thing is sometimes true in the opening of a story. The main character is actively engaged in following some intent, but we don't know immediately what his purpose is. Curiosity carries us along until we find out.

Urgency, immediacy

Purpose also lends the advantage of immediacy. We don't know what the main problem of the novel will be, but this is leading toward it and provides something which must be done *right now*. A problem which can be postponed is not conducive to suspense. Urgency—if possible, a time limit—increases suspense.

Any problem implies a goal which the main character is seeking to reach. The main goal of the story must be desperately important to the character's happiness. Sometimes life or death must depend upon its successful achievement. (Most readers would still like to see things turn out well in a story.) But not all story goals, problems, and purposes can be equally important. A minor purpose needs to last for only a scene, and then we go on to other things. We hold the interest while the heroine picks up the phone and tries to get her mother on the line. Almost any small purpose which provides action and may lead to bigger things will hold the interest, build suspense. If you find that the purpose or immediate goal is a weak one, don't stretch it too far. Limit it to a single scene. It will grow tiresome, for instance, if Leigh keeps on trying to phone.

Cross-purposes and conflict

Purpose—that attempt to resolve—is something that works for you constantly in many ways. It is a good idea to know what the purposes of your other characters are in every scene (whether you tell the reader or not) so that you understand exactly what your main character is up against. Your opposition, your "villain," also has a problem, a purpose, a goal, and because of these he will furnish conflict. As a writer you must be aware of these elements and set them in your main character's path, threaten him with them. Without purpose and cross-purpose it is too easy for your story to drift, rudderless.

Purpose which leads to achievement (or defeat) is the obvious kind. But there are scenes in which you may find it difficult to have the main character take outward action. Which leads us to the purpose of merely resisting someone or something. Digging in your heels and refusing to accept what another character wants to achieve through you, or wants to convince you of, is still an attempt to resolve something:

Leigh is antagonistic toward her mother. She has no sympathy or feeling for her (or so she thinks). Her father's friend likes Laura Worth very much. Leigh does not want to be caught by what she regards as his sentimentality, and she attempts to resolve this problem by resisting his sympathy for Laura. She can do nothing except resist it, but resistance means an inner conflict, and this gives interest to your scene.

As every beginning writer is told, there are three kinds of conflict in fiction: Man against man, man against himself, man against nature. I may use all three in a novel. I certainly use the first two. In this story, Leigh finds herself in conflict with her mother, with the man Laura has married, with other characters in Laura's house, and with her father's friend. She also finds herself very much in conflict with her own ambivalent feelings about her mother. These conflicts lead to new problems, new purposes—and to the eventual goal of reconciliation between the two women, as well as the end of a physical threat to both women.

So make sure that your main character's purpose is opposed in nearly every scene. This opposition, or conflict, may be intense, or it may be the quiet kind. Variety is needed. How *much* does your main character want to solve his problem, against what opposition, to reach his goal? What will it cost him if he doesn't succeed? This cost may not be so very great in the beginning, but as the story develops, the main character must find himself trapped (by circumstances, by other people, by his own emotions), so that he can't run away but must stand and fight. Out of these things conflict grows. A problem you can easily turn your back on doesn't lead to strong story purposes and a life-or-death goal. And unless your character has the courage to fight, conflict will do you no good.

How strong is the opposition which makes a solution far from easy? Conflict is especially dramatic when opposite traits clash. Leigh finds herself a very different person from her mother and the seeds of conflict are there to be cultivated in many scenes. There are decisions to be made and the wrong ones will cost her everything. She is surrounded, cornered. She has to act. As tension mounts, other characters force purpose upon her.

As you go from one problem to the next, you must always have in mind an immediate purpose for your main character. The threat of failure which will destroy the main character's happiness should increase, and there should be strong opposition on all sides to raise this threat. Such threats must always be real. If your opposition is only a misunderstanding that could be cleared up at any point, that isn't strong enough. No danger must ever be faked.

There is something to remember, however, when you are raising opposition and conflict, defeating your main character's purposes, keeping him from solving his problems. Too much of this can become monotonous. I have read books which were so filled with continuous disasters that the story became too depressing and was no longer any fun to read. High tension that never lets down can become as monotonous as no tension at all. Interest lags, and we don't care what the next disaster will bring. There must always be the relief of an interlacing of hope. There are times when purposes succeed warmly and everything seems to be improving so that we can reach toward the ultimate goal of happiness. There is more trouble to come, of course, and we don't reach that goal until the end of the novel, but there has been relief from tension, and now we can fight again. Of course, even in these quiet scenes, your main character must still have a problem, a purpose, a goal.

Involved observer

Is there any time in a piece of fiction when there is an exception, and your main character may lack a purpose and have nothing immediate that he is trying to do something about? Yes, that can happen, though it is to be approached warily. There is a scene toward the end of *Listen for the Whisperer* when Leigh, Laura, and several other characters go to see a play at Bergen's National Theater. This is not Leigh's scene—it is Laura's. It belongs to the famous movie star who has not emerged in public for twenty years and is now sitting dramatically in a theater box for all the world to see. Leigh is filled with anxiety about her mother and about what has been happening in Laura's house. All sorts of problems remain, but she does not try to do anything herself in this scene. The purpose is all Laura's, though we aren't sure what it is. Leigh is swept along, temporarily aghast and helpless, dreading what may happen.

This shift in purpose to Laura carries the reader along. We want to know what she is up to, what she means to do, and how this will affect Leigh. So we don't mind becoming an observer through Leigh for this scene. The viewpoint doesn't shift. However, it is best to use this device only when necessary and when it can be made effective. It is too easy to excuse yourself from the hard work of giving your main character a purpose by having him sit around and watch the other characters follow their purposes. If he is to be a watcher temporarily, you must be sure that he is deeply and emotionally involved in what is happening. Much must hang in the balance for your hero, so that what other characters do affects him critically.

It is a good exercise to watch this matter of purpose in your fiction reading. Too often, in a scene that drags, you will find that there is nothing the main character is *attempting to resolve.* In a scene where interest is high, you will usually find that such an attempt is being made.

Problem, Purpose, Conflict, Goal. Use them. Think about them while you are in the planning phase of your novel; keep these elements at the back of your mind to guide you while you write. When you have written a scene, make sure they are all there, or that if one or another is missing, it is intentional and the effect is what you want.

If you follow this course you are much more likely to make sure your reader will keep turning those pages.

23

THE DETECTIVE NOVEL

by Catherine Aird

THERE are four main categories of the detective novel. The writer has therefore to decide first of all which type of detective novel he is going to write. This is an important decision.

Fact and invention

If you are the sort of person who enjoys reading old newspaper files, tracking down facts and looking up authentic background material, then *real life crime* may be your choice. This is a story based on actual fact and researched by the author. It can be historic (in the sense of being of a different time from the present) or contemporary.

A Private Disgrace by Victoria Lincoln is a recently published book about that old, old—but endlessly interesting—story of Lizzie Borden. Another excellent example of Real Life Crime is *How Charles Bravo Died,* by Yseult Bridges. This is a modern book which chronicles the death in 1876 in London of Charles Bravo, barrister-at-law, aged 30, and at the same time paints a fascinating picture of the social, medical and legal background of the times.

The crime, of course, does not have to be old. *In Cold Blood* by Truman Capote and *Beyond Belief* by Emlyn Williams both concern events still fresh in all our minds.

Here *the story exists*. The art lies in the presentation.

If you are still interested in handling (sometimes dusty) old records or if you are fortunate enough to know (of) an astute criminal investigator, there is also the detective novel based on a *real life detective*. Sherlock Holmes was modeled on a certain Dr. Joseph Bell of the Edinburgh Royal Infirmary, Scotland, a man noted for his acute powers of observation and accurate deduction.

Robert Van Gulik (who died only recently) has written a series of detective stories about a certain Judge Dee who flourished in China about the year 660 A.D. (Van Gulik was a Dutchman, Netherlands Ambassador to Japan, who wrote in English about ancient China—a breathtaking feat of intellect.)

Here *the main character exists* and the story has to be built around him.

The principal drawback to both these forms of the detective novel is rather the same as that experienced by Mrs. Beaton in her famous cookery book when advising on the making of hare pie: "First, catch your hare. . . ."

Their great advantage is that truth may well be stranger than fiction while fiction is not allowed to be as strange as truth.

The third category is *fiction based on fact*.

Josephine Tey's entertaining mystery, *The Franchise Affair*, was an up-to-date version of a notorious eighteenth-century *cause célèbre* put into a twentieth-century setting and also offering "a guess at the solution of a famous riddle." Nicholas Blake's *The Tangled Web* is a fictional modern reconstruction of an Edwardian murder case. (This can also be done in the opposite direction. A true story that might be libelous or otherwise dangerous to tell in a modern setting sometimes can be put with more safety into an historical background. William Shakespeare was known to have done this.)

Here *the main plot exists* and the background has to be written round it.

The fourth category of the detective novel is *pure fiction.*

The structure of the first three varieties mentioned is obviously already determined, but in pure fiction *the crime, the detective, and the plot* have all to be invented by the author.

Advance planning

How does he go about it?

I would suggest that the easiest way is by sitting down and taking four calculated decisions before you start to write.

First, the reason the criminal has for committing the crime.

These days, the crime is almost always murder, and in my view the kernel of the plot is usually the reason the murderer has for doing the murder.

In real life I have no doubt that people are done to death every day because they sniff or snore or grumble or are mean. In detective fiction the reason must be a more substantial one. It is worth your while to compile a list of "good" reasons for murder—gain, lust, revenge, fear, blackmail, jealousy, power . . . and this is not exhaustive. King Henry VIII went in for judicial murder in order to get (or beget!) an heir.

Second, the background.

The field is wide, though the advantages of choosing a background familiar to you are obvious. On the other hand, a total setting that has to be researched leads one "to fresh woods, and pastures new." The background is an important decision. Emma Lathen has written a series of fascinating books, using as background, New York's world of high finance. Because this is not familiar to the average reader, the authentic details in the background add to reader interest. The same can be said for the works of Harry Kemelman, *Friday the Rabbi Slept Late, Saturday the Rabbi Went Hungry,* and *Monday the Rabbi Took Off,* where the religious background is important.

Third, the means and method of the murder.

As the duelists used to say: name your weapon. You have a very wide field from which to make your choice. Except for the fact that "No undiscovered poisons are permitted" (Monsignor Ronald Knox's advice), you can make your selection from the entire armory of the centuries, the world's arsenal, the complete pharmacopoeia—to say nothing of all those instruments which could conceivably be described as blunt. After that come the sharp ones—the carving knife, the ax, the butcher's steel . . . the list is endless, but it will be tempered by your earlier choice of background. So name your weapon, and if it's a gun, go right back and read Dornford Yates for really first-class writing about what happens when you pull the trigger.

Fourth, the part which the murderer has to play in the plot.

This is, I think, one of the most difficult decisions of all. It has to be a convincing part. He or she has to be one of the main characters and has also to make an appearance early on in the story. Time spent on considering this point is not wasted.

Situation writing

I myself find I can begin to write when I have taken the above four decisions on motive, milieu, means and method, and murderer. ("Apt alliteration's artful aid," as Charles Churchill put it.)

But if you find this approach too formal, there is another. It is particularly useful if you are one of those writers who find themselves stimulated by the actual process of writing—who find a blank page produces a blank mind, in fact.

This is what is known as "situation" writing. Let us suppose, for instance, that your mystery is to be about a well-established, moderately prominent man who disappears. Your first chapter might well begin:

"How So-and-So spent the last Thursday in June was to be closely examined in every detail by everyone afterwards. By his wife, his secretary, his business associates, the police. . . . It was apparently absolutely normal in every way. He went to work, dictated some letters, asked his secretary to remind him to buy his wife a birthday present, ran through a speech he was to deliver that evening"—and so on.

You can get as far as the end of the first chapter ("and then he completely disappeared") without having made up your mind whether So-and-So is victim or villain, alive or dead or why he has disappeared, though by writing and thinking as you go along, you will have begun to have some idea.

You will also have collected two good chapter endings (the disappearance *and* the finding of So-and-So, alive or dead). You can also discover that it isn't his wife's birthday and make that the first significant finding of your detective.

This obviously isn't everyone's method of writing, but there are some writers whom it helps over the first hurdle. You have to be prepared to go back occasionally and alter what you've written and also not to let characters who come into the story late (i.e., when you have just thought of them) throw the plot out of balance. I would recommend this method of working as always worth a trial; you may be one of those writers who find it just right.

Rules and conventions

Now to the book itself.

First and most important thing the writer has to help him is the fact that the purely fictional detective novel is still written within a convention, though naturally not every writer keeps all of the rules all of the time. It is a convention which has been changed and modified since Wilkie Collins first published *The Moonstone* exactly one hundred years ago—but not changed as much as you might imagine.

The most important tenet of it is still that virtue triumphs. Just as in romantic fiction everyone lives happily ever after, so in detective fiction good always succeeds over bad. (Someone somewhere is probably already engaged on a thesis postulating that the detective story is the modern equivalent of the medieval morality play.)

Furthermore, while in real life we presume nearly all murderers to be insane—or at the very least temporarily deranged—in fiction the fiction is maintained that they are as sane as you and I (sic). In other words, your murderer cannot turn out to be insane to the extent of acting so irrationally that the reader cannot be expected to work out the logic of his actions.

There still remain some decisions, of course.

Whether you make your detective professional or amateur will be governed by your knowledge of and feeling for police procedures.

How many suspects you need is a matter of not having too many (say, more than six)—which makes for confusion—or too few (say, two)—which doesn't leave you room in which to maneuver.

To try to keep the murders down to one is, I think, unnecessarily limiting. At the same time, more than three takes the book out of the detective novel class. Killing off the chief suspect two-thirds of the way through will often open up the plot.

A couple of blind alleys at strategic points are very useful.

A sub-plot or theme running along in a subdued, secondary way is very handy when a change of scene is indicated. (This is a good place to use knowledge of a favorite subject or occupation, if it doesn't figure in the main plot.)

Good and bad advice

Now to begin writing.

Some of the best advice I ever read was on this question of beginning a detective story: Do not introduce the body on page one. As a reader, I must confess to liking it there. As a writer, you lose a good chapter or two while you build up the background. After all, if you're playing fair with the reader—and you should always play fair with the reader—he will feel confident that sooner or later a body will be discovered.

Some of the worst advice which was ever given me was "to take your main character and never let him out of your sight" (i.e., off the page). This is very restricting.

Once you have started writing, you will find that something called "thematic apperception" sets in. This, as I interpret it, is an heightened awareness to all things appertaining to your selected theme.

I chose a convent for the background for my first book, *The Religious Body* (a pun: the body was of a nun).

I was delighted when reading an otherwise exceedingly dull report on the wool trade, to come across a note to the effect that the wool from black sheep was used to make the cloth for nun's veiling. I don't think any writer exists who couldn't make ironic use of that fact.

Had this item come my way before—or after—the time of writing that particular book, it would not have had any special significance for me. Thematic apperception, then, can be described as an important bonus which comes to the writer after he has decided to write on a particular subject.

Now that you have decided upon the type of detective novel which appeals to you, have made up your mind about the salient features of the plot and have your book underway—your eyes and ears alert for useful material and most of the conventions observed—what then?

There is the infinitely more important matter of finishing it. I have found that from the point of view of useful experience one indifferent but *completed* detective novel is worth half a dozen good but discarded beginnings. The end product may or may not be salable, but the benefit to the subsequent novel you may write is immeasurable.

24

WHEN YOU WRITE HISTORICAL FICTION

by Norah Lofts

I THINK it was Maugham who once said that you didn't go out and choose a story, the story came and found you. For "story" read "historical character," and I suppose that for the chosen few, the same thing holds true. We have all heard of the writer who could neither eat nor sleep until he had spent years studying up on and writing about some historical character with whom he had an obsession. We have also all heard about historical novels written, as it were, under dictation from the vast Beyond, and of writers so far possessed by their subjects that their handwriting comes to resemble that of the dear departed.

Nice work, as they say, if you can get it; but I am now assuming that you, like me, are one of the lesser breed who must make the choice and make it alone.

Character hunt

The first thing which must be faced is the fact that whatever character you choose will be wrong. You choose a fairly well-known character from history, and nobody wishes to read another single word about him or her; everybody read a book dealing with him/her only last year, last month, last week. You choose a character never, so far as you know, put into a work of fiction, and you find that nobody knows anything about him/her; nor does anyone wish to. The unknown is profoundly distrusted. You will also be extremely lucky if, when you are correcting the final proofs of your novel, somebody who got a head start doesn't bring out a book dealing with your character. This John-the-Baptist book is hailed as something brilliantly original, an exploration of unknown territory. Your book, emerging three months later will attract terms like *carbon copy* or *feeble imitation*.

In this, please refrain from weeping over your typewriter; salt water has a detrimental effect upon metal. The day will come when the agony abates somewhat, as Macaulay said, and you'll be off on another character hunt.

You cannot choose correctly, but you can choose carefully. Rather like marriage—in fact singularly like marriage in that for a period of time you have to live with this character.

In more leisurely days, in country places, a girl contemplating marriage would be told, "You should summer and winter him first." A nice, pithy way of implying that it takes about a year to study a character in depth. I am now, as a result of hard experience, inclined to think that the rule applies as much to a fictional character as to a potential husband/wife.

He/she is going to be your constant companion, will go to bed with you and face you first thing in the morning, or, worse still, in those night watches. He/she will usurp the place of your family and your friends. It is therefore as well to choose a character congenial to you, not necessarily one for whom you have blind admiration, but one whose flaws and follies you are capable of understanding and regarding with some degree of sympathy. You must, I truly believe, be *en rapport*. I will even stick my neck out and mention the word *sex*. I will not go so far as to say that no man ever wrote a good historical novel about a woman, or a woman about a man, but Nature will have her say. The number of men able to write convincingly about the horror of an unwanted pregnancy, the number of women capable of describing the joy of leading an army into battle could be counted on the fingers of one mutilated, frostbitten hand. The same could, I know, be said of writing in the contemporary field, but the historical novel is subject to a scrutiny which contemporary novels escape. The contemporary novel stands up to be measured against a changing, fluid background; the historical novel stands against the yardstick of the written record.

Here again the choice must be carefully made. The question must be faced: How much information is available on this subject? Where is it? In what language?

Presumably all those good solid history books and biographies and those other "basic sources" used for research offer what they think is the truth. But even when one has allowed for prejudice, for propaganda, some staggering discrepancies remain; even dates can vary. If I may for a moment sink into the egotism which I have so far tried to avoid, I can give a concrete example. Anne Boleyn, briefly Queen of England, died on the block in the Tower of London on a May morning in the year of our Lord 1536. She was accused and convicted of adultery—in a queen, high treason—with a number of young men, one her brother. I wanted—or perhaps I should say that I thought it would make a better story—the young men to die first, so that to misery over her own fate should be added remorse over theirs. But one account said firmly that she was executed first. Puzzled, I hied myself over to the University Library in Cambridge and there consulted the Calendar of State Papers. They are housed in a solemn room; the other four inhabitants seemed from their appearance to have been dead for quite a long time, so when I found, to my joy, that Anne was the last to be executed so that the story pattern fell into place, I was compelled to restrain my cries of satisfaction.

Different worlds

I offer the tentative suggestion that what is called reader identification is more important in an historical novel than in a contemporary one, because the background of a new historical novel is unfamiliar to the reader, and he cannot, therefore, identify with the *situation*. A contemporary novel dealing with the problem of unemployment, the housing shortage, an unhappy marriage does not make much demand upon the reader's imagination and could be told quite satisfactorily through the medium of puppet figures. Asked to summarize, one can say, it is a novel about a man who is unemployed, a woman who has no home, a couple who are unhappily married.

The historical novel must inevitably deal with situations far less easily understood, situations which are so alien to anything known to us that they can only be partially comprehended through the character involved. Puppet figures here will not serve. The reader must identify strongly with a character in order to visualize a world so completely different from his own. Most readers—I'm one myself and some of my best friends are readers—like to be in sympathy with the character; again not necessarily in blind admiration or even approbation, but with an understanding of motive. If you select a "bad" character, select one for whose badness there is some valid excuse: faulty upbringing, thwarted love, overweening ambition. If you choose to write about a "good" character, choose one with a few human weaknesses.

Whether the facility to slip into another person's skin is inborn or can be acquired, I wouldn't like to say. I can very clearly remember that when I was five years old I heard blindness discussed, and I spent the whole of the next day going about with my eyes shut, trying to find out how it felt to be blind; and even now, when I'm old enough to know better, I suffer extravagantly from other people's ills and woes. It hurts me to see anybody going into the dentist's. A holiday in Spain and Italy was the most fiendishly miserable experience: I identified myself with every underfed, overladen horse and donkey I saw.

Escape route

I don't know what kind of fan letters other writers collect; mine are, without exception, thank-you letters, saying in this way or that, that something written by me has helped somebody to escape for an hour or two from circumstances that were harrowing, distressing, or merely dull. The letter writers are of both sexes and all ages, intellectuals and harassed housewives who say that their greatest joy is to take home one of my books and lose themselves for a while in reading it. I indulged in some mental arithmetic: if one in ten people has made the effort to write me, I must over the years have provided an escape route for thousands of people. I said to myself, "I'm a public benefactor; that's what I am!"

This trick of the trade is really very simple: If you want to show somebody something, you must first see it yourself; if you want to help people to escape, you must have the route ready; if you wish to fire another person's imagination, you must use your own as the trigger.

The brew of fiction

For those wishing to transport their readers, as against entertaining or informing them, the first rule, I think, is that formulated by somebody addicted to fox hunting—which I am not, but it is a sound rule. He said, giving advice on how to tackle a formidable fence, "Throw your heart over; the horse will follow." I am sure that throwing your heart over is the first essential; but it is not enough. You must first know what is beyond the fence; this knowledge is gained either by experience, or from reading. On any subject about which I wish to write I read prodigiously. I love reading anyway. Most of the information thus obtained I never use, or I use it in such a compressed, transmuted form that it is imperceptible. Twelve years of teaching taught me that most people are congenitally averse to being instructed. Very few readers wish for bare facts, and those who do seldom read fiction; fiction readers enjoy atmosphere, and that is something that can only be brewed from facts which the writer has so thoroughly absorbed that he has *forgotten that he knows them*. This, though I say it myself, is a profound truth. You can, if you wish, put a marrow bone, some vegetables and seasoning into a soup plate, but it isn't soup.

Another thing which is essential for what I call imaginative writing is a patient flexibility. There are, I know—and I respect them—people who plan a book from A to Z and know exactly what is going to happen, and how many words, spared writers' cramp or some other deterrent, they can produce each day. Their motive power is a tame beast of burden, standing haltered in the stable. Imagination is a wild-ranging, far more tricky mount. Here I come to one of my examples, and if it sounds egotistic, remember I'm only trying to *help*.

A few years back, I sat down one morning facing as tough an assignment as ever any writer faced. I was about to begin a book about the first Christmas. I'd done a lot of preliminary reading about the history and the geography, the flora, the climate, the political and economic problems of Judea in the twenty-fourth year of Augustus Caesar's reign. I proposed to begin the book with Mary and the Archangel Gabriel. I had all that is necessary for me, a blank wall to stare at, a clean piece of paper in the typewriter. The inner screen of my mind stayed, for some time, as blank as the wall and the paper. When, at last, somebody moved across it, it was nobody that I was then prepared for. It was an old man in a dirty, wadded cotton robe, briskly climbing some stone stairs that ran, spiralwise, inside the wall of a high tower, topped with glass. I remembered being told years ago by a South Korean woman that Korea had the first observatory in the world. I recognized, if I may use the word in this connection, the old man; Melchior, the astronomer, the first to see the Star and realize its significance.

I said to myself, Oh, so this is where we start, is it? We'll leave the Annunciation for another day. And that was, for a time, my last really conscious thought. I threw myself over and was in Korea, feeling the chill of a March morning during a slow thaw. I was an old man who had devoted his life to astronomy, frittered away a fortune and now owned nothing but what he knew, his tower and his instruments, an ancient female slave named Senya, and a pig half dead from starvation. I lived in his skin for some hours, typing quickly and badly, getting down everything I could about him while I was there. (One can always chop and re-arrange later on.) By the time that I felt a change of focus was needed, I knew enough—from him—about old Senya to make the change of skin dead easy. She was old and hungry, angry with her master because his impracticality had brought them both to the verge of starvation, yet determined to find food from somewhere because she was loyal and because half a century earlier she had loved him. So then I had another blissful hour or two with her, being her, seeing with her eyes, sharing her savage misery when a malicious trick was played upon her. I became so much at one with her that I knew with the utmost certainty that when the time came for her to kill the pig she would slash its throat three times, one for each of the people who had tricked her.

And so, more or less taking what presents itself, I deal with all my characters, one by one.

The world they live in

Having chosen a character congenial to yourself and likely to be acceptable to the reader, a character about whom some information is available in a form which you can use, it is not enough to know virtually all there is to be known about him/her. This character did not exist in a vacuum or operate against a dead backdrop of events. Other people were concerned and about them something must be known, too. Christopher Columbus, to take an obvious example, would be a good subject for an historical novel—a man through whose eyes the reader could see the world as the scholars of the time believed it to be, flat, with a terrible abyss awaiting the fellow who ventured too far, and as Columbus saw it, a globe on which by sailing west he would come to the rich and fabled East. But he could never have set out on his momentous voyage but for Isabella, Queen of Castile; and he could never have completed it without the aid of the common seaman, the mutinous, doubting fellow who accepted this desperate venture as an alternative to rotting in jail. Any novel about Columbus must take the Queen and the deckhand into account.

I am completely unable to write about what is called "real" life. I am aware of, and concerned with, contemporary problems; I'm neither unobservant nor inexperienced. I should, by all reasonable reckonings, be able to produce a topical book. But that would bore me, literally, I think, to death. In my real life I shop and cook and make beds; to write about such things would be to serve two life sentences, running concurrently. When I do write about the twentieth century—mainly in short stories—I must always have a fantastic element, a ghost, a bit of black magic, an exotic setting in some place that I have never seen. And this—*be warned*—prevents me from being recognized as a serious writer. On the other hand, when I project, I do it thoroughly and make mention of the stinks and injustices as well as the laces and ruffles and tossing plumes of the past, and therefore I cannot qualify as a romantic writer. Between the stools there is one place—on the floor. But as Bunyan said, "He that is down need fear no fall."

I am in full sympathy with this very human desire for the characters with whom one has been identifying oneself to live happily ever after and am always sorry when the logic of the story dictates otherwise. But a happy ending cannot simply be stuck on. I believe in playing fair with the reader; a story that is to end happily must have glimmers of hope, just as one that is to end badly has threatening shadows.

Escapism, to which I freely admit, is nowadays almost a dirty word. But it serves its purpose; time and time again it has saved me, and through me, others. There is a woman, still alive and now, happily, free, who spent twelve years in a detention camp. No visitors, no reading or writing materials for twelve years. When she was freed, she wrote to me and said that she had saved her own sanity and that of several other women by telling and retelling those of my stories that she had read before her incarceration, and that when she left, other women were still telling the stories. If that kind of tribute seems to you, gentle reader, worth more than the more glittering rewards in the writing game, just go ahead and throw your heart over.

25

THE ELUSIVE PLOT

by Dorothy Eden

I WILL begin by saying that I dislike the word "gothic." It seems nowadays that a writer needs only an old house and an elderly eccentric character (doesn't half the world live in old houses of one kind or another, and don't most people grow a little eccentric in old age? There is nothing remarkable or rare about these things.) to be labeled a gothic novelist.

Being a writer who writes two kinds of books, the short suspense and the longer novel which is not remotely gothic, I would prefer to be labeled simply a novelist. However, in this computerized age, categories seem inevitable, and I expect my reputation as a gothic writer will continue.

And let me add that I thoroughly enjoy writing this kind of tense atmospheric story. The atmosphere is enormously important to me, and begins before the story. In *An Afternoon Walk,* the hot swooning summer day was what suggested the behavior of the characters. It had to be like that. Ella and Kitty grew out of the hazy golden afternoon. The atmosphere gave them the extra dimension they needed to become real to me. So that was the point at which I began, on a hot haunted day, and the plot developed from there.

Jigsaw puzzle

I find plotting extremely difficult. I let things and images drop into my mind, until a shadowy story forms. This is a lovely, easy dreaming period that makes me keep postponing the real work, i.e., getting an outline of the story onto paper. When I finally get down to that, I am inclined to type out the outline several times, while it clarifies. I list possible incidents, I name my characters and make notes about their appearance, their nature, their motivation. They must appear vividly in my mind. If they don't, they will eventually shrivel up and disappear.

Apart from two or three background characters necessary for dressing up a scene (the daily help, the doctor, the schoolteacher, etc.), I never use anyone who hasn't a vital part to play in the story. For, remember, this is a jigsaw puzzle, and every part must fit. I always know, of course, how the story will end, although I never follow a rigid path towards that end. I highlight the way by several obligatory signposts, but when they are ready to do so, I allow my characters to take over their own scenes.

When I say "when they are ready to do so," I mean this literally. There is always a period, sometimes brief, sometimes much too long, but always disheartening, when my characters obstinately remain strangers and shadows. I struggle with them; I threaten to give them up and send them back into limbo. Sometimes this struggle goes on for one or two hundred pages. But I know that, just as I won't let them go, they won't let me go. They lurk like ghostly images in the back of my mind, until suddenly, in a scene, a paragraph, even a sentence, they break through. From then on, my major troubles are over. I am willingly possessed.

I might add here that names are enormously important to me, and sometimes by changing a name I see a character more clearly.

As to the chief character, necessarily the heroine in these romantic suspense novels, it is a drawback that she must be rather vague and dreamy, almost, I am sorry to say, stupid. Otherwise she would get to the bottom of the mysterious happenings by the third chapter, at least. She must be young, vulnerable, sensitive, emotional and extremely susceptible to atmosphere. She doesn't even need to be brave, although a certain amount of spirit is called for. But she is definitely not a hardheaded, logical young woman.

Another problem in this permissive modern society is that obstacles to true love, such as the hero's being already married, are no longer valid. Alas, the mad wife locked up in the attic has gone forever. Therefore, our young lady must be a little brainwashed to make her behavior plausible. This, in an age of increasing ingenuity in psychological torture, is not difficult to suggest, and the plot can be shaped to this end.

I consider that all plots of gothic novels are farfetched, but the secret is in making the background so interesting and unusual, the action so vivid, and the characters so alive that the reader is swept along on an uncritical tide. Involvement is the word, for both reader and author. And I can assure you that if the author has remained uninvolved, the reader will also suffer from this very easily communicated disease, and care little what happens to Lucy or Sarah or whomever.

I myself, as I have said, remain uninvolved, or only half involved, until my characters begin to talk to me. If this felicitous state of affairs doesn't happen, then I regretfully put my notes away in a drawer, perhaps forever, perhaps to be resurrected a year or two later, when the story may come to life.

Evoking a period

The long, partly historical novels that I write are another matter entirely. I particularly like evoking a period, and being able to dispense with the dreamy and rather too-pure heroine. I can select the kind of house suitable to the period, and then have a marvelous time filling it with the kind of people whom I am sure once lived there. In these novels, happiness is not necessary, and love can be as variable as clouds in a rainy summer. There must be a strong theme; it can be business, a lawsuit, family feuds. But for me it is always a working out of human emotions over a long period, the progress of a marriage, or the growing up of a family.

I adore writing about families. I suddenly know how many children there will be and exactly what they will be like. The children evolve from the atmosphere of the home. And in that respect, I love the claustrophobia of Victorian houses, the repressed emotions, the boredom, the cruelties, the intensely stylized pattern of living. It is a breeding ground for sudden uncontrolled passions. I sometimes think I was once a Victorian if only because I love William Morris wallpaper and button-backed Victorian chairs.

This kind of novel is inclined to go on forever. I can indulge myself with deathbed scenes, and balance things by producing new babies. In a minuscule way, it is playing God. It is worrying and traumatic because I can never see the shape of the book until it is nearly finished, and I go through phases of elation and despair. But it is constantly absorbing, and I could never contemplate any other way of life.

The compulsive art

I suspect that the role of being purely and simply a storyteller is slightly despised nowadays. But to young writers I would suggest that this attitude is wrong on two counts. A good story is always sought after and salable—important, if you want to live by your work. And from the days of the *Arabian Nights,* storytelling has been a compulsive art, both for teller and listener alike. I do not think this is going to change, simply because human nature does not basically change.

So I would advise would-be writers not to be too obsessed by gimmicks or fashions, above all not to slavishly copy a successful writer. Be yourself, create good strong characters and open your mind to them, let them behave within the pattern of the personality you give them. Above all, write about something with which you are familiar and can communicate.

A writer is only a pen on paper, a manuscript, a voice through which his characters speak. But try to make it an individual voice.

26

WRITING THE CAREER NOVEL

by Marjorie Mueller Freer

IF YOU would like to master the art and craft of novel writing, the teen-age career novel poses a challenging as well as specific area. As in the adult novel, characterizations in the young adult career romance for girls 11–16 need to be dimensional; the settings, realistically presented; the problems confronting the heroine, difficult of solution; and the style including dialogue and narration, as expertly handled as in books for the mature reader. The major difference between this and the adult novel is that here the main characters are teenagers, while the rest of the cast involves people with whom the girl would be in contact in family, educational, social or work situations. Also, the particular career featured should be woven in naturally as part of the story.

Entertainment plus

Although the underlying purpose of the career novel is vocational guidance, it is equally important that the story be entertaining in its own right, with a top length of 50,000 words, which can be read at one sitting. The knowledgeable setting-forth of a particular career is the plus factor.

If you have not actually participated in a particular field in which you wish to interest an editor, play the reporter and researcher. Meanwhile, the answers to the following questions (in writing) will set in motion your own career novel:

1. *Do you have a particular point of view you want to air?* While still in college, I was distressed by the emptiness in the lives of many older women who had raised families and then led lives without challenge or direction. Thus was born the philosophy basic to all my career books: to insure against future frustrations, every girl should develop a particular career talent before she marries—either one that could be carried on at home while she raises a family, or resumed when her children no longer require a large share of her attention. While all my novels from *Roberta, Interior Decorator* through *A School for Suzanne* have this as a basic philosophy, each book also has its individual theme. In *Roberta* it is: No matter how great the difficulties, in order to achieve a dream, hold it high. In *Suzanne* it is: Have the courage to change your mind if the goal you have been pursuing is the wrong one.

To bring your theme to the level of consciousness, fold a paper in half lengthwise, and, over a period of several days, on the left-hand side, leaving space in between each entry, make a list of attitudes in other people that make you indignant. On the right-hand side, express in a sentence the positive point of view, the attitude you agree with. As an example of an indignation, you could include, "People who give up a goal as soon as they encounter opposition or difficulty." The positive would be, "Although one encounters setbacks and frustrations, one needs purposeful thinking and action to head towards a desired goal."

2. *Is there a specific locale, a place and region personally known to you where you would like to set your novel?* Since I am a Connecticut Yankee by residence, I use specific areas in

Connecticut as the major setting for many of my novels. *Orchids for April* (horticulture) features the Connecticut River Valley; *House of Holly* (gift shops and mail order), the Housatonic Valley. Other additional settings in the various books include places I know firsthand—London, Edinburgh, Munich, the Bavarian Alps, New York City, Grand Rapids and Holland, Michigan. In *Roberta,* Roberta's private tour through a furniture factory in Holland is one I took. In *Gay Enterprises* (culinary careers which include restaurant stations like salads or desserts, catering, selling food specialties by mail or running a bakery or restaurant), Gay's ultimate enthusiasm for Block Island, Rhode Island, is the way I feel about the island. On the other hand, Mark Logan's passion for Alaska which dominates his life and breaks up his romance with Holly Elliot in *House of Holly* was based on six months of reading all the personal-experience books I could find on Alaska. Field trips and research reading are part of the fun of doing a book.

3. *What time period should be used?* Since a well-written career novel could have a life expectancy of twenty years, the time is an elastic "today" which would not include specific current national or international events, current catchwords, or characters like hippies.

4. *What career or careers do you know through actual participation or because of family or friends?* Is it a career many girls might follow? Has it been overdone? (Nursing) While my publisher already had issued a career novel on teaching, I had another point of view which was presented in *A School for Suzanne,* the story of a young actress turned reluctant teacher. She came to see teaching as the greatest career challenge she had ever faced, since in this field she could give her students a feeling of self-worth and also help them become self-motivating.

5. *Are you an expert on a subject which you would like to use in some way in your novel, as the hobby of one of the characters or as the featured career?* Gay in *Gay Enterprises* (culinary arts)

is a passionate sailor. Knowing a sport like sailing through first-hand experience helps lend authentic local color to your writing. In this instance, it also provided a dramatic and unusual first meeting between Gay and two young men who were going to figure prominently in her future.

6. *As you start thinking in terms of a main character in a particular setting and a particular career, is the girl or isn't she already motivated in terms of the career?* Either approach will work. Originally Gay has no strong career drive, although she likes to cook and bake. In contrast, Roberta has a major motivation to become a decorator, but her father insists that she first master a quickly salable skill like secretarial work so she can be self-supporting if anything happens to him. But even in her initial confrontation with her father, the many facets of decorating are pointed out:

> "Of course there's always work in a decorating shop. Besides that, I could teach or lecture on decorating. Miss Allison also said that I could write about interior decorating for magazines or newspapers, have my own decorating business after I worked for someone else, or open a decorating shop in a department store."

7. *Who, initially, are the other characters involved with the main character?* In Gay's case, these include her mother, who is living on Long Island; her father, who is living on Block Island; her married friends, Betty and Bob Terrigel, who run a private school in New London and invite her for a sailing weekend; and the young men aboard the yawl which almost runs her down in the midnight dark of a stormy night.

8. *As you think in terms of various settings in which your main character will be involved, can you think of other characters who will make their first appearance in the opening chapters of the story?* In the case of Gay, this includes her father, whom she goes to visit on Block Island, and her best friend Susy, who comes on a surprise visit.

Try to visualize each character for your reader through the impressions of your main or viewpoint character:

A short while later when the steamer had docked, Gay went ashore, and there, thinner than when she had last seen him, and deeply tanned by the wind and sun, stood her father. She spotted him first. . . . In the months since he had come to the island, bitterly resenting as she had his stubborn stand on coming here to live, she had almost forgotten how charming he could be or how distinguished he looked with the streak of white through his still dark hair. Even her hurt feelings that he hadn't taken time out to come to her graduation faded into the background.

Characters can also be characterized through the dialogue of other people, as in *Showcase for Diane* when Diane reports to her mother on an interview she has done with a ship model maker:

"What was Captain Faraday like?" her mother wanted to know.

"Well—" Still with her coat on Diane paused to organize her impression. "Stephen Faraday is a big hunk of man—as tall as Dad and with the bluest eyes. And he wore a blue shirt that made them seem even bluer. . . . He isn't what you'd call a braggy kind of person—he doesn't talk much about himself. What he's interested in are his models. He really opened up and talked about them."

9. *Have you worked out the past as well as the present and the future of each character?* In a looseleaf notebook, divide two facing pages into horizontal thirds for each character. Set down what you know about him or her in each time period. For the past, include notes on nationality and family background, places where character lived, physical home, home life, schooling, sparetime occupation, important people, training, successes, failures. For the future, tentatively project events that might take place, people with whom he or she might be involved. (In the case of Captain Faraday's future, I knew that he was going to marry Diane. Since this was the first teen career novel to show the problems of a young married career girl, the wedding and the

linking of the two futures took place halfway through the book.) The longest part of the work on a career novel or any long piece of fiction is getting to know the characters on paper. Put down daily thoughts on each character; add as many double-spread pages as necessary.

10. *Do you have the specifics for your settings?* These can come from observation, from memory, or from research. Make it a habit at all times to carry with you 3 x 5 cards or a small notebook so that you capture on paper graphic word pictures.

11. *Are you making the difficulties your main character faces sufficiently challenging?* In *Orchids for April*, the heroine interested in horticulture, who needs a fixed base of operations to establish her plants, is literally uprooted when her mother, who is forever house shopping, finds yet another place to which she moves the family. In *Tours by Terry*, Terry is always planning trips for other people, but one crisis after another prevents her from going on a trip of her own. When she does manage a vacation abroad, another ship collides with hers and the passengers have to take to the life-boats. Romantically, also, there is a difficult choice for her to make from among three young men. The harder you make things for your main character, the better the book. Also, in the career novel, the contrapuntal effect of romantic versus career complications heightens the tension and suspense.

12. *And speaking of suspense, are you planning on writing your career novel as suspensefully and entertainingly as something you yourself would enjoy reading?* Once you know your characters, the setting, and the initial situation, you can start the first draft. Don't try to force your characters into a preconceived plot or story line. The personality of your main character, her particular handling of problems, and people who oppose and befriend her, shape the actual story. If you need the security of working from a synopsis or chronological listing of situations,

follow this method, but if a certain scene anywhere in the book cries out to be written out of sequence, get it down on paper. Whatever your method, let the transcription be fun, let each encounter between people reveal more about them or someone else important to the story, or forward the action itself. But even though you may write many of your scenes out of sequence, save the writing of your climactic or final scene until last so you have something towards which you can build. While the final outcome, career and romantic, should be successful and happy, the story itself should illustrate that competence in a career and recognition are not easily achieved—that they require considerable practice, study, hard work, and the ability to weather disappointments. In this way, you can demonstrate that no worthwhile goal is easily achieved.

On your way

As for your own goal of writing the career novel, this, too, can be achieved by following through on the dozen suggestions discussed above, devoting a section of your notebook to thinking through each area on paper. Even with a full-time position or a busy life as executive director of a family, write every day, taking advantage of each small section of free time. Also, go to the library for reference books and research; take necessary field trips to check settings and various phases of the career in action; or interview people in connection with the career or a related career necessary to your story. (When I was working on *Roberta, Interior Decorator* and touring the factory in Holland, Michigan, which turned out fine 18th-century furniture reproductions, my guide was a furniture designer, an occupation about which I needed firsthand background for the hero.) Most of all, enjoy the delight of getting to know the book people you are creating. Once you have sufficiently internalized them, you'll be in the happy state of taking dictation from them, a sign that your career novel is really on its way.

27

PLOTS AND PEOPLE IN MYSTERY NOVELS

by Hillary Waugh

PLOT construction is something I suspect many modern novelists pay little attention to. If challenged, they might even insist that a book doesn't need a plot, that the novel has escaped from the prison of a story line. I would also suspect that authors with such views are more lazy than enlightened. Constructing a good, solid plot is tedious work; it's much more fun to play with characters.

But there is pleasure in plotting too, and it's probably the mystery writer who knows this better than anyone else. While plot is no longer sufficient to sustain a mystery novel all by itself, it still is the book's main *raison d'être* and lays the heaviest claim on the author's attention. As a result, there is no better training ground for the art of plotting than the mystery. And when one has mastered this art and become experienced in its disciplines, he can dominate, control and handle plots as a skilled musician dominates, controls and handles his instrument. This is when plotting becomes fun—when the structure of an intricately conceived story can produce the intellectual pleasure of a subtle chess combination.

But let's start at the beginning. A novel is first an entity. All parts bear on all other parts. Thus we can't lift out this thing called plot and expect it to detach itself cleanly. Clinging things will come with it. Background, for one, characters for another. We should cut those free before going on.

Background isn't much of a problem, for it has a relatively minor effect on plot. A story will, of course, follow one line of action if its setting is New York City, and a different one if it's rural England. The problems of transport, the problems of privacy, of obtaining goods, of terrain, of virtually all of life will vary markedly between such places, and the story will have to vary to solve them.

Motivation and behavior

Such strictures affect only the surface of a story, however. What is basic to the plot and what will not change is the behavior of the characters. A given man's response to a stimulus will be the same in England as in New York, and the only variable is the means at his disposal to respond with.

It is character that has the affecting influence on plot. A given man may respond the same way to the same stimulus regardless of locale, but a different man will respond to the same stimulus in a different way. Twenty men will respond in twenty different ways.

This business of character is a major stumbling block in plotting, and the way an author handles it separates the would-be writer from the professional. The would-be writer remains a would-be because he makes the mistake of letting his story move his characters. The professional knows it's the other way around. The characters move the story. That's the first big lesson and the first big task, and at the back of a writer's mind at all times should be the cry, "Motivate, motivate, motivate!"

Let's talk about that for a moment. Everything every character says and does must be consistent with his personality. Granted. Next, those consistent responses, actions and reactions must advance the story. It is the only way the story can be told.

It is what the story is. But there is more yet. This action that moves the story was triggered by a cause, and the cause should also be relevant to that story. In a good plot there is nothing extraneous.

Suppose that the exigencies of the plot require that Jones accidentally bump into Brown as he is leaving his downtown office. There has to be a logical reason for Jones's being downtown at that particular time. Nor will it do to say he went down to buy a pair of shoes or mail a letter. What does he need the pair of shoes for and why buy them now? Or who's the letter to and why can't he mail it in the corner letterbox? And, in any case, what do shoes or letters have to do with the story we're telling?

If his action isn't a relevant factor, then it's a contrivance, and the author is saying to the reader, "I'm too lazy to solve the problem of getting Jones downtown legitimately, so I'm going to rig it."

And what is meant by "legitimately"? Simply: That the reason that brings Jones downtown had, has, or will have some bearing on the story.

The aim of the game

Now, having recognized the impact of characters on the motivation of stories, let us get to the business of the story-making itself. The first aim of the game, of course, is reader involvement—that quality that keeps him turning the pages. Some people call it "reader urgency." To me it's simply, "suspense." This doesn't mean the story has to be an action drama. Perilous Pauline doesn't have to be hanging from a cliff at the end of every chapter. All that is required to keep the suspense up and the reader reading is two things: 1. The reader must not know what is going to happen next. 2. He must want to find out.

Taking up the second point first, the reader will only want to find out if he cares about or identifies with the characters. Thus there must be still another dimension and purpose to the people in the story than merely the motivation of the plot. They must be heroes and villains, liked, detested, feared or scorned. This is what a book is really all about, and that motivation business we were discussing never should reach the reader's awareness. That's structural support and only the author is supposed to know it's there.

But enough about character. We want to talk about plot so we'll assume the reader cares about the hero's future, and we'll concern ourselves with the first point, the element of suspense. Let us consider the following: The fair damsel is a prisoner in the moated castle; the hero and his outnumbered band of intrepid men seek to rescue her.

Given this situation, the reader is not sure whether the hero will succeed or fail. Therein lies the suspense, and both reader and author know this. The reader can relax, therefore, during the hero's effort to swim the moat, scale the walls, elude guards and reach the fair damsel's chamber. He knows the hero will encounter only token danger in this stage of the adventure. (Only an abysmal plotter would have the hero captured *before* he reached the girl.) The real trouble, the reader knows, will arise when the hero tries to escape with her. (There's a 100% guarantee that he can't do it without having someone raise the alarm.)

This is a basic suspense setup. It's legitimate, but it's garden variety suspense, very predictable, and very uninspired. That's the kind of plotting I'd have to jazz up in some way. I don't want my readers sitting back thinking they know what my moves are going to be. I'll lull them into sitting back only when I'm ready to pull the chair out from under them. And after I've pulled out enough chairs, the readers will be (hopefully) conditioned the way I want them: To sit on the edges of those chairs.

To go back to that hero swimming the moat and scaling the walls to rescue fair maiden: He eludes the guards. So far so good. He reaches the heroine as promised, and now the reader anticipates those suspense-filled pages while the hero tries to get her safely out of the castle. But now we'll pull a switch and have her flatly refuse to go with him!

A curve like that will not only jolt the reader; it will completely disorient him. Now he has *no* idea where the story is going next. Presumably he now also can't wait to find out!

It goes without saying that the reason for the damsel's refusal must be absolutely valid so that when she explains herself, the reader will acknowledge that her decision was, at worst, logical, at best, inescapable. Ideally—and this is where I like to play games with the reader—a clue has already been planted in the text so that the discerning reader could have predicted that response. The ideal in the plotting game is to keep the reader guessing what will happen next, at the same time secretly weaving into the story all the clues that would tell him. This is where the challenge and the fun lie.

Reader satisfaction

There's more to good plotting, however, than playing games with the reader or keeping him guessing, interested or excited. A good story should offer him intellectual satisfaction at the same time. He should feel, when he closes the final cover of a book, that the reading of it has been a rewarding experience and not a waste of time. There has to be meat in a book. It should be packed with content. Thus, no plaudits for plotting can be earned for producing mere one-purpose scenes. Everything that happens in a book should have at least two reasons for being there. And I mean in addition to the suspense motive that keeps the reader reading. (All scenes are assumed to have that or you're not a writer.) Two additional reasons are desired—at least two.

And if the author can work in three or four, so much the better.

Here's a sample case. Suppose an author wants to put a bed-room scene in his story. Boy and girl will make love as explicitly as the house rules of his particular publishing company will permit. The purpose? To titillate the reader. This, I have to con-cede, is a legitimate purpose. The author's aim, after all, is to keep the reader turning pages and titillation will do it as well as suspense. (I suppose my main objection to maintaining reader interest through titillation is that it doesn't require any skill, and even bad writing can get published if it's pornographic enough.)

Now, using this example, assume that a bedroom scene is to be included in the story. If its only purpose is titillation, that is very bad. It has no more business there than suddenly having a man go over Niagara Falls in a barrel to inject suspense. As we said before, there should be at least two reasons besides reader interest to justify every scene in a story.

So we have to give this bedroom bit some meaning. Perhaps we can say that it reveals something of the character of the couple involved. This we can make it do, and now we're on less shaky ground. However, it's a pretty big scene for very little character insight, unless we reveal something about their be-havior that will have a future bearing on the story! If we can do that, then this scene becomes a must. Now we're full-fledged legitimate; we have a valid purpose for invading the bedroom and not staying out in the hall.

But that's only one purpose, and we want more than that. What else can that scene do for us? For one thing, if we happen to be writing a mystery novel, this serves as an alibi for the pair. If they're with each other in the bedroom, they can't be killing victim number two. There's a second purpose.

There's no point in using bedroom capers for an alibi unless we can make capital of the fact that it's bedroom capers rather than, say, a trip to the amusement park. So if the amorous duo should have to reveal their indiscretions to save their hides, we're locking this scene in as an integral part of the book.

There is still more we can do. When it's discovered what the couple have been up to, other people are going to be motivated as a result. Perhaps the revelation will move the villain of the piece to embark on a course that will ultimately lead to his destruction. If so, our hot little love scene is indispensable. It has to be in there, and the author can even defend it as artistic if he wants.

Meanwhile, though the reader won't find it out until the end of the book, that torrid little interlude, which he found so enjoyable that he read through it without thinking, really held the key clue to the mystery, and he was conned into forgetting to pay attention!

That is plotting in depth and, to me, is the only way to do it and where the fun lies. The result is a tight, well-integrated story that moves ever forward, and an author, when he has worked out a scheme like that, can say he's got a book. To me, however, that is still not enough. Plot is important but there is something even more important. I mean the characters that make the story happen. They are what I want to play up, not the story.

My tendency, therefore, is to strive first for that solid, integrated plot with its box of surprises, then hang it up as a backdrop and have another story—the real story—take place in front of it.

This story will be about the development of a man's character, perhaps, or its degeneration, or the change in the relationship of two or more people to each other or toward life or whatever. In its most elementary form, of course, it's the ups and downs of a boy-girl romance.

There are, besides boys and girls, all kinds of personal relationships which can be explored and presented against the backdrop of the storyline, but the writer must take care, of course, that the relationships develop in the context of that backdrop.

Though the focus may rest on the relationships rather than on the storyline, the two interrelate. They do more than that. They fuse.

As I said earlier, a book is an entity. All things connect with all things.

28

SCIENCE FICTION: SHORT STORY AND NOVEL

by Harry Harrison

THE western novel is about the west, the historical novel is about history, the crime novel is about crime. The science fiction novel is *not* about science.

There are people who like to list all of the inventions that were written about first in science fiction, but this is thinking after the act. An awful lot of gadgetry is proposed in science fiction by writers who know their technology, and it would be strange if some of it did not prove workable at some time. This is completely incidental. Science fiction is about the impact of science upon people, and upon our environment and society.

It is very hard to give a single definition that will adequately describe *all* science fiction, so I shall not attempt it. It is enough if we realize what science fiction does. First, and most important, science fiction deals with today and tomorrow. All other fiction is about yesterday. Take almost any mainstream short story or novel. With a simple change of props, horses instead of autos, it could have taken place at any time during the last hundred years—because these writers are most interested in the eternal verities of interpersonal relationships. Even if "today" is mentioned in the book, or if this concept is in the author's mind, it is "yesterday" by the time the book is published.

Science fiction holds the opposite view. If the story takes place "today," it is the real today, even by the time it sees print, because it is about the existing world that has been changed in every way by the arrival of science on the world scene. If the story is about tomorrow, it is about the continued alterations and results of these changes. Science is the inescapable bedrock of science fiction.

In the paleolithic science fiction days, the hard sciences dominated the field: chemistry, physics, biology, and the like. The wonders of the new things that could be invented and discovered were of the utmost importance. The rocket story was about how the ship was put together in the cellar, and the story ended when ("with a licking tongue of lambent flame . . .") it blasted off. If you read about a rocket today, it will probably be treated as just another vehicle, as prosaic as the Boeing 707 is now, and the story will concern itself with the passengers aboard it. The softer sciences are being admitted to science fiction, and you will find stories based upon sociology, psychology, anthropology, political science—anything and everything.

Scientific method and science fiction

The basic attitude of the science fiction author must be humanistic. He must feel that man is perfectible, that human nature can be changed, that this will not come about through wishing or praying, but by the application of intelligence, using the tools that the scientific method has given us. Once this is thoroughly understood, there will be no question about how science *fact* blends into science *fiction*.

The facts of science are there, all around us, inescapable. The science fiction author buys all of the scientific magazines and books that he can afford because he is fascinated by the ceaseless discoveries and the endless permutations of nature. There is even material galore in the daily press. I have a clipping on my wall with the headline "DIRTY AIR MAY CAUSE ICE AGE": EXPERT. Isn't that a plot for a story? A few months ago, there was an article about how the Marines in Vietnam use dowsing rods to locate mines. This story plots itself: the contrast between the old soldier who doesn't believe this and the rookie who does.

Or take the announcement that flatworms fed on their intelligent and chopped up brothers became smarter themselves. Curt Siodmak read that and wrote *Hauser's Memory*.

And how about the frightening overpopulation and overconsumption figures? I read them and applied them to New York City in the year 2000, and wrote "Make Room! Make Room!"

The list of extrapolations from new knowledge could be extended. (Science fiction has borrowed the term *extrapolation* from mathematics and made it its own: using present knowledge to extend a trend or possibility into the future.) Of equal importance is the "what if" type of plotting that can be traced right back to H. G. Wells and his, "What if pigs had wings?" Brian Aldiss said, "What if no more children were born into the world?" Then he wrote *Greybeard*. Robert Heinlein said, "What if we used the moon as a penal colony?" Then he wrote *The Moon Is a Harsh Mistress*. Daniel Keyes said, "What if we could raise a moron's I.Q. by chemical methods?" Then he wrote his novel *Flowers for Algernon* (*Charly* in the movie version).

In order to write science fiction, one must not only like science fiction but must like science as well—some one science, any science, all science; the science fiction author must be a *fan* of science. He must realize that there are no monster brains lurking in computers, ready to destroy us all, just as there are no secrets that mankind "should not know." The scientific method is mankind's crowning achievement. It is the only really new thing in the entire universe. With it our race of hairless apes can talk around the world in a fraction of a second—or can refine a few pounds of a particularly heavy kind of rock and blow up that world. If you don't think this is the most fascinating thing to ever come down the pike—then you should not consider writing science fiction.

Concept is king

Science fiction is idea-oriented. The idea comes first—and is many times the hero—and the story follows. The complexity of the idea is what determines the length of the story. A single concept produces a short story. It might be argued that most science fiction short stories are back-plotted, i.e., the ending is known in advance, then the story is filled in to reach the desired ending. Or the sequence is reversed and they are front-plotted, with a "what-if" statement, then a solution. There is little or no character development, because the characters are there to illuminate the concept. The basic story is not about the characters as people. The story is *concept*-oriented, not person-oriented. One, or at most two, of the characters will be fleshed out with personalities. The rest will be cardboard props with labels (laboratory assistant, soldier, second pilot), who do their bit and vanish.

Only in the science fiction novel, and in the longer intermediate lengths, can character be developed to any degree. Even then, rounded and real as the people may be, the concept is king. John Wyndham had real people in *Day of the Triffids,* yet their names are forgotten while his strange plants lurk in memory. Can you remember the name of a character in any science fiction story or novel you have read recently? Now try this with *Gone With the Wind,* or *Crime and Punishment,* or any other general novel that you recall with warmth.

There are exceptions, of course, to all these rules and statements, as well as an entire school of science fiction writers, often referred to as the "New Wave," who would deny everything I have said. But these new writers would all admit that they write science fiction because they first read and enjoyed the basic stuff. You have to learn the rules before you can break them.

As an editor, I can truthfully say that there is very little good science fiction around in any length, old or new wave. As a writer, I can say that good science fiction is not easy to write. Of course the bad stuff is just about as simple to do as hack westerns—and is just about as important.

Where the science fiction short story is a vehicle for a single idea or concept, the novel, when it is not just a short story written long, can not only explore more complex concepts, but can show interrelationships. Ecology has far more interconnections than are possible among all of the characters in *War and Peace*. An ecological concept would have to be handled in the form of a novel. All of the "earth destroyed" novels are ecological, as are the multi-generation starship novels.

New worlds

The "world created" is also a novel-length concept. This is rarely found outside of science fiction—*Islandia* and the Tolkien books are the only examples that come to mind—yet this label could be applied to at least 9 out of 10 novels inside the field. (Or more. I just went to my unsorted-science fiction-novels shelf, and the first twenty out of twenty books are "world created" novels.) In the science fiction field, this concept is as old as H. G. Wells, the man who invented modern science fiction books such as *The Sleeper Awakes* and *The Shape of Things to Come*. A first-class science fiction writer can invent a world, down to the smallest detail—or generate the illusion that the smallest detail has been revealed—then populate it and set a story in it that could take place in no other possible world. This, I believe, is one of the reasons for the continuing, and expanding, interest in science fiction. The western is in the west, and the murder mystery has a corpse, and we have been there many times before. But, from time to time, in the best science fiction novels, the reader will have a chance to enter a wholly new and logical world and to watch an interesting story take place there. No other form of fiction can make this statement!

I wish there were an easy formula that I could give to tell just how to write the science fiction novel, or the short story. There is none. As a first step, the prospective science fiction writer must seriously *like* the stuff. Then he must accept the idea that we live in a changing world, not a repetitive, generation-unto-generation feudalistic one. Change in itself—like science—is neither good nor bad. It is just there. Then he must accept the concept that we can change change, that all things are possible (whether probable or not is another matter). Then he must read an awful lot of science fiction, both old and new, to see what has been done and what is being done. Then he must read a lot of *non*-science fiction to understand what good writing is, because so much of science fiction is so terribly written. Then he must apply seat to chair and fingers to typewriter and create something that never existed before.

Then, and only then, he may have written a salable piece of science fiction. Maybe.

Still, there is very little competition at the top. Or at the bottom either, for that matter. It is certainly worth the try.

29

I LIVE MY NOVEL

by Amelia Walden

FOR me, the writing of a novel is an intensely personal experience. I live my novel. Sometimes I sing it, sometimes I weep it. But the second in which that first sentence is banged out, I enter another world. It is the only world I care about until that other agonizing second when I can type "Last Page" on the final sheet of manuscript.

Let me tell you how it begins. There is this thing called creative chemistry. It is not much different from the girl-boy, man-woman chemistry when two people feel an instantaneous involvement. Only in the case of the writer and the novel, it is an intellectual emotion.

The key word is *fascination*. I get fascinated—sometimes by a character; other times by a place or a theme; sometimes by a group of people, as in my book, *What Happened to Candy Carmichael?,* in which the story centered around a clique of international mod jet-setters, all famous in their fields, all tenderly young, all rebels and bent on self-destruction. Who wouldn't be fascinated by such a bunch?

The fascination acts as a goad. It bedevils me. I feel the first

symptoms of that terrible disease, *novelitis*. You see, if you don't
have to write it, you never will. I have to.

Then this is how it happens.

I start with people—the people who are going to get real flesh
and bones, real blood in their veins. The story people are what
I am talking about. I live with them mentally a few days, maybe
longer than that—a few weeks, a couple of months. I make the
atmosphere of my thoughts pleasant and congenial for them, and
they reciprocate by revealing themselves, their tastes and preferences, their backgrounds, their motives—especially their motives—their uncertainties, fears, drives—whatever, all of it, the
whole kit and caboodle.

Soon I am ready for two concrete steps: The first is to find illustrations, or pictures, from the huge file I have collected over the
years from magazines, advertisements, et cetera, of likenesses that
seem pretty much like the story people who have moved in on me.
Quite possibly it would not work for a single other novelist. I can
only say it works for me, and my editors like it. It gets the characters across to them, especially if they are visual-minded, which,
interestingly enough, many editors are. This first step is fun.
The second is more concrete and much harder work.,

The prospectus

I learned it from my work in the theater. I use the Aristotelian
method of probing my characters and setting them down on
paper in the form of a character analysis. This includes a description in great detail: physical, psychological, emotional, intellectual. It sets down the history of the character from birth till the
time I've met him or her. It gives—and this I consider most important of all—the character's SPINE, that is, his driving motivation in life. And also his FATAL FLAW—the trait that is going to
make for his development, if he licks the flaw, or his disintegra-
tion, if he does not surmount it.

I do this for every character which the novel will include.

Quite a feat, yes, if the novel includes something like twenty-odd characters as in *Candy Carmichael* or *The Case of the Diamond Eye*.

This bit of intellectual gymnastics I have dubbed "A Prospectus." It includes, along with the character analyses, a rundown of the settings, the major conflicts (the drama of the book), by all means a terse statement of the theme and an inkling of the plotline. Plotting is not the *bête noire* it appears to be to so many beginners. Plotting is exciting and really quite effortless once you lay the groundwork indicated above. Ninety-nine times out of a hundred, the characters will write the novel for you, they will take care of the story line or the plot or whatever you want to call it.

I have been called a novelist who is long on "story" and cooks up great plots. Nonsense. I simply hand it over to my characters, have faith in their validity, and let them have a whirl. Of course, if your characters are *not valid,* then you are in trouble from the start. Nothing will go right, including the plot.

Now let's get back to novel writing.

The prospectus is complete and is sent off to the editor. While the editorial staff is having a go at it—they like this, don't like that; they think maybe you ought to cut out this character or strengthen that one—the writer buckles down to research.

Research

If you traveled a lot when you were young as I did, you can take a refresher course or a quick trip, armchair or otherwise, to bring you up-to-date. You have to soak in the settings, no mistake about that. The smallest detail is all-important in whatever country you have selected. You have to research the plumbing, how it works or doesn't; the telephone systems; the foods; the transportation systems. I work with a map of Rome or Lisbon or Paris or London pasted up in front of me as my characters romp through one of my suspense novels. Also, in these suspense stories, I have had to become familiar with technology. This too can be fascinating, but it has to be accurate in every detail. In the course of writing these hefty suspense yarns, I have acquired a pretty substantial "smattering of ignorance" about such subjects as the laser, oceanography, earthquakes, orchids, Interpol, the diamond industry from blue-earth mining to cutting and designing, scuba diving, how to maintain and sail a yacht, the industrial peculiarities of Milan, the lure of the Algarve, the charms of Northumberland, bullfighting, plastic surgery, Grand Prix racing and the oil industry. I could go on and on.

One has to know how to read, of course, as well as how to observe. Speed reading is, I should think, a must for any prospective serious novelist. Also, the knack of knowing where to get the kind of information which you can obtain only by going to the sources. People have been enormously helpful to me, but you do have to know how to approach them: Honey will get you more than vinegar, and people generally love to help a writer. A young writer should develop eclectic tastes in friendships. You will need to know a lot of people in many different fields and walks of life.

So . . . our research (I call it the honeymoon period) is well launched. The prospectus is returned and happily accepted by the editors.

Methods

Now you have a perfect right to ask: But how do you *write* the book? What are your work methods?

Here goes.

Once started, I work on my novel every single day until it is finished. And I do mean every day. That includes weekends. *"Wait for inspiration?"* That is for the birds. If I had *waited* for inspiration, I would never have written one single chapter. No. The thing is discipline. You've heard it a million times, and a million times it is true. Every day you must get to that old typewriter (you may prefer longhand or a tape recorder). You sit at your desk, and you sit and sit and sit until that first sentence gets down on paper. You know by now that I am speaking only for myself, but I can truthfully say that the first sentence is always the hardest for me. After that, the going is not always easy, but at least I am going. I don't struggle and labor over *how* I am saying it. Leave that to writers who are style-conscious —and let them win the prizes. I just let the stuff *flow*. After all, with over forty published novels behind me, I feel entitled to some fun in the game. Sure, it's work, backbreaking work, often nerve-racking, but it ought to be some fun, too. I insist that some of it be pure joy, times when I am saying just what I want to say through the characters. Perhaps this may not prove to be the best part of the novel, but as stated above, I do think anyone who decides to go in for the grueling job of professional writing should be privileged to get some of the protests or anger or injustices or sheer rage bottled up inside him off his chest.

If you want to know how much I can write in one session, I aim for a completed chapter a day. This isn't always possible when the chapters run long. Let's say, eight pages is a good day's work. I will seldom let myself get away with less. Sometimes I can do it in a few hours, say three or four. Sometimes I have made myself stay at that infuriating desk for eight or ten hours, and not up every ten minutes to see if the mailman has been here, either!

Self-criticism

I revise and edit my own stuff, relentlessly, before I will let any editor have a squint at it. I am professionally proud in this respect. I do not stand in awe of my own writing. It is sometimes good, sometimes bad, and sometimes horrible. I often overwrite and cut mercilessly. Once finished, I fret and fume to get the exactly right word. I am very tough on myself. My editors know it. Nothing any critic could ever say in a review would be more severe than I would be on my own finished job—even after it is published.

Thus I never read my reviews. I am simply not interested. My publishers know this. I believe reviews are largely personal opinions. Besides, I could point out to the critics some flaws which perhaps they have overlooked, so why bother? Forty reviewers reviewing the same book will all disagree. This could be most confusing to a writer. I think a writer should write because he wants to, because he *has* to write. He has something to say and has to get it down in cold print. He has to share, to tell others how the view is from his particular bridge. "Look," he says, "this is life, the way I see it, and these are people, the way they appear to me." Life is wonderful, miserable, joyous, sad, noble, and vicious. This feeling is inside me, you, all of us. We have to get it out where it can be heard and seen and, perhaps, do some good. We don't write for the critics. We write for ourselves, and each other.

Of course, writing for money is rather nice, too. But that's a whole new chapter. Don't you agree?

30

THE THRILLER IS A NOVEL

by Ellis Peters

It's quite true that it employs an accelerated pace, severely edits its selection of details for effect, and adopts minor refinements of technique all its own. Nonetheless, the fact remains a fact: the thriller is a novel.

On the face of it, a fairly obvious statement. But does everyone agree with it? In a world where thrillers are hygienically segregated from so-called "straight" novels, given to other reviewers, and allotted about one-twentieth the amount of review space, we can hardly afford to take general consent for granted. Nor do all thriller writers subscribe to the axiom. There is still a school which holds that the thriller is and must be a pure puzzle, and that any deviation is heresy.

Now the pure puzzle is not and cannot be a novel, because it has nothing to do with real life, but is a contrived exercise for the mind, and demands a cast all—or almost all—equally expendable, in order to preserve the secret to the last page, and if possible to the last line. And this, too, of course, is of the nature of the thriller. We want to keep our secrets. We want to surprise the reader in the last line if we can; but not at any price. And even the word "surprise" is here used in a strictly limited sense.

213

Speaking for myself, if my readers don't react to the solution with a deep release of satisfaction, approval and fulfillment; if they don't think, consciously or subconsciously, "Of course, that's right, that's inevitable!"—then the book's a failure. Simply because, as far as I'm concerned, if the thriller isn't a novel, it's nothing at all.

And what if readers find the final surprise no surprise, but discover to their own satisfaction "who-done-it" somewhat earlier than I wanted them to—does that also make the book a failure? It does flaw the performance, of course, but not to the same extent. I'd rather have it that way than the other, for it means, at any rate, that this book was real enough, true enough, enough of a novel, to enable the perceptive reader to know quite surely which of its characters could and which could not have committed that particular crime in those particular circumstances. But it also means that I've failed, against these self-imposed odds, to pull off the puzzle and preserve the mystery to the end.

The unforgivable flaw

Only Allah created perfection! In spite of some superlative performances by various authors in the past and the present, I suspect that the genuinely perfect thriller—by my rules, of course! —has never yet been written, and possibly never will be. So far from causing us to sell our typewriters in despair, this circumstance provides a challenge that keeps us writing. Once you have written one thriller, you can't stop, if you happen to see the art my way. There is always the dazzling possibility that you may be the one, that you may pull it off in the teeth of all the conditions that make it flatly impossible. What is merely difficult the thriller writer performs annually, if not oftener. The impossible is another matter.

For the truth is that the thriller is a paradox. It must be a mystery. And it must be a novel. And it is virtually schizophrenia to aim at both. But for the dedicated author nothing less is conceivable. To lower your sights is unthinkable. You might as well take to the modern "straight" novel, currently subsiding soggily into the morass of the non-novel.

For consider the definition. According to the *Concise Oxford Dictionary,* the novel is "a fictitious prose narrative of volume length portraying characters and actions representative of real life in continuous plot." Narrative? Characters and actions representative of real life? Continuous plot? Granted that "real life" is a very wide canvas, taking in the reality of man's fantasies and dreams and withdrawals no less than his overt actions and frequently deceptive words, do we really get satisfaction on this level from the current novel? And how often?

But the thriller is more closely bound to the tradition and the law. It cannot possibly dispense with narrative and continuous plot, or even pretend (more than once!) that they are expendable. Its field of choice is defined within its responses to that other ingredient, "characters and actions representative of real life." And as for me, I go with the *Concise Oxford Dictionary,* all the way. The novel is bound by respect for the true observation of the action and reaction between characters and circumstances, involved with every creature it creates, and in honor bound not to lie or falsify for its own ends. So is the thriller, being itself, for good or ill, a novel. If you have been unlucky enough to create a complex, agonized, bewildered character who cannot possibly react to the circumstances in which he finds himself but in one absolute, awkward and damned inconvenient way, too bad! You're stuck with him, and with his reaction. If you force him out of his nature, you've killed both him and your book. Nobody will ever forgive you—or at any rate, you'll never forgive yourself, which is the same thing.

The trap, the dilemma

Beginning a book, however completely planned in advance—and for the thriller this pre-planning is absolutely essential, down to the finest detail, though the actual writing will modify the plan according to its own organic needs—is plain hell. You know your characters then only by repute, as it were, as if someone had described an individual to you, and you were just about to meet him in person for the first time. This is a very different matter from knowing him through your own senses, by sight and sound and touch. You write his first utterances, even his description, very gingerly, feeling your way; and suddenly he says something which you know to be in character, and you type it down furiously and respond to it warmly, and you're off. Or he is, rather! He can lead you a dance, after that, but let him. Follow him every step of the way. He'll show you exactly what he is, and God help you if you lie about any part of it, or in any circumstances try to make him behave in a way in which he does not instinctively behave. That's essentially what I mean by saying that the thriller is a novel. The truth about people is the truth about events, about life, about every mortal thing. Lie about one thing, and everything goes sour.

But you see, don't you, the trap you're setting for yourself? The more truthfully and solidly you set each character up to view, three-dimensional, calculable (to the limited extent that any man is calculable), and open to sympathy, the better your readers will know him, and the more you are limiting your own field of action where the mystery is concerned. Not a bit of use creating ten rounded, knowable people, and then thinking you can knock off any one of them at random on the last page, and say, "This is the murderer." Your readers will rise up in wrath and give you the lie. Because they know the man by this time, and they know such a solution is not right. This wasn't a thing he would do, given the circumstances, given the incentive, and given the kind of man he has been shown to be. In fact, you're a liar. And you yourself will know that indeed you are. And you won't like the feeling.

Now this is a dilemma which the pure puzzle of former days

evades. It doesn't aspire to be a novel; it aims at something quite different, a mental titilation which has its own pleasures and rewards. It knows what it wants, and sets out the field accordingly, with a cast of carefully constructed plastic characters, brilliantly deployed but in very shallow depth, so that every man-jack in the cast is expendable. Thus the puzzle itself can be as complex and marvelous as the author chooses, and prolonged tantalizingly until the last line, and nobody is going to be able to say that the puppet shot down in the finale could not possibly have done the deed. He could. Any one of them could. They were designed to that end.

It is a perfectly respectable and clearly-stated end, and has produced many a brilliant tour de force. But for good or ill, it is not my end. A book about half-people is not for me. If I have written such books, they were simply failures on my part. What I want is to make my people live, breathe, speak, act with such conviction that the reader may know them as he knows his own kin. So the thriller I always set out to write—win or lose—is stuck with a cast of characters as intimately known to the readers as their brothers and sisters, maybe better. Sometimes, it's true, the author can legitimately hold in reserve a few ambivalent characters, the ones no one would ever really know, even in the flesh, but they are few and far between. And yet he has a mystery to preserve if he can.

The test

This is the real fascination of the thriller, the constant challenge that won't let you get away once you've tasted blood. To do the impossible! To show the reader every inflection of every character's personality, and yet come up at the end of everything with a solution that both startles and rings true. Here is the murderer, you say to your public. Go back and match up every word he speaks, every move he makes, even every glimpse vouch-safed you into his thoughts. Go ahead and check. Did he lie at this stage? Have I misled you as to what he meant here—if only you had interpreted it correctly? Is he not the same man throughout, however troubled and devious? Is this solution truth, or isn't it?

And if, at this point, you should ever find your reader reacting with an explosion of understanding deep within his own mind, and saying, "Yes, yes, yes!" in a fury of affirmation, while at the same time dazzled by your revelation, then believe me, my friend, you may well have written that hypothetical perfect thriller which would also be in the fullest sense a novel. That's what we're all aiming at with every shot—or many of us, at any rate, and myself certainly. We make the whole thing difficult for ourselves, if not impossible, as long as we see the thriller as a novel. We also make it endlessly worthwhile, endlessly fascinating and alluring.

To travel hopefully, after all, really is better than to arrive!

31

WRITING HISTORICAL NOVELS

by Jane Aiken Hodge

HISTORICAL novels are like icebergs. There is (or should be) more to them than meets the eye. A dear friend, and eminent literary agent, once told me that the secret of success was to do a vast amount of research, and then let practically none of it show. I think this is very sound advice to the beginner in the field, or to anyone else, for that matter. The reader does not want to be bothered with learned disquisitions on the customs or events of the period in which the story is set, but he must have confidence that you, the author, know all about them. And the only way to achieve this, is, quite simply, to do so. Then you can slide in the casual little detail that makes for conviction, and it will work.

Research

The first thing to do, then, if you really want to write an historical novel, is to choose your subject and period, and make up your mind to a good spell of research before you even start writing. Obviously, your task will be easier if you choose a period about which you already know something: at least you will have an idea of where to begin in your reading. Then, while your characters are growing in your mind and their story is taking shape, you can be studying the background of their lives. Obviously, you will need some idea of roughly how much time your story is going to cover, though I myself find this one of the most unpredictable factors; characters will take the law into their own hands and come to their personal crises either sooner or later than one anticipates. For my novel, *Savannah Purchase,* I collected a great deal of fascinating detail about President Monroe's visit to Savannah in 1819, and a fire and plague the next year, only to have the story wind itself up almost immediately after Monroe arrived. But it is still better to do too much research than too little. You need, for instance, to know all about your character's past, before the actual story opens, so that you can start work more or less at the birth dates of your hero and heroine. If, for instance, you were setting a book in France under Napoleon, you would need to remember all the time that your characters had been born and grown up during the horrors of the French Revolution.

First, you will need a general history book for a very broad framework of events, and then, if you are lucky, its references and bibliography will lead you outward into the absolutely essential secondary reading: diaries, letters, travel books and even novels and plays of your period. For you will soon find that the kind of framework your history book gives is far too general for your purpose. You want to know much more than that such and such a battle was fought on such a date, or that the prime minister was assassinated, or the government fell. You want to know what books were being published, what plays were being produced, the kind of thing people were talking about. And for this, the best source is obviously contemporary newspapers and magazines, if they exist.

If you set your story much further back than, say, 1800, you are going to have to do without these. Your task will be practically simpler but imaginatively more difficult. I have never gone much farther back than 1800, for all kinds of reasons, so that what I am saying applies mainly to the historical novel set in comparatively recent times. For earlier periods, I would recommend a study of some of the masters in the field. There is Mary Renault, who uses the first person to evoke so effectively the atmosphere of ancient Greece; or Maurice Druon with his amazing chronicle of the early kings of France; or Shelley Mydans' spellbinding (and brilliantly researched) life of Thomas Becket, *Thomas*. All of these, by the way, are based on stories already in existence, either in history or in myth. For the remoter periods, I think one is more likely to succeed with this kind of book than with straight fiction. The greater the difference between the lives of imaginary characters and ours, the more difficult the problem of making them seem real, or getting your readers involved with them. It is interesting to note that many successful authors of fiction set in remote times write for children or young adults. A straight adventure story can carry conviction, while a story for adults, dependent on the interaction of characters for its crises, might not.

Language and dialogue

Dialogue is a major problem in writing historical fiction. If you set your novel in a period or place so remote that the characters do not speak English, your task will be comparatively simple. You should not, of course, use modern slang and should keep an eye on the kinds of metaphors and similes your characters use. Here again the first step is to read any literature that may exist of the time you have chosen. If you are going to set your book in ancient Greece, read Homer; if in pre-conquest England, read *Beowulf*. This will help you to avoid the pitfalls of using phrases based on the apparatus of modern living. People could not be shocked in classical times, because electricity had not been discovered: I suppose they would be thunderstruck instead. In the same way, in writing about times before 1900, you must translate metaphors based on the motor car into terms of the carriage or the horse.

In some ways, the question of language gets more difficult as you get nearer to the present day. Your reader will know more about the way your characters really talked. If you write a book about Henry the Eighth and have him say, "Cool it," to an hysterical wife, your reader will probably be surprised. On the other hand, if you make Henry talk as he actually would have done, you probably won't have any readers. You need to achieve a compromise, with just enough easy, typical phrases of the time to suggest it, but not enough to stick your reader. Shelley Mydans' *Thomas* is outstanding in this respect.

I find that a useful kind of two-handed dodge to give verisimilitude in dialogue is to use it as much as possible to convey the historical background. Instead of using straight paragraphs of historical information, I let my characters talk about what is going on, thus getting essential information across to the reader in a comparatively painless way (remember how Alice liked conversations) and at the same time placing the speakers firmly in their period. In order to be able to do this, you will almost certainly find, as I do, that you need to make yourself an outline or diagram of your period, covering both major and minor events. Otherwise, it is all too easy to have your hero and heroine carry on an interesting conversation about something that is not, in fact, going to happen for several months. This is a particular hazard where information from abroad is concerned. For instance, in writing *Here Comes a Candle,* which is set at the time of the War of 1812 between Great Britain and the United States, I had to keep remembering that it took up to six months for news to cross the Atlantic. It was also useful to remember that the bloody Battle of New Orleans was actually fought some time after the War of 1812 had technically ended.

Choosing your time

Altogether, if you are eager to get started on your historical novel and reluctant to spend more than, say, six months on research first, I would strongly recommend choosing a time not too far from the present. I have so far stuck firmly to the early nineteenth century, partly because it is a fascinating and eventful period, with Napoleon rampaging over Europe, and partly because the language is close enough to ours so that one can get by with a minimum of what I tend to call "pish tushery." In fact, I use less and less, conveying period much more by what the characters talk about and what they do: fans and snuff-boxes and quizzing glasses, instead of cigarettes and matches.

This is very much a matter of personal preference. Georgette Heyer, who has set many of her delicious books in the early nineteenth century, has invented what I am tempted to call a language of her own, except that I am sure it is all (or very nearly all) drawn from genuine contemporary sources. It is just that she uses it far more thickly than people actually did at the time. You have only to compare a speech in one of her books with one of Jane Austen's to see what I mean. Jane Austen, who had a very sound suspicion of slang and metaphor, reads like a modern author compared with Georgette Heyer. This, in fact, is one of the great charms of Miss Heyer's books. She uses her special language to brilliant comic effect, but I think it would be a rash author who would try to imitate her in this or in her increasingly—perhaps excessively—lavish use of period detail.

This, again, is a question of taste. I like to think that the reader will care about my heroine and identify with her, and, with this in mind, I tend to play down the ways in which she is different from a modern girl. Obviously, one must have some idea of what she looked like, and, from time to time, of how she was dressed, but by and large I think readers should be allowed to build their own hero and heroine. Clothes, if they are mentioned, should be significant, as part of the action, not as careful, setpiece descriptions. On the other hand, the author must never forget about them. There are limits to what even the most active heroine (and I like my heroine active) can do if she is dressed in full Regency rig. It was a great relief, when I wrote *Greek Wedding*, to dress my heroine in Turkish trousers for about half the time, and later as a Greek boy. And then, of course, when she did get into a proper dress, it was an event.

Heroes are more difficult still, partly because Georgette Heyer has done them so often and so well. I have vowed never to use another many-caped greatcoat, just as I hope never to have another governess. This, by the way, is a real problem of historical romances. How do you get your hero and heroine together in a world of strict chaperonage? And, having achieved this, by some sleight of hand, how do you then keep them apart? There are all kinds of answers. In writing *Maulever Hall*, where the heroine was a protégée of the hero's mother, I made him a politician, constantly rushing off to London to try to pass the Reform Bill. In *The Winding Stair*, the hero was a secret agent and got sent back to England, leaving the heroine to make the best of things in Portugal, where he had landed her. In *Marry in Haste*, the hero was accidentally exported to Brazil, which left such a gap that a lively subplot developed with an unexpected secondary hero.

And that, I suppose, is what makes writing historical novels such fun as well as such hard work. The constant interplay between the real and the imaginary time-scheme adds enormously to the stress, and consequently to the satisfaction of the writing. The whole business is delightfully full of setbacks and surprises, and it is a rare book that ends as one has planned. But when it comes to the crunch, fiction must always give way to fact. If you betray your reader once, he will never trust you again.

32

WRITE ME AN ADVENTURE NOVEL

by Bruce Cassiday

THE last author I asked to write me an adventure novel looked at me as if I had been marooned on another planet for a hundred years and said:

"The adventure novel is dead."

He walked away, shaking his head, and needless to say, he did not write me my adventure novel.

But he was wrong. The adventure novel is not dead; it has never been more alive and flourishing, nor, ironically, has it ever been less recognized. It has proliferated into so many different forms that it is probably read more than any other kind of novel, but, at the same time, the average reader never thinks of "adventure" except in relation to *Treasure Island* or *Tom Sawyer*.

We define escape novels today as historical novels, mystery novels, gothic novels, spy novels, war novels, science fiction novels, cold war novels, Western novels, and so on, and never think of them as offshoots of the age-old adventure novel.

Yet Hammond Innes' *The Wreck of the Mary Deare*, Alistair MacLean's *Ice Station Zebra*, Desmond Bagley's *Landslide* and many others in this pure category are widely read today.

225

Possibly because of its exotic setting and its international flavor, the novel of adventure, rooted in Homer's *Odyssey* and related to Defoe's *Robinson Crusoe*, has found its most effective expression yet in our nuclear age.

What distinguishes the pure adventure novel from its hybrid contemporaries?

This usually male-oriented entertainment essentially celebrates a perilous and bold undertaking in an exotic locale, where hazards are constantly met and the issues hang upon unforeseen events. The enterprise concerns the quest for a fantastically valuable object, and the hazards encountered include human antagonists, natural phenomena, and modern technological disasters which impede the progress of the hero. A strongly formulated story line lends support to overt action; conflict pits man against man and man against nature; the four main ingredients of the adventure novel are a hero, a villain, a prize, and a technology.

The hero

In the mythological epic, the hero ventures out into the world, encounters dangers and terrifying experiences, and returns home in some greatly improved human form, the prototype of the national figure: Ulysses, Jason, Aeneas.

The American adventure hero has never really been defined. Is he Robert Jordan in Ernest Hemingway's *For Whom the Bell Tolls*, blowing up the bridge in Spain? Is he Tom Joad in John Steinbeck's *The Grapes of Wrath*, seeking a home in California after Oklahoma crumbles to dust? Is he Captain Ahab of the *Pequod* in Herman Melville's *Moby Dick*, bent on exacting vengeance on the White Whale?

No. Jordan was obsessed with proving himself a man. Joad was obsessed with social reform. Ahab was simply mad.

Is he the anti-hero, Yossarian in Joseph Heller's *Catch-22*, signing a separate peace with World War II and turning his back on the madness and folly about him? Or is he the super-hero,

James Bond in Ian Fleming's *Goldfinger*, foiling the takeover of the world's gold supply, and offering his splendid body to all those girls?

No.

A super-hero like James Bond is important not because he represents the ultimate and utmost in the male image, but because by his very invincibility he points up the fallacy of the idol. The anti-hero like Yossarian is important in forcefully pointing up the foibles and idiocies of our time. Like the super-hero he satirizes, he, too, is an extreme symbol at the other end of the human pole. Both serve as remote razor edges of "the curve."

The hero of today's adventure novel is a combination of heroes from all the adventure genres: detective, spy, fighter, mountain climber, scientist, seaman, cowboy—in short, the male adventurer, neither too big for life, nor too small for adulation. But he, like Ulysses, has one dominant trait: "ingenuity." And he has embellished his cunning with modern technological know-how.

For instance, the protagonist of Berkely Mather's *The Gold of Malabar* must (1) break a complicated map code like a scientist-detective, (2) disguise himself and infiltrate alien country like a spy, (3) take on single-handedly a group of enemy thugs like a fighter, (4) ride a horse like a cowboy, (5) climb a mountain like a professional, (6) sail a boat like a seaman—all within the confines of a single adventure.

The villain

No story is stronger than its villain. When the hero sets himself on a course of action, usually in the pursuit of some valuable object, other men, strong, evil, and amoral, challenge him for its possession. As with the mythical Jason, who had to overcome countless villains to get the Golden Fleece, Jason today must contend with the Sirens and Harpies of today.

In the race for fame and fortune, every other contender is an enemy, a creature unsympathetic to the hero. Villains abound in our world. Because they, too, are shrewd and worldly-wise, they present formidable opposition.

Interestingly enough, the central villain of many an adventure novel is a countryman of the hero, in spite of the fact that the action takes place in some remote corner of the world. The hirelings and associates of the villain on the other hand usually come from the background where the action occurs.

The villain must be shrewd, cunning, and more unscrupulous than the hero; and he must be in possession of at least one elementary fact the hero does not have, to provide him with temporary superiority. Eventually, the hero must destroy the villain by ingenuity, technological knowledge, or courage—or a combination of all three.

For example, in *The Mountain of the Blind* by John Creasey, the hero is trailed by an evil mining tycoon whose strange secret compels him to keep the hero out of a Central African country, and who pursues, threatens, burns out, and shoots the hero in that order. In *Northward the Coast,* by Edward Lindall, the hero is pursued by a sadistic politico, by a minion of the law, *and* by a tribe of headhunting aborigines—close parallels to Jason's adversaries. And the hero is hunted by car, by airplane, by ship, and by radio!

The prize

The object most frequently sought by the hero in the adventure novel is gold, but instead of gold, the object can be diamonds, or rare metals, or almost anything the novelist's imagination can substitute from our nuclear-age grab bag. In Desmond Bagley's *The Golden Keel,* Mussolini's wartime treasure—five million dollars in bullion, gems, and rare gold coins, lost in his abortive flight in 1945—is the object of the hero's quest. In Hammond Innes' *The Blue Ice,* it is a vast mineral deposit under a glacier in Norway, and *Ice Station Zebra* deals with the recovery of a satellite missile tracker.

And what motivates the hero to go in search of a "prize" undoubtedly not equal to the amount of money he could make at home in a big business deal? Classic motivations are strong ones: honor, fear, glory. But we live in unheroic times today, and for a man to subject himself to pain and discomfort simply to assert his honor is, by our lights, ridiculous. Even to challenge fear is deemed inadvisable; it is expedient to run. And glory is a word in the dictionary, quaint and interesting, but of another era.

Something drives the hero to prove himself; proof of virility is not an end in itself. Something within the hero, something within the writer, something within the reader is at work here—and perhaps it cannot be truly defined except as the kind of stubborn male pride that makes a man grow a beard in defiance of convention.

Technology

The American reader of fiction is a practical man, neither a dreamer nor a thinker, but a tinkerer with gadgets—not words. For this reason, one of the most important elements of the adventure novel is technological accuracy.

A good adventure novel features at least one modern technology somewhere in its pages, usually as background for the dramatic action. The technology covered must be colorful, correct, and realistic. For example:

Mining operations, lumbering, whaling, meteorology and diamond mining occur in five representative books.

Because adventure presupposes long journeys, the writer must present technological exactitude in travel. If the hero sails a boat, he must report the nautical facts correctly. If he flies an airplane, he must do so with skill. If he is involved in operating earth-moving equipment, he must use the proper terminology.

Today's reader demands a more scientific approach to the description of natural phenomena than during Homer's time, when gods inspired the terrors.

In Hammond Innes' *The Strode Venturer,* the hero is buffeted about by a strange Indian Ocean current called a "boiling sea," accompanied by noxious sulphurous vapor rising from the ocean. Pumice appears on the surface of the water: the world quivers and seems on the verge of self-destruction. A newly-formed volcanic island then sinks—actually disappears from sight!

The hero of *The River of Diamonds,* by Geoffrey Jenkins, is attacked underwater by a giant "monster" made up of a fantastic number of Siphonophora (of the variety known as Portuguese men-of-war); individuals are linked together into a colony and compose a completely new organism of great size. In the same story, the hero is warned of imminent death by a hideous phenomenon called The Bells of St. Mary's, which presages an enormous inundation by poisonous methane gas.

In mythology, the hero is frequently saved from disaster in the nick of time by the intervention of his favorite god: this is the device of *deus ex machina,* "God out of a machine," favored by the epic writer. The modern hero does not escape with the help of the gods; he escapes by his own ingenuity, quite like Ulysses—the more amazing and ingenious the escape the better —often making use of electronics and other highly sophisticated technical devices.

High in the Andes Mountains the hero of Desmond Bagley's *High Citadel* defends a party of plane-crash survivors from an army of revolutionaries by fashioning ingenious replicas of medieval weapons out of parts of rusted steel, rubber, and leather: the trebuchet and the two crossbows he makes help him hold the enemy at bay.

Technological savvy is closely related to another element of the story line of the adventure novel, a portion closely paralleling a standard convention of the old epic: battle scenes described vividly, with catalogues of arms. Guns, laser beams, grenades, nuclear warheads, torpedoes, bombs, bows and arrows, *plastique* —all are grist for the author's mill.

A list of weapons will give you an idea of the extent and type. You might run across: A water-cooled Spandau; an air-cooled Hotchkiss; a 7.65 millimeter Borchardt; a 12-bore shotgun; a single-barreled bolt-action rifle; a Purdey .300 Magnum; a 7.2 millimeter Mannlicher automatic; a Molotov cocktail (very popular); and many more.

Exotic backgrounds

In no other type of novel today is the exotic so necessary as in the novel of adventure. American men have ventured into strange parts of the globe fighting in World War II, Korea, and Vietnam, and today, as readers, they are eager to see more of the world. No longer will they be satisfied with stories set in the same old street where they live.

For this reason, the reader of novels is eager and ready to experience vicarious adventure in exotic places, countries which in the jet age are really not so far off as they seem.

The advantage enjoyed by the adventure novelist is obvious. He has a ready-made audience for his exotic backgrounds. But he must present foreign locales with skill and precision. Dialogue makes the modern novel move swiftly and surely, and here the author can use language most effectively, inserting carefully in the speech of the characters strange foreign words easily understood in context.

And he can make the physical geography of the country— the houses, the roads, the mountains, the rivers, and the general atmosphere (called "color" in the writing trade)—an integral part of the dramatic action.

A quick rundown will give you an idea of the variety of locales in a handful of adventure novels:

The North Pole; the Atlantic Ocean; the South Pole; India's Malabar Coast; the Maldive Archipelago; the Andes Mountains; the wilds of British Columbia.

These are the trappings of the Nuclear-Age Odyssey, then: a protagonist; antagonists; a quest; fascinating technologies; ingenious weaponry; natural phenomena; exotic locales.

They are the heart and soul of the modern adventure novel. And because technology fascinates the reader as well as the writer, it becomes the *ne plus ultra* of the modern Odyssey. Classic monsters, storms, and obstacles transform themselves easily into recognizable modern phenomena.

In these realms the writer today holds the power to capture and define the spirit of the nuclear age, and it is for these insights into the modern world that the adventure novel is read.

33

WRITING PAPERBACK ORIGINALS

by Mona Williams

AT some point every writer, beginner or professional, reaches a kind of roadblock, in or outside of himself, and asks himself this question: Would changing my medium change my luck? If I reached another audience would it be more *my* audience?

This is especially true today of magazine fiction writers, both striving and long-established, not only because so few stories are published now in the high-paying magazines, but because the editors seem nervous and unsure of their fiction policies. Presenting facts, they are fearless; they will calmly feature articles informing their readers what percentage of mothers (according to the latest poll) provide their high-school daughters with the Pill; they will tell you how many virgins (or how few) reach the altar. But to publish a story on the same subjects is different. Stories arouse emotions; fictional characters are much more real than the faceless people in case histories. This revelation can make a fiction writer feel pretty powerful, but it can be baffling, too.

Last spring I wrote a story called "The Double Bed," about a boy and a girl living together. It was rejected by *Cosmopolitan* as "too folksy and conventional" for them, and also by *Redbook*, who wrote a rather agitated letter regretting that it was "too far out" for them *now*—maybe they could see it again next year!

I had reached a roadblock; I felt I was through with short-story writing—it had become too chancy. Neither I nor the editors knew just what was right for these times. I would reach for another audience. This had happened to me before, and whenever it did I wrote a book—most recently two softcover originals.

A sense of freedom

After the restrictions of magazine writing, the first thing a writer feels, once he has decided to do a book, is a sense of freedom. We are, of course, writing as always, we hope, for an audience. Nonetheless, the first person we must please and interest is ourself. We can go through our notebook (whether we keep it in our desk or in our head) for never-used story ideas, situations, and characters, and *we* will decide what we want to write now and what will fit the times and the market. Many nuggets of plot and theme, rich with possibilities, set aside again and again as never quite right for any magazine, look quite different to us now.

I recall this sense of freedom as especially strong when I had written a few thousand words of (what I then expected to be) a novelette. Suddenly I decided it must be a novel.* No longer need I water it down to be acceptable to a woman's magazine. I could write it my way! The basis of this freedom is simple: when you write a book, it will, if it's any good, find its own audience.

The difference between magazine fare and books is the difference between the Blue Plate Special and ordering a la carte. If you order oysters and apple pie, it is because that's what you like —not just because they come with the dinner, not because they come with the magazine. If a reader browses through a bookstore

* This became *The Company Girls,* a Gold Medal Fawcett paperback original (1965).

or picks out a volume from a paperback rack, it's because he sees something he expects will please his individual taste. Good! The first contact is made; the writer has attracted his own kind of reader. That's one advantage—there are others.

Paperbacks and magazines are accustomed to co-existing. In most outlets—grocery stores, drug stores, airports and railway stations—they are only a rack apart. But step from one to the other, from the glossy array of magazine covers, mostly devoted to news, informative articles, features and personality pieces, to the softcovers and we make a happy discovery. In paperbacks, fiction still outnumbers everything else. So this is where they all went, the fiction devourers, the lovely people who still believe that the best reading of all is a good story! We feel wanted again, because this is what we can give them. This is our own thing— to dream up characters and situations in which a reader can lose himself, that will *involve* him as nonfiction writing can never do.

To write a first novel that will interest a major publishing house, to compete with all those big names on hardcovers, seems a formidable project. But a paperback? Would that be so difficult to produce when it's only a rack away from what you've been doing?

The changeover

If you have never before done a book-length, there may be more of a jump here than you had expected. Basically, it involves change of pace; you can't get all steamed up and write a novel off the top of a mood as you have written short pieces. When you are writing a book, you must *settle into it*.

Imagine a long journey (there are no *real* "long" ones now that planes take you anywhere over a hundred miles, so imagine it). All I have to do is remember—twenty years ago our family, with three young children, usually a dog, too, used to drive from one coast to the other twice a year. With all the stops it took over a week. No one settled into the trip the first day. But gradually the pace took hold. By the start of the third day, even the baby and the dog knew we weren't going to get there by nightfall. Moving from short story writing to novels takes this kind of adjustment. If you don't feel this wrench of adjustment, it probably means that novels are right for you; what you thought of all along as short stories were really bits and pieces of novels.

For most writers there is a certain category that is natural to them; instinctively their stories adapt themselves to fit those limits. I wrote a great number of novelettes for the big women's magazines—"Complete Novel in One Issue" the cover proclaimed them. Actually, they were only a third the length of an ordinary novel—twenty to thirty thousand words. When I wrote my first book, *The Marriage,* it wasn't easy for me to change pace, to go into the feeling and action deeply enough to triple that wordage. This book was published first in a briefer version in a mass-circulation women's magazine under the title, "Never Own Me." I then expanded it to book length, my first experience with real change of pace, since I was working with the same material. It had a third life in paperback, under the title, *The Passion of Amy Styron.*

Some writers never can make this changeover. I think of J. D. Salinger and John Cheever, both fine writers, full of insight; yet when they attempt a book-length, it comes out more like strung-together short pieces. On the other hand, the rare short story that Thomas Wolfe wrote was rather like a little chunk chewed off a novel.

I don't think any writer should stretch himself too far from his natural bent to compress or to expand. It is easy to know which is natural to you. Ask yourself this: when you rewrite, do you cut or fill out? I clearly do the latter. My first draft is skeletal; all my rewriting is fleshing out. I had two books pub-

lished during a single year—*Voices in the Dark,* a narrative poem
or "spoken novel" published in hardcover by Doubleday (116
pages); and the other, *Celia,* a paperback original published by
Dell, which in 188 pages hurries one poor woman through three
husbands and four lovers. Though utterly different in appeal
and content, what these books have in common is that both
would have far more stature if they were fleshed out to three
times their present length.

I couldn't do it, and this is my limitation. The great writers
have such a wealth of talent that it gushes out of them; rewriting
must be a pruning of too much richness, and if it hurts too much,
their editors will do it.

Pluses in paperbacks . . .

Although I have mentioned some advantages of writing paperback originals, there is another important one: Most paperbacks
are written by professionals who are more or less nameless. This
cuts down on the competition—name authors are not attracted
to this field, so publishers like Dell and Avon welcome and *seek*
writers who can meet the requirements of the paperback original
market.

If you decide to try the paperback original field, the following is the best plan. Block out your story and write a five- or
six-page outline. Then, unless you are a well-known writer, do
a couple of sample chapters, probably the first chapter and another that will fit in later, in the midst of the action. Now the
editor will be able to judge your material and have some idea
of how you will handle it. Find out which publishers buy originals of the kind you can write and submit your outline to them.
What you are aiming for is not just a green light but a contract
and a good big advance against royalties.

To receive such a substantial vote of confidence on the basis
of an outline, before the actual novel is even begun, as I did

on *Celia,* my last novel for Dell (they knew my writing so didn't require a sample), is like having a launching pad and a booster to set you off. You don't feel nearly as alone as you usually do when you and your typewriter take off into empty space. Somebody down there is monitoring your flight, some editor has written you a buddy-like letter saying that he is assigned to you and your book, and if you have any problems you must feel free to consult him. Even the discipline feels good; re-entry is set for a specific time (it says so in the contract), so that's one decision you don't have to make.

There are still plenty of decisions that are all yours, mostly technical: Are you going to stick with one viewpoint or move around getting inside several people's skins? Or will you keep your distance from all the characters and just observe and write down what you see? Are you going to tell your own story, or will you let the dialogue tell it, as John O'Hara does? The great thing is that you are *capable* of making all these decisions and you know it—otherwise you wouldn't have that contract.

. . . and a few minuses

It's only fair to remind you of something else—the unrewarding side of writing paperbacks. Even the most successful paperback originals lack something. You already know what it is: the fanfare, the kind of special excitement that accompanies the publication of a hardcover—the autograph parties, reviews, publicity clippings, the warm glow of presenting family and friends with your author's copies, the personal inscription you proudly write inside. Here is your hardcover book, solid and heavy in your hand; there is your picture on the jacket.

But in a paperback, there is no picture on the jacket; you can stuff the book into a pocket. You don't say much to your friends about it, but you see it on the stands, and it costs so little, it's humiliating.

Still, there are compensations. There is the honest satisfaction of knowing you are a pro, and that your publisher is thinking of your book, not in terms of how many thousand it may sell, but how many tens or even hundreds of thousands. Then you think of all those strange pockets your little book is stuffed into, and you feel a very private small excitement all your own.

34

WRITING FOR CHILDREN

by Irene Hunt

ANY writer, whether he writes for children or adults, must face and answer the questions posed by Goethe to would-be writers:

Do I have something to say?
Is what I have to say worth saying?
How best can I go about saying this thing which I consider to be worth the saying?

Any fictional writing if it lays claim to being literature must leave the reader with a clearer picture, a deeper understanding of some aspect of human behavior, of human needs—a more profound knowledge of the human heart, if you will.

Thus the writer must find his answer to the question "Do I have something worthwhile to say?" by discovering what aspects of human behavior he wishes to explore.

Will it be the courage of a child in overcoming his inner fears, in overcoming a hostile environment, in overcoming physical or emotional handicaps? Will it be a child's perceptions of the adult world around him? Will it be the insights of a young person into his own behavior? Will it be the interplay between environment and human needs?

There are an infinite number of problems which beset the family of man, and they lie waiting for us to present them in a new light—to clarify and illuminate them through our own originality.

When the question of what one is going to say has been resolved, the writer must decide how best he can say it—what characters, what situations he can create which will provide the best setting for the ideas which are the core of his writing.

Armstrong Sperry, in writing of courage which overcame a terrible fear, chose the terrors of the sea, of storms, of primitive savages to illuminate his theme in *Call It Courage*.

Scott O'Dell pointed up another kind of courage, the courage to live, to survive, in his Robinson Crusoe-like story, *Island of the Blue Dolphins*.

E. B. White and Kenneth Grahame chose fantasy—a fantasy accurately reflecting human values—and where is the child who can miss the dignity and compassion of some of their characters, the bumbling foolishness of others?

An affinity for childhood

Now, a look at the qualifications of the writer himself—the man or woman who aspires to write for that vast crowd of young readers and who aspires to write wisely and well for the audience he has chosen. First, his ability to write for children involves a close affinity with his own childhood, and if he has this, it follows that he will have that same affinity for childhood in general. He must remember! He must remember the anxieties and uncertainties; he must remember the loneliness of being teased or misunderstood. He must remember the dreams, the perplexities, the sudden flashes of joy over something that seemed trivial to adults. He must remember his reaction to tastes, to smell, to colors; his love of a kind hand, his fear of a harsh mouth. He must remember the imaginary companions, the wonderful secret places where he could be alone, the hoarding of nondescript material in an old box—guarding it, rearranging it, caring greatly for it without quite knowing why.

This affinity for our own childhood and for that of others is something that not all of us possess; it is, I sometimes think, as final an attribute as the color of our eyes or the shape of our ears. If we don't have blue eyes or brown, we don't, and there isn't much we can do about it. If we don't understand childhood, we don't, and I doubt if we can ever develop that understanding. This quality is not correlated with either age or intelligence; some great scholars have it, some don't. Some people of twenty have it; some have already lost it at that early age. Some people of sixty or eighty have it; others of the same age do not.

Writers of adult literature are sometimes dismayed when they have turned from their own field to that of children's literature. They often find that they do not know how to speak to children, that they are unable to establish the bond of sympathy which they had believed would be so easy to do. They have found they long since have left their childhood behind them and that they are aliens in a community of readers who sense their kinship with one writer without ever quite realizing that it is present, and who sense equally well the lack of kinship with another writer.

People who have forgotten their own youth tend to carry with them a picture of rosy childhood, protected from all evil, bathed in love and security and winsome innocence. Those of us who remember the anxieties, the anger, the fear—sometimes the cruelties which we perpetrated and have never been able to forget— we are the ones who know that childhood is not always a period suffused in a rosy glow. And those of us who remember the delight at a word of praise, or the sound of a birdsong; the sweet comfort of being understood, the heady excitement of running against the wind, the sense of security in hearing a mother singing at her work—we are the ones who know that childhood delight is not all a matter of camping trips or toys, parties or the approval of peer groups.

A matter of respect

Another point which the writer for children must keep in mind is that he must have respect for his audience. Can he lend dignity to a child of seven or nine—or is he one who would say, "No child of such an age can possibly have felt grief or fear or anxiety with such intensity?"

And again, is the writer in tune with that bittersweet period of life which we call adolescence, or does he believe that adolescents are concerned with nothing more than getting a date or getting on the football team or romping around camp for the summer? Worse still, is he one of those writers who have great fun in depicting adolescents as callow, silly, uproariously funny to the "sophisticated" adult? How naïve can such writers be? Have they completely forgotten the sensitivity, the bewilderment, the groping for beauty and truth that are so often characteristic of these years—the years which, I often think, may be described by the words which Dickens used to describe the closing years of the eighteenth century—"It was the best of times, it was the worst of times; it was the age of wisdom, it was the age of foolishness."

Children have dignity—they appreciate respect for that dignity. Children perceive and evaluate, they feel intensely and they look for answers to the many questions with which a capricious society often baffles them. If the writer for children does not remember this, he will soon need to turn to another field.

Preaching and teaching

Closely associated with respect for childhood is the ability to write without preaching. This is difficult. As parents, we are inclined to preach. As teachers, we are very much inclined to preach. And as writers, we still feel the urge. We want to spell the idea out. We're afraid the immature mind may not be aware of the pearls we are offering it. We want to say, "And so you see, boys and girls, if children do this or that, then these or those results are going to ensue." Paul Hazard in his great book, *Books, Children and Men,* has this to say on the subject: "A glance of the eyes, a thrust of the thumb is all they need. They sense the coming of a sermon and they skip it with dexterity."

Preaching is not the only cardinal sin either. There is the matter of the author feeling that he must be instructive. We like to say—implicitly, of course—"I know that you selected this book because you thought it was fiction, but you're going to get a little lesson in science or history or anthropology on the side."

There is nothing wrong with children learning something of science or history or anthropology in a book of fiction. BUT—and this is a very important BUT—it is up to the author to make this kind of information so much a part of the story, to endow it with so much of human interest, that it is an integral part of the story. When a child picks up a book from the shelves devoted to fiction, he has a right to expect a story. He heartily resents the intrusion of what he perceives as a "classroom bit" interfering with that story. He doesn't mind if it's a part of the story; *Johnny Tremain,* for example, contains a wealth of history concerning the American Revolution, but that history *is* the story of Johnny Tremain—it *is* the story, and not a fringe benefit.

Again I quote Paul Hazard when he writes of some of the early works of what was whimsically called children's literature: "To admire an oak for its beauty was considered time wasted; children needed to be able to calculate what the oak might yield in board feet when it was cut into planks."

What interests children?

Next, an author must be true to himself. If he has a story to tell, he must tell it without worrying whether it will appeal to children of seven or ten or sixteen. Incidentally, if it is a good story for a child of seven, it is in all probability a good story for any age. Take Rebecca Caudill's *A Certain Small Shepherd,* for example—take *Winnie the Pooh,* take *Charlotte's Web*—what age group will like these stories? Any age from seven to ninety, provided the reader has learned to love excellent literature.

I feel that the writer who has a story lurking around in his mind and heart should present it as *he* sees fit. He should be allowed to forget vocabulary and taboo subjects; he should close his ears to the chorus of "children are no longer interested in this or that." One educator told me with a finality that left little room for doubt, that children would never read a story of the Civil War. "They are fed up with it," she said firmly. Of course, what she meant was that *she* was fed up with it. I have more than a hundred letters from children all over the country who have read and have told me that they loved my book, *Across Five Aprils.*

Other members of this free-advice chorus have told me, "If your book is written in the first person, you might just as well throw it away right now. Children simply *won't* read books written in the first person." Oh, won't they? Have a look at *Huckleberry Finn,* at *Treasure Island,* at *Island of the Blue Dolphins,* at *Onion John,* at *It's Like This, Cat.* And my own *Up a Road Slowly* is doing pretty well. My advice to writers is: Ignore the chorus, and write as you please. Children are interested in almost any subject, written in either first or third person, if it is presented in an interesting context, if it is written honestly and well.

There is no need to be upset if we feel that we are dealing with a subject that has often been dealt with before. Some authors strain very hard to be original, confusing novelty with originality, forgetting that it is what you as an author bring to the subject that constitutes originality. Flaubert, Tolstoy and Thackeray used the same, time-worn theme: woman's self-destruction. And yet, Emma Bovary, Anna Karenina and Becky Sharp stand out as different, as unique, as sharply drawn as if each had participated in a situation never described before—products of their specific creator's originality.

I feel that originality is that special blend of color and contrast, that quality of vigor or poetic mood, that depth of characterization with which the writer presents his story. Novelty is only an arresting factor; originality is the quality which gives a book endurance. In children's literature, *Alice in Wonderland* is a shining example of novelty. But it is not novelty that makes this book great. It is not Alice's unusual acquaintances or her experiences with changing size or her encounters with frightening incidents which make the book a great one. It is the satire, the wry wisdom, the impish lashing out at certain stupidities of society which give the book greatness—it is the quality which only Lewis Carroll could give that situation—that very personal and private attribute of a writer which is his originality.

Individuality

Young writers are often concerned with style—they wonder how they can develop that concept which is so elusive, which does not easily lend itself to definition. Style, it seems to me, is an outpouring of the writer's self—his perceptions of life, his grace or lack of grace, his courage or his whining self-pity, his humility and compassion or his cynicism and arrogance.

Think of the delicacy of Katherine Mansfield, the robust humor of Mark Twain, the gentle wistfulness of Kenneth Grahame, the sweet, prim morality and great warmth of Louisa May Alcott. Each has a style all his own because each one has poured out a part of himself, the kind of person he was or is, into his writing.

The young or beginning writer cannot copy a style authentically any more than he can *be* the person whose style he admires. He may be influenced by another's style in that he has read and admired the writings of an author until he has come to accept that person's viewpoint. But if he is wise, he will not seek to emulate another writer's work; he will set himself to the task of telling his own story as clearly, as honestly, as gracefully as he possibly can. When he has worked for a while, he may suddenly discover that he, too, has expressed some inner feelings in a way that people will speak of as a particular style.

In conclusion, I would say that our concern over children's books is justifiable and understandable. There is a great need for excellence in children's literature just as there is a need for excellence in all other aspects of education. To train a nation of readers, of people who have at an early age commenced to deal with ideas, who have come to recognize a system of values which includes such concepts as insight, compassion and understanding of human behavior—to do this carries a responsibility which is of towering importance. For whether a child becomes a scientist or a housewife, a mathematician or a mechanic, a teacher, a businessman, a statesman, a factory worker, a farmer, these values are basic to his fulfillment as a human being.

We must remember that children are not born with these values. Their understanding and appreciation of literature and of life do not suddenly spring full-grown like Athene from the forehead of Zeus. It comes from reading and discussing and learning to love good books; it comes from guidance in discovering wisdom and beauty; it comes because authors and teachers, librarians and parents are providing the books of wisdom, of beauty and joy, for these young learners. The good books, the gay, the sad, the wise ones, are providing a basis for a nation of readers, a nation of people who understand themselves and those around them a little better. We do not learn courage, humility, compassion, honor or human decency from penny lectures or from a special unit in the classroom. We learn those things through the people around us—we learn them largely from the behavior of those characters who march through the pages of our books.

35

WRITING ACTION FICTION

by Desmond Bagley

IF being in the mainstream of a tradition that goes back thousands of years is considered old-fashioned, then I must confess that I am indeed a square fellow, because I consider myself to be first, last, and always a storyteller. I am old-fashioned enough to believe that a story should have a beginning, a middle, and an end.

The telling of stories probably began back in the caves when Ug, his belly comfortably full of meat, said, "Glug, tell us a story."

Glug considered for a while, and then began, "Well, once upon a time . . . ."

Glug's stories would often, but not invariably, end: "And they all lived happily ever after." Thus we have a beginning and an end, and stuck in the middle there is, of course, the middle.

Three-part structure

It is no accident that the classic drama developed a three-act structure. Act I displays to us the characters and the situation in which they find themselves, tells us who they are, their relationship to each other, what they are doing and where they are doing it. Act II develops and complicates the opening situation in various interesting ways. The author of the drama seems to be painting himself into a corner, and our attention is held by figuring how he intends to get himself out. Act III is the denouement; all the complications and problems inherent in the opening situation, and magnified in the development, are solved.

This three-part structure may be seen in the sonata form of the first movement of a classical symphony. It is also to be seen in chess where there is the opening, the middle game and the end game, each requiring its own form of play. The three-part structure itself seems to be psychologically satisfying.

The cardinal tenet in all fiction writing is that characterization is more important than plot. This may seem an odd statement coming from a writer of action fiction, a genre in which strong plotting is considered to be the prime necessity. Nevertheless it is true. There are no original plots; Shakespeare mined his stories from Holinshed's *Chronicles,* and *West Side Story* was a retelling of *Romeo and Juliet.*

Because a novel is primarily about people, it stands or falls by its characterization. The dream folk who populate the pages of your book must be human beings with past histories and hopes for the future. Even though the previous life of even a minor character is never referred to in the book, it must be present in the writer's mind so that he is able to regard his creation, and so to present him, as a rounded human being. I think it was in this connection that Hemingway once remarked, "What you leave out of a book is more important than what you put in."

I choose a background that is interesting to me personally and, if possible, I do my research on the ground as I did when I went to Iceland to research my novel *Running Blind.* I treat the background as a character in its own right. This, to me, is most important. The plot that was worked out in *Running Blind* came directly from the terrain and the peculiar social institutions of Iceland, and I do not think that specific plot could have been set in any other country. This tends to give the story a free-flowing spontaneity that is hard to achieve otherwise.

So I have a group of interesting people set in an interesting landscape. I have no plot. This is not to say that I do not have a theme, which must not be confused with plot, although it often is. The theme of *Running Blind* was the sheer damned stupidity of international espionage; the theme of *Landslide* was the search for personal identity; that of *The Vivero Letter* was of the danger of using vanity to cure a punctured ego.

The theme, then, is the core of the book—it is what you want to say—and out of the interaction of the characters, the environment, and the theme comes the plot. I know how the book starts because I have already set up the initial situation, and I know, rather vaguely, how I would like it to end. Between beginning and end there are 250 sheets of blank paper—the all-important middle.

Cliff-hanging for writer and reader

The only time I wrote the synopsis of a book before attacking the typewriter was the time the book never got written. When I finished the synopsis, my unconscious mind must have decided that I had finished the book, and I lost interest. So in the day-to-day writing I never know what I am going to put on paper next. My wife, who reads my work as a nightly cliff-hanger, often asks, "What is going to happen now?" My invariable answer is a shrug and, "Damned if I know. I'll find out tomorrow."

This way of writing is, at least, a prophylactic against *telegraphing,* which does not let the reader figure out, in reading Chapter Two, what is going to happen in Chapter Six. In the writing of action fiction this is a mortal sin, but if *I* don't know what I'm going to write tomorrow, how the devil is the reader expected to guess? And, again, it helps spontaneity.

When a potential reader enters a bookstore or a library he

will take down a book, glance at the blurb, and then inspect the first page. It is here we find the writer's main problem—how to get the reader to turn that page. And not only that page but the next page and the next until he has come to the end of the book.

This ability to grab the reader's attention is a flair which some writers possess naturally. Dickens certainly had it. How else can you explain the thousands of people who crowded the New York docks awaiting the next issue of *Household Words* so they could find out just what had happened to Little Nell? A flair it may be, but a little thought can find an underlying technique.

I characterize this as the *hook*. On that first page a character must do or say something, or the opening situation must be such that the reader is impelled to ask himself, "What happens next?" You have planted a hook. It may not be removed until page 20 or page 192, when that particular situation is resolved, but before then, another hook must be planted, and so right through the book. There must always be at least one—and preferably more—hooks to catch the reader's attention.

A single example should suffice. On the first page of *Running Blind,* the first-person narrator is shown standing on a lonely road in Iceland, a corpse at his feet, a blood-stained knife in his hand, admitting that he has deprived a person of life.

There is not just one hook here, but many. To begin with, by the conventions of the action fiction genre, any first-person narrator is automatically the hero, and heroes don't go around slaughtering people indiscriminately—at least, mine don't. So the reader immediately asks, "How come?"

Since the narrator is apprehensive about the possible approach of a car, the reader asks, "What's going to happen to the body?" Then he also asks, *"How* did it happen?" and, again, *"Why* did it happen?" Four barbed hooks in the reader's imagination, and the reader must turn that page to get the answers to his questions.

Because I write action fiction, the hooks in this example tend to be bloody, but in *any* kind of fiction if no hooks are jabbed into the reader's imagination and if the reader is presented with an uninteresting first page—or any page, for that matter—then that page will not be turned and, as a writer, you are dead.

You may have noticed that in the above example the book has started *in medias res*—in the middle of the action. You don't *have* to start at the beginning because you can always cover that by a flashback. Using flashbacks is not recommended for the beginning writer because this technique is fraught with technical difficulties mostly concerned with maintaining tension.

Good versus evil

At this point I can imagine the reader of this piece saying to himself, "That's all very well, but what about the plot? Where does it come from?"

The answer to that is simple. If you choose your characters carefully then the opening situation will have built-in tensions, and the whole aim of the book is to relieve these tensions. While the action novel may be simplistic, the underlying philosophy is of graver moment and is nothing less than the eternal battle of good against evil. If, as usually happens, good wins out, then the tensions are relieved. It is worth pointing out, however, that the tensions are also relieved if evil wins.

So the plot grows from the initial situation in an organic way. The characters interact with each other and are constrained by the environment in which the action takes place. The unfolding plot must be strictly in keeping with the motivations of the characters and the premises inherent in the opening situation, which is another reason why I do not favor the writing of a synopsis. All too often, a character is called upon to behave in a way called for by the synopsis which is not in line with the way he has developed in the book, and the reader immediately frowns and says, "But he wouldn't do that!"

When that happens you break the magic spell of the willing suspension of disbelief, disillusion sets in because the reader believes himself to have been cheated, and the book is tossed aside unread, which is a sad thing to happen to any book.

I do not think that in the writing of action fiction there need be any strict adherence to real life probability. Plausibility is enough, provided that the premises of the opening situation and the integrity of the characters as you have drawn them are not violated. To paraphrase Shakespeare: "To thine own characters be true, and then thou canst not be false to any reader."

And when all is done and you come to the end, you will find to your surprise that you have a pretty taut and well-plotted book, the better written because the action has derived entirely from the natural drives of the characters and has not been imposed as a preconceived and somewhat artificial schema.

I would say that these are *personal* notes on the writing of action fiction. If the examples quoted are from my own books it is because I know my own books best and because I know just why I have used one technique in one book and a different technique in another. Again, my method of writing may appear to be idiosyncratic in the extreme. All writers differ in the way they write; though my way may be peculiar, it works for me.

36

BUILDING FOUR-DIMENSIONAL PEOPLE IN SCIENCE FICTION

by John Brunner

THE idea that a man is made out of mud may be a workable rule for a sculptor shaping a clay figure, but a writer struggling to create believable characters in a novel is employing altogether more tenuous materials than clay, and a science fiction writer attempting the same task finds the job even more difficult than does the writer of contemporary fiction.

For decades the complaint has been leveled against science fiction that its marvelous alien and future worlds have been inhabited only by cardboard cut-outs; at best, their populations have included not characters but Characters with the capital C—grand eccentrics or supermen.

There is a good technical reason why this should be a justifiable charge. Stop and think for a moment about all the influences which make you and me different even from our own grandparents, let alone people as far removed from us in time as King Alfred or Julius Caesar. Our nature hasn't basically altered, but our attitudes have been turned topsy-turvy by Freud and Kinsey, automobiles, television and the hydrogen bomb.

Different assumptions

Some of these changes have been so radical that it's small wonder the majority of science fiction writers, already burdened with the complexity of societies revolutionized by automation, or expanded like an inflating balloon by the discovery of interstellar flight, have chickened out when it came to populating their marvelous new universes; they have been content to transplant present-day men and women to Arcturus Four. Take even such a fundamental matter as relationships between the sexes. Our ideal modern marriage has practically nothing in common with the ideal Victorian marriage, apart from involving a husband and a wife. Yet only a handful of writers (Frederik Pohl in *Day Million,* Fritz Leiber in *Nice Girl with Five Husbands,* and a few others) have exploited the certainty that change isn't going to stop with us and attempted to depict other possible kinds of marriage.

Naturally, the problem is a tricky one—the moment you set a story even a single generation ahead of our time, you're by definition dealing with people whose prejudices and preferences are no longer the same as ours. But the fact that the problem has been solved shows that it's worth taking more trouble over than most science fiction writers, even nowadays, seem to feel.

It has been solved? Oh, yes—and not only by science fiction writers, but also by writers of historical novels facing precisely the same job of taking the reader out of his regular environment and into one where people operate by different assumptions. In *Coromandel!* John Masters performed the astonishing feat of creating a genuine pre-Freudian man for his hero—someone immune from the doubts about ourselves which we feel because we know about the existence of the subconscious mind. And Mary Renault, particularly in *The King Must Die* (a book that is, incidentally, very popular with science fiction fans), has also depicted brilliantly convincing alien worlds . . . not less alien for being distant from us by going back in time rather than into the future.

Key principles

Granted, when writing historical fiction, one has a skeleton to support the flesh of one's story, whereas inventing a whole new future world may take one completely away from known facts. Yet adherence to a relatively small number of key principles can make all the difference between a bunch of cut-outs in cardboard and convincingly warm-blooded characters.

First, and by far the most important: *be consistent.* Try to draw the same analogy between yourself and the man who's accustomed to walking on a dozen different planets, and yourself and a remote ancestor who knew nothing of jet airliners but had his horizons bounded by the progress of a tired horse. Characterization, after all, consists in providing a set of clues for the reader, and there are what one might term "constellations of characteristics" from which two or three can be selected—with care—in order to hint at the whole person.

The most blatant example of this that I can call to mind is the apocryphal advice given by an old Hollywood hand to an aspiring writer of Western scripts, concerning the introduction of the villain: "He should get off the stagecoach and kick the nearest dog." With all respect to writers of B pictures, in science fiction that simply won't do; there are places on Earth now, such as Greece, where kicking or stoning a dog is a highly acceptable social act because dogs run in packs, descend at night on towns to steal food, sometimes attack children and are carriers of hydrophobia!

But it is exactly that kind of unexpected, non-contemporary insight which can most readily be called on to help make a character in science fiction stand up on the page. An author who is expert at this technique is Philip K. Dick. Consider how he introduces the key character of David Lantano in *The Penultimate Truth* (Belmont Books). Lantano first appears at work—an unusual job, matching the future world he lives in; he's very good at it, he's polite and well-mannered toward the colleague he's meeting for the first time, and apart from his professional skill seems unexceptional. Then, like a bolt of lightning, we discover that he is daily risking his life to stake out a claim in a dangerously radioactive area left abandoned after nuclear war, and suddenly he leaps up off the page so solid, so real, one could touch him because we have been given one ingeniously selected glimpse into his personality, and all that's necessary to imagine a man radiates from that central point—ambition, hunger for power, disregard of well-meant advice, persistence in the face of appalling peril.

Constellation of characteristics

There indeed is a "constellation of characteristics" which need not be spelled out to the reader, yet because of the approach which the author has chosen, we view it from the standpoint of the future world where Lantano lives, not from our own familiar environment.

This leads into the second key principle to be kept in mind when elaborating characters for a science fiction story. *The reader must be given a point of contact.* A shining example of the fact that it's a mistake to make characters in science fiction totally different from ourselves can be found in Neil R. Jones's "Professor Jameson" stories, where most of the characters are numbered, not named, and hence are as interchangeable as bacteria.

To my mind, even such respected works as William Golding's *The Inheritors* and Brian Aldiss's *The Long Afternoon of Earth* exhibit this flaw; while they are unarguably consistent within themselves, the characters in these books are too remote from us to afford the chance of identification with them; hence, readers don't very much care what becomes of them.

A way of getting around this difficulty while retaining the desired quality of a good match between the character and the non-contemporary setting he inhabits can be found by endowing him with some virtue or failing which is effectively universal. If I may be forgiven for citing my own work: I ran up against this problem when writing *Stand on Zanzibar* (Doubleday). One of the leading characters is a Negro vice-president of a multi-billion-dollar corporation in the New York of 2010. Obviously, with the fantastic changes currently going on in the status of the world's colored people, he's not going to be a one-for-one equivalent of someone in today—indeed, of *anyone* in today!

Yet for plot purposes he had to be a Negro and professionally very successful.

So I introduced him by way of a dreadful disappointment—the fulfillment of an ambition which had haunted him since childhood and which he expected to give him immense satisfaction, but which changing circumstances turned to ashes. That left the poor guy bewildered and upset, and in just the right frame of mind for him to re-assess the surroundings in which he lived. Automatically, therefore, it afforded a convincing opportunity for the reader to discover how he and his world were interacting.

We've all experienced that kind of disappointment, but the detail in this case was special. This trick, device, gimmick, whatever one terms it, is versatile, flexible, and adaptable to fields other than science fiction (indeed to any kind of fiction with an exotic locale), but it's in science fiction that it is most indispensable.

And the third key principle to bear in mind can be summed up essentially: *think hard, but don't stop feeling.* It was once said of E. E. Smith's galaxy-roaming hero Kimball Kinnison (featured in adventures as dazzling as a fireworks display but having no more depth than a raindrop), "I wish he'd do something human for a change—like catching cold!"

So your heroes can out-think a computer and conquer the Spican Spider People single-handed? Fine; anything goes in science fiction. But remember that this doesn't define a person. It could equally depict a machine. Regardless of what supernal powers the guy possesses, he's also going to feel hungry or cold, like music or have an illogical distaste for the color green or— or *something*. For men are not rational beings, they are rational animals, and judging by the slowness of evolution, it's going to be much longer than we dare try to see ahead before they give up these instinctive reactions.

Consider Lincoln Powell in Alfred Bester's *The Demolished Man,* a skilled mind reader hunting down a killer so brilliant that he nearly—but not quite—manages to get away with his crime. Powell suffers from a fondness for practical jokes which sometimes get him into serious trouble; he has a girl friend whom he doesn't want to marry although she is hopelessly in love with him. And so on. He stands up and is believed.

So too, I hope, is Gerald Howson in my own book *The Whole Man.* He is a crippled dwarf, gifted with fantastic psionic ability, but he wishes he could trade all his talents for the chance of looking other men straight in the face and walking down the street without a limp.

People are many-sided creatures, and as time goes by, we become more, and more, and *more* complex, chiefly for the simple reason that we learn about more subjects on which we can hold opinions. In his hilarious comedy *The Remarkable Flirgleflip,* William Tenn pictured an expert on Martian art, with a well-paid job at a future university and a splendid academic reputation, who on being accidentally shipped back to the twentieth century could find no other job but washing dishes.

Which means, of course, that it's even worse to populate a

science fiction story with flat wooden puppets than it is to do so in a contemporary story! Yet month by month the science fiction magazines produce puppets whose joints can practically be heard creaking!

Points of human contact

How then can these key principles be applied to *your* science fiction novel?

Well, let's assume that you've already taken the kind of trouble one must take in writing any sort of fiction. . . . No? You were too busy working out the mechanics of the interstellar drive? Hm-m! Then try this little exercise: ask yourself what your hero would do if he found himself in a dull everyday situation. What would he say, for instance, if his spacesuit weren't returned from the laundry, but he got one intended for a hyperthyroid giant instead? You hadn't thought about having his spacesuit cleaned? But you should have! We are already infinitely more fastidious about grime and stale perspiration than our ancestors; our descendants are likely to be even more persnickety. And unless you know exactly what your hero would say, whether he'd be polite or sharp, long-suffering or furious, you can't claim to have visualized him as a character.

Of course, you're at liberty to have disposable spacesuits, thrown away after a single wearing, or anything else you choose, but remember that every single item your hero depends upon will be something he has an *attitude* toward, just as we have attitudes toward our furniture, cars, TV sets and cigarettes. Come to think of it, what's his opinion on the current social problems of his day, regardless of their connection with the plot? Does he approve of Thubans manufacturing imitation Martians for sale as pets? If not, is it on abstract principle or is it because he likes Martians more than Thubans?

These, naturally, are superficial and indeed absurd, extreme cases of the problem. Nonetheless, they indicate the right approach. Ask yourself frankly whether your last rejection was due to plot weakness, or whether it failed through lack of characterization. Remember: in science fiction, there's no need for characters to be physically human, but they must still offer the reader that point of contact I mentioned above, whatever form they've been given. A perfect instance of this is the nostalgia for the good old days which haunts the robot Jenkins in Clifford Simak's *City*, and makes him more memorable as a personality than the human beings or even the dogs in the same book.

Check your characters out against this list:

(a) Can I imagine him stepping offstage into another setting?

(b) Would his reaction in that setting build him up more solidly in the actual story I have here?

(c) Is that other setting one which forms a consistent part of the world he's living in?

(d) Do his reactions here in the story enable the reader to guess what he'd do outside it?

When you have four yeses, it's time to retype the story and ship it out again, and you'll stand a far better chance of a sale than you did before.

37

HOW TO KEEP THE READER ON THE EDGE OF THE CHAIR

by Joan Aiken

> Is the night chilly and dark?
> The night is chilly, and not dark.
> The thin grey cloud is spread on high
> It covers, but not hides, the sky.

OBSERVE how cunningly Coleridge sets the scene for something nasty to happen. He understates, he plays down. Nothing *seems* very bad; but as one small, carefully qualified detail is added to another, each harmless in itself, the reader begins to notice a feeling of menace; there is an unnatural element about the almost obsessive moderateness of every assertion that Coleridge is making. The cock crows, but it crows drowsily; even the mastiff bitch, woken by the castle clock, makes answer in "sixteen short howls, not over loud." Coleridge is anxious to pretend that everything is quite normal, but he lets us see that he is pretending too hard.

> The moon is behind, and at the full
> And yet she seems both small and dull
> 'Tis a month before the month of May
> And spring comes slowly up this way . . .

He is almost apologetic about it. There is no storm, no drama;
everything is very subdued; everything can be accounted for;
nothing is wrong; not *exactly*.

> She stole along; she nothing spoke
> The sighs she heaved were soft and low
> And nought was green upon the oak
> But moss and rarest mistletoe . . .

Presently this very moderation, this very understatement, begin
to play on the reader's nerves. All the negatives create an atmosphere of tension, of expectation.

> The night is chill; the forest bare
> Is it the wind that moaneth bleak?
> There is not wind enough in the air
> To move away the ringlet curl
> From the lovely lady's cheek . . .

The lovely lady is Christabel, gone out to pray for her lover in
the midnight forest. The trappings are pure gothic: the remote
forest hall (somewhere in the English Lake District; the names
Dungeon Ghyll and Witch's Lair are later irrelevantly tossed in
for a bit of gratuitous creepiness), the night scene and the unsus-
pecting simple-hearted heroine whose betrothed knight is off at
the wars and not available to protect her, are all staple ingredients of the contemporary gothic novel. Coleridge gets down to
business at once. In the midnight wood, Christabel finds a woe-
begone lady who tells a cock-and-bull story of having been ab-
ducted by five ravishers on white steeds; innocent Christabel hos-
pitably leads home the lady who loses no time in putting the
come-hither on Sir Leoline the Baron rich. But things look bad
for Christabel; the strange lady's eyes turn to serpents' eyes when
she looks at the poor girl, who straightway falls under a hypnotic
spell and can't reveal the sinister knowledge she has acquired
about the visitor. Meanwhile, the only possible ally, Bracy the

bard, has been dispatched in search of the lady's father, who is alleged to live a long way off on the Scottish border.

The scene is set for dark doings at Langdale Hall, in fact. A paperback blurb for one of my novels (and a few thousand others) —"Who was trying to enslave her body and destroy her mind? She woke to terror . . ."—would do equally well for Christabel.

Unfortunately, we shall never know what was to happen to her, for Coleridge (though the person from Porlock doesn't seem to have been responsible this time) did not finish the poem. But what a good beginning it is: a first-class example of how an atmosphere of horror and anticipation can be achieved, not by loud bangs and vampire shrieks, but by a series of careful, gentle touches.

Henry James achieves the same effect in *The Turn of the Screw*. If you analyze that story, remarkably little actually takes place: two ghosts are seen from time to time—sometimes a man staring through a window, sometimes a woman gazing steadily across a lake. But what power these apparitions have! Part of their horror lies in the silent suddenness with which they appear and disappear—no spooky atmospheric preliminaries, just the flat event itself, unnerving as a blown fuse. "There again, against the glass . . . was the hideous author of our woe—the white face of damnation." "She rose erect on the spot my friend and I had lately quitted." Very much of the horror, too, lies in the moderate, reasonable tone in which the whole story is told.

Frightening your reader

Both Henry James and Coleridge were accomplished professionals; both knew just what they were about. It is interesting that in each of these examples the writer can be seen quite consciously and deliberately making it plain that he is out to scare the reader, right from the start. Coleridge does it in his opening lines:

'Tis the middle of night by the castle clock
And the owls have awakened the crowing cock
Tu-whit—tu-whoo . . . etc.

Midnight—castle—owl-calls: the sequence is as good as a key-signature to indicate that the reader must be prepared for supernatural occurrences. Henry James does it even more directly; by his formal story-within-a-story framework, he gives himself the chance of announcing in advance that his tale is a horrible one, that it concerns the fate of two children, so that the reader is put into a receptive frame of mind. (If not in a receptive frame of mind, presumably he shuts the book.)

So the first step in frightening your reader is to *tell* him that you are going to frighten him—though not in terms so specific as to impair the effect of the fright itself when it finally arrives. (Relative to this, I have had one or two arguments with publishers, some of whom have a disastrous habit of giving away far too much plot in a thriller blurb: "At the end of a long and gripping chase the heroine discovers that the children have been safe all the time at the house of a neighbor," one blurb blithely revealed, raising my blood pressure to a dangerous level, since the heroine's uncertainty and terror about her children formed the whole fulcrum of my lever for keeping the reader up in the air.)

Tell your reader then; give him some idea what is in store.

"Hale knew, before he had been in Brighton three hours that they meant to murder him," Graham Greene begins *Brighton Rock*. And by page 23, sure enough, Hale has been murdered, not crudely in front of the reader, but offstage. The knowledge that his death has been so easily, so speedily arranged, is a kind of salesman's sample, a demonstration of what may yet occur to other characters.

I opened one of my thrillers with the sentence, "Hari Lupac was waiting for the girl he was going to murder," and then went

on edging my way up to this murder for the whole book, ending
with the girl's escape in the last line. I don't think it's my best
book, though it's hard to judge the fright-content of one's own
suspense stories—to oneself the mechanism shows so plainly—but
several readers have told me they found that one really frightening.

Distinguishing suspense from horror

The early warning may occur obliquely. Le Fanu's *Uncle Silas,*
another prototype gothic, starts well in tradition, with the se-
cluded country mansion. "It was winter . . . great gusts were
rattling at the windows . . . fire blazing in a sombre old room."
Things don't really start to go wrong until the arrival of the
sinister governess, Madame de la Rougierre, who is first seen
outside the window in the moonlight, "curtseying extraordinarily
low and rather fantastically." Sinister hints about Uncle Silas
then begin to be dropped: Maud's father keeps insisting that his
brother has been unjustly accused, Cousin Monica reveals that
he was suspected of a murder. Furthermore, she gives a warning
to Maud not to let the governess tamper with her food and ve-
hemently objects to the arrangement whereby, at her father's
death, Maud is sent to live with Uncle Silas, heir to the estate
should Maud die before coming of age. Anyone but the heroine
of a gothic would take fright, but not Maud, not even when she
meets Uncle Silas, with his gentle, cold voice, long hair of the
purest silver, face like marble, thin-lipped smile, and habitual
contraction resembling a scowl—a classic wicked uncle if ever
there was one—not even then does she lose her simple trust.

Uncle Silas has some gripping moments, but I find *The Turn
of the Screw* infinitely more frightening, because the threat remains indefinite. The final twist, both in *The Turn of the Screw*
and *Christabel,* lies in the reader's total uncertainty as to what
can possibly happen; in each case an evil supernatural force is in

pursuit of an innocent victim, but what can this sinister power actually do? The writer doesn't say, and it is the sense of nameless menace, unformulated threat, that really has power to chill the blood. Demonic possession is a terrifying conception, and it is this that both stories are hinting at, but in each case the suggestion is kept, as it were, tucked up the writer's sleeve. This keeping-back, this fear of the unknown, is what differentiates suspense from horror. Horror is specific, fear is indefinite. I don't at all decry the horror genre but I personally find suspense more interesting, both to read and to write; also more of a challenge.

Suspense unlimited

Once you have prepared your reader to have his hair raised, the range of possible suspense is unlimited. But there are various tried and reliable threat situations—the failed rescue, for instance. *Uncle Silas* has a good example of this, when the scheming uncle sends away honest Doctor Bryerly, who realizes Maud's danger and tries to extricate her: "I heard that dismallest of sounds, the retreating footsteps of a true friend, *lost*." An even better example occurs in a short story by Michael Joyce, "Perchance to Dream": the hero is trapped in a dark house with his mad brother-in-law, a chemist who has been conducting sinister experiments on his wife and child. The police are summoned, but they arrive too late, the madman has run amok with an ax and is lurking in the front hall. So the police, after vainly knocking, *go away again;* it is a terrible moment when the hero realizes that he is not going to be able to summon them back.

A variation of this, sometimes a stage later in time, is the exposure of an appeal for help; up to this moment hero and villain have been conducting their maneuvers with a pretense of amity, without the admission that their interests are opposed, the villain gradually gaining ascendancy. Then, the hero (or heroine) sends out a help call. Maud, for instance, sends a message to her cousin, which is intercepted. "[Uncle Silas] rose like a spectre with a white scowl. 'Then how do you account for that?' he shrieked, smiting my open letter, face upward upon the table."

I used this device in my children's novel, *The Wolves of Willoughby Chase*. In it, the orphans appeal to their father's lawyer for help; their letter is intercepted by the wicked governess. Some readers have told me they found this a "bad moment." This comes partly, I think, from having the orphans found out and partly from the concept, "now she [the governess] *knows* I know how wicked she is," which for some psychological reason is always particularly frightening.

Hero/heroine discovered by villain in a compromising situation is always a moment of acute tension. In *Appointment with Yesterday*, Celia Fremlin has a woman sorting through old newspapers. She looks up and realizes that her husband is watching her through the window. A simple-sounding scene, but it has power to frighten you down to your socks. Why? Celia Fremlin has used plot-inversion to heighten suspense: The author opens the book with her heroine on the run, evidently fleeing from some appalling denouement relating to her husband. Then, in a series of flashbacks alternated with the chronological progress of the plot, the story returns to the start of the marriage. Miss Fremlin can be as leisurely as she pleases in the build-up of tension; she is confident of the reader's confidence in *her*.

Villains

Stevenson, who was a master hand at creating fear situations, made use of two infallible ingredients in *Treasure Island*—a child, and a crippled villain. Indeed, *Treasure Island* has two villains with physical disabilities, Blind Pew, whose entry into the book is a most terrifying scene, and Long John Silver. Why should a disabled villain be more frightening than one with all his faculties intact? I suppose it must be some atavistic streak in us: We perhaps feel that a physically handicapped person may have developed supernormal powers, may be a warlock, may feel supernormal malice and vindictiveness because of his physical inferiority. Or—Freudians would say—we fear him because we are afraid of being overtaken by the same misfortune; it is a castration fear. Whatever the reason, handicapped villains have held the stage from classic times: the one-eyed Cyclops, lame Vulcan, Richard Crookback (used by Shakespeare in *Richard III* and also by Stevenson in *The Black Arrow*), one-handed Captain Hook, one-legged Long John, Castro in Conrad's *Romance*. Mary Stewart has one of her villains (in *Nine Coaches Waiting*) confined to a wheelchair. The villain of *Jamaica Inn* is an albino. In one of Stevenson's most terrifying scenes, two boys are pursued by a blind leper; the combination of blindness and leprosy is almost too bloodcurdling. And yet, if one could think the matter over rationally, what could a blind leper, what could a man in a wheelchair actually *do*? But one can't think it over rationally; that is the worst part of it. A Jekyll-Hyde personality split, or a moronic villain, as in James Hadley Chase's *No Orchids for Miss Blandish,* or in William Faulkner's *Sanctuary,* are all terrifying and unpredictable. But a writer should be sparing with mad villains; the temptation to make them go off the rails at the end of the novel is partly a kind of laziness. The villain is being bested, but the writer wants him to battle on as long as possible, against whatever odds. It is more ethical, though harder work, to have the villain defiant on logical grounds, not just a crazy refusal to give in.

A child villain or a senile villain can be equally terrifying. In his story, "Miriam," Truman Capote created an appalling little girl. And in his book, *The Man Who Was Thursday,* G. K. Chesterton had a horrifying, dilapidated old man whose power to terrify lay in the fact that, although he seemed so old he was almost falling to bits, he could nevertheless manage to keep chasing the hero: supernatural fear again. (In fact Chesterton was cheating, because his old man turned out to be a young man in disguise, but it was a good fright while it lasted).

Of course an essential ingredient in a fear situation is a central character with whom the reader can empathize. A child is excellent, as Henry James demonstrated in *The Turn of the Screw*; or a defenseless person, such as the paralysed heroine in Hilda Lawrence's *Duet for Four Hands*; or an old, incapable person— the old blind man in Elizabeth Fenwick's *A Friend for Mary Rose*. Hugh Walpole, in *Kind Lady*, has a masterly example in the old woman terrorized by the gang. This is also an example of the "enclosed-world" fear situation. The enclosed world can be literal: an island, a prison, an old people's home, an asylum, an occupied country; or it may be cut off not by physical barriers but mental ones. Moral subjugation can achieve this, or straight threat—a protection racket, for instance, where the enclosed world appears to form part of the world at large, but the barriers are really set up by the central character's fear of reprisals if he tries to appeal for help.

Graham Greene's Brighton is an enclosed world. So is the whole world in *The Man Who Was Thursday*, the whole of England in Wilkie Collins' *The Woman in White*. Chesterton and Wilkie Collins achieve their effects by apparently omniscient, omnipresent villains, who seem to have total knowledge of what their opponents are likely to do next; but readers now are more skeptical of this device than they were in the nineteenth century.

Creating fear

These are all technical ways of creating suspense, but there are two basic essentials without which I am sure it is impossible to create a really convincing fear situation. The first is conflict between good and evil. Fear situations are fundamentally primitive and simple. As soon as the conflict shifts to a different level, to disputed loyalty, for instance, or betrayal, or choice of allegiance, the issues become more sophisticated, and fear is replaced by anxiety.

The second essential is that at some point, no matter how long ago, the writer must in some degree have felt this fear himself. Writing is on a par with acting. The actor can't, obviously, feel the emotion all the time he is portraying it, but he must act out of experience; he must have the capacity to feel or he won't convince. In the same way, the writer will fail to frighten his reader unless he really knows what he is talking about.

Fear is not the only suspense situation. Hope is another. Will the pilot be able to land the crippled plane? Will the supplies arrive in time? Will the gas leak be discovered before it is too late? Will the prisoner be rescued? Will the poison be found before someone swallows it? Time, weather, adverse circumstances —not a human agency—are the agency.

But that is another story. We are concerned here purely with the fear type of suspense situation, a most challenging and interesting form of mystery.

It is a good exercise for a writer to work out the minimum props he needs to give the reader a genuine cold prickle: A man is standing in a phone booth on a deserted street; the phone starts to ring. This terrifies the man. Why? And how can it be made to terrify the reader, too? By what artful steps can one approach that phone booth so that the ring can seem an almost unbearable climax?

38

WRITING A MYSTERY

by Patricia Moyes

THERE is a story, probably apocryphal, of an author who was engaged to lecture to university students on the art of writing. Surveying the packed hall, he started by saying, "Hands up, anybody who would like to be an author." Every hand shot up. "Then," said the author, "why are you wasting time here? Go home and start writing." And he walked out of the hall.

I must say straight away that I have much sympathy for his point of view. Writing, like all creative acts, consists of three parts: talent, technique and hard work. All three are absolutely essential to produce worthwhile work: no two alone will do. Talent, of course, can never be taught. Hard work must be self-imposed. Technique? Well, now, I'm not sure. Even technique in writing is an intensely personal thing, and every writer must hammer out his own. Heaven forbid that rules of technique should be laid down, rigidly taught and conscientiously applied.

I do think, however, that benefit can be derived from studying the various techniques used by practicing writers, as well as their actual methods of work—not in order to imitate them, but to absorb ideas from which one's own original technique can evolve.

Stylistic technique can, of course, be studied by reading the published work of authors whom one admires, and, as it were, taking the paragraphs and chapters apart to find out what makes them tick. Mere reading of the books will not, however, tell you how the author set about the planning of his work. So if it is of any interest, I will tell you the system I use. Of course, it is not the only system, and perhaps not a very good one, but it works for me.

Since I write detective stories, I have of necessity to work within a more rigid plot framework than does an ordinary novelist. The problem is to maintain this meticulous plotting without allowing it to restrict unduly the freedom of movement and expression of the characters. This entails planning.

Plotting and planning

Personally, I use setting and background as the starting point for all my books, and I am a great believer in the fact that the author should have a genuinely deep knowledge of any subject on which he bases a book. I know that there are people who can go on a two-week package tour of Turkey, and come home to write a book with a vividly authentic Turkish background. I am not one of them. For example, I lived in Holland for nearly five years before I felt that I knew the place and the people in sufficient depth to start writing about them. To my mind, a conducted tour and a couple of reference books just will not do.

As for characters, and places mentioned in less depth, I rely on a distillation of personal experience. This means that life takes on an added interest, because every single thing that happens to me, every person I meet, every place I visit, is grist to the mill. I have a bad memory in the usual sense; I muddle up names and faces and places; but I do seem to have a good general memory for the mood and smell and *feel* of places, and for the conversation, dress and so on of various types of people. It is to this mass of digested experience that I turn, often years later, for the raw material of my books.

Having decided on a setting, I then sit down to think up a crime plot which essentially belongs to and grows out of that background. For example, in my novel *Dead Men Don't Ski,* the crime arises out of dope-smuggling by ski; in *Murder à la Mode,* it is the pirating of Paris dress designs; in *Death and the Dutch Uncle,* it is the constitution of permanent international legal bodies, and points of international law—and so on. I would consider it cheating my readers if I took pains to create an authentic background of, say, an archeological dig or a big-game safari, simply in order to accommodate a plot in which A murders B in order to marry B's wife—a situation which could as well take place in Hampstead or Pittsburgh.

It is at this stage that I produce what I call the skeleton of the book—and extremely skeletal it is. In a school exercise book, I write down the answers to certain basic questions. Who is to be murdered? By whom? How? Why? And—very important, this—how is my detective going to unravel the mystery? That is to say, the principal clues are worked out well in advance, and dropped into the book, like currants into a cake, at intervals as the writing proceeds.

This sketchy outline now becomes my bible for the writing of the book. I refer to it constantly, and pretty soon I know it by heart. It is absolutely rigid, and no deviation from it can ever be allowed. It is the framework, and if it is tampered with or twisted, the whole fabric of the work will collapse, like a badly built house.

Next, I write down in the same exercise book a list of characters, with their names, ages and occupations. It is amusing, later on, to come across some of these lists and to see how in the actual book some characters have been dropped altogether, some have been merged, and many have changed their names. The exceptions, of course, are those controlled by the "skeleton"—the murderer, the victim and the detective.

It is this very rigidity of basic structure which allows me to play around quite freely with the other characters, and the happenings, subplots and red herrings which form the decoration of the work. It gives me the elbow room which, I hope, stops the book from being strangled by its own plot.

Surprising yourself and the reader

Peter Ustinov—with whom I worked for many years and who taught me so much—used to say that if an author doesn't take himself by surprise, he can hardly hope to surprise his readers. I have found this to be perfectly true. Characters who start out nebulously as names on my original list begin to develop real lives of their own as the writing proceeds, and wills of their own, too. They frequently astonish me by behaving in ways which I had not foreseen at all. They must be allowed to do this, for if they are rammed into the straitjacket of a too rigid plot, they simply die as people. Without wishing to stray into the realms of theology, I have always felt that the problem of free will versus predestination has an excellent analogy here. The author is the maker of his book: He creates his people, and he has a pretty good idea of what he intends them to do, but, as I said, unless he respects their personalities and lets them develop in their own way, he defeats his own ends. He is all-powerful, he can *make* them act any way he chooses, but if he does he will find himself maneuvering lifeless puppets instead of real people.

Now, I am ready to start writing, and here the self-discipline of hard work is really essential. I know very few writers who actually enjoy writing, although, of course, none of us would want to do anything else. The paralyzing fear of the white sheet of paper with nothing on it; the knowledge that for every single word of the book there is just one right word and a million wrong ones; the terrible slowness of writing compared with the speed of reading, which makes one's own work seem an endless, dragging bore—I think that all writers experience these horrors. The only thing to do is, like a tightrope walker, not to look down into the abyss of possible failure. Keep on going, get to the other side somehow. Tell yourself that you can revise, rewrite, or burn the manuscript if it turns out as badly as you fear. Just push on somehow until that marvelous moment of triumph when you write THE END.

Of course, there are days when one works well, even easily, and others when the words just will not come. I think these bad days should be worked through. I often force myself to sit at my desk for several hours, even if the result is only a couple of paragraphs squeezed out painfully. Sometimes, strangely enough, these turn out to be the best parts of the book. In any case, it's no use just sitting about waiting for inspiration. On the days when the magic fluid is flowing, take full advantage of it and write like mad. When it isn't, have a go all the same.

Actually, in spite of my gloomy forebodings when writing, I do very little revision. What I do is to read through the book once, quickly, to make sure that the shape is right. Then I go through it again, correcting careless slips like the use of the same word twice in a paragraph, and, most importantly, cutting whenever I possibly can.

I believe that some writers take strong exception to a single word of their work being cut out. My own feeling is different. I will never, if I can help it, allow *anybody else* to cut a word of my books, but I am a regular butcher myself, always slashing out unnecessary lines, and I find that the more pared down they are, the better. Recently, I was asked for permission to cut 10,000 words from one of my books for the British paperback edition, for technical publishing reasons. The publishers were slightly surprised, I think, when I said that I would gladly consent, provided I did the cutting myself. The result, in my opinion, is a book which has lost nothing and gained a good deal in speed and tautness. I wish I had written it like that in the first place.

No loose ends

Some aspects of writing are mysterious, even to the author. For instance, I have often found that an object or event thrown in near the beginning of a book purely for fun, becomes, to my surprise, a vital plot link at the end. I don't believe that this is either coincidence or magic, but the fact that my subconscious mind, unknown to me, has been mulling over the book and tidying up its loose ends. In a detective story, there must be no loose ends and no cheating. The reader must be supplied with all the clues, so that he can work out the solution to the mystery if he has a mind to; and everything that happens in the course of the story must be explained adequately by the end. I sometimes think that this scrupulous fairness is becoming an outmoded virtue, and it certainly makes more work for the writer; but I know from my mail that many readers appreciate it.

Let the last word again come from Peter Ustinov. When I was starting on my writing career, he said to me, "Above all, make your own mistakes, not other people's." It's the best advice I ever had, and I am glad to pass it on.

39

WHEN YOU WRITE A GOTHIC

by Elsie Lee

IN THE first place and despite fifteen of my novels so advertised, I do not write gothics. A real gothic is *The Castle of Otranto* by Horace Walpole, which is so outrageously bad as to be hilarious entertainment. Today, "gothic" is a publisher's category for novels of romantic suspense: fewer corpses than a murder mystery, but more frightened shivers than a straight love story. There are certain other specifications, such as scary old houses located atop seaside cliffs and gloomy local legends of death or disaster. The heroine cannot be more than thirty—nineteen to twenty-three is better—and she must be a virgin unless respectably widowed; in other words, there is no sex. In general, the time of the story is left vague, to avoid inconvenient questions such as "Why didn't she phone the police?" Basic plots are simple: girl finds herself in unfamiliar surroundings, becomes aware of menacing undercurrent, and grows progressively more scared for eight chapters—during which there are at least two men, the hero and the anti-hero. She doesn't know which is which until the penultimate chapter, which must contain some really perilous experience. Hero saves girl; they leave the island (or burning house) forever—and there you are: a gothic.

The novels I write are better described as fairy tales for grown-ups—primarily women (although the occasional husband-in-bed-with-a-cold has found my stories bearable). That is because I am writing about today, modern houses, and intelligent people. The situations in my books are always possible, though not probable, and resolved by the heroine's common sense and quick wits. There is not much terror, not many shivers, and little violence in my books. I despise that convenient hit on the head; I've used it only twice in my fifteen books. Equally, I despise stupid little nitwits who stick their necks out, asking for trouble.

My heroine often recognizes the puzzle very quickly and puts the pieces together to solve it. She always gets into the final dangerous situation quite logically. In her place, my readers would have tried to save the burning castle, or rescue the stepson, too. They also would have dashed over to the main house for a forgotten paper, thinking the villain was still in Richmond.

What attracts *me* is the possible-but-not-probable situation. What if I inherited a house full of antiques in a rampantly segregationist locality . . . or suspected a woman's two sons wanted to kill her . . . or discovered the titled head of a Scottish clan was an impostor—what would I do?

Planning a gothic

I begin planning a gothic very vaguely, by deciding on the background on the basis of "where haven't I been that would be fun to write about?" *Anything* can spark this step. My father's German dictionary suggested a castle on the Rhine; the snapshot of a house in the Channel Islands became Ivorstone Manor in Ireland; a scholarly tome on Norsemen wound up as an archaeological dig near Stockholm. At the same time, I may find that a friend's specialized knowledge will suggest my heroine's occupation. Thus, one of my heroines was a free-lance fabric designer, and another was the head of a photographic library.

The main characters

Once I've decided *where* the story is to take place or *what* my heroine will be, I invent a general plot. Why does my heroine go to this place? What could happen, either because of the surroundings or as a result of the heroine's special knowledge? Who are the people she meets, and which of them has a hidden secret she will eventually unravel? All of this must be absolutely logical.

My heroine is always an intelligent, educated young American woman who works for a living, and often has some special knowledge or talent unknown to the others. I vary physical appearances —if she was a tall Bostonian blonde in my last book, she's a small New York redhead in this one. If she was a secretary, now she's head of personnel. If she had a family, now she doesn't.

My hero is always a stalwart, solid male, usually ten to fifteen years older than the heroine—which makes it possible for him to underestimate her at first because of her youth, yet believable that he'd fall in love with her later. Otherwise, the heroes can be Americans or foreign, medium height to six-foot-five, sometimes rich and titled—but they all *work* at something, whether as captains of industry or consultants for our government.

The main characters are always wholly imaginary, and few of them are either beautiful or outstandingly romantic—except in each other's eyes. These are real people, you see—they are easy for readers to identify with. I suppose I may have some readers of authentic beauty, but most of them probably have eye-colored eyes and hair-colored hair, and it's pleasant for them to dream that in the heroine's place, they could nab a prince, too.

At this point, I have three main characters in a locality: the hero, the heroine, and the villain—plus a secret. Then I work out the major details of the puzzle, going backward from the final perilous situation in which the heroine is rescued by the hero. I think this is essential: *you* must know the denouement before you start writing, in order to get there. It does not matter if your readers know from the clues you have planted that something will occur at the whirlpool or the watchtower. In fact, the reader will feel cheated unless something does happen after such clues, because in the end, everything must be logically explained.

Next come the red herrings. Sometimes it is the hero himself who arouses the heroine's suspicions by being too anxious to remove her from potential danger; or the hero may be dubious about the heroine's motives. Or the red herrings may be minor characters—a surly family servant, an overfriendly relative, or a stranger who is overly curious, for example, about the name on the heroine's luggage or where she is staying. In all cases, you must have a satisfactory explanation for putting these characters into your book, as you must for all seemingly extraneous incidents. That is to say, you may not introduce so much as a pet mouse unless it will further the story. Nor may you emphasize an unusual skill of the heroine's, unless you plan to use it to resolve the final peril.

Names and family trees

My next step is choosing names for the main characters. I use one of those "What to Name the Baby" books—and I think about the meanings of the names. I deliberately look for names that will stand out and set the mood of the story. Readers will remember a girl named Holly, Megan, Bianca, Sable. . . . I also consider the sound of the heroine's married name. I can see a Miss Quain in an advertising agency becoming Sigrid Quain Penberthy, for example. If your mind goes blank, use a telephone directory—but avoid the letter M. If I had a nickel for every time the heroine is Mary, and the hero Derek Marsland, I wouldn't need to write another book.

Names of the minor characters are much less important, although I try to avoid duplicating initials. If the butler is Paul, for example, I do not name the chauffeur Peter, but call him Robert or Edgar. I take the time to search out the proper foreign spelling of names for local characters, all of which contributes to a convincing background.

After choosing names, I draw up rough family trees for the hero and the heroine to show how old the various members of the family were during major events in the book. I often find this useful, since it frequently turns out at this stage of the writing that the heroine's father would have been only fourteen years old or away at war when she was conceived. It is probably to avoid this that so many gothic writers make the time period of their novels vague. Then they can ignore electricity and indoor plumbing. But I write my novels about contemporary people in possible-but-improbable situations, and my readers are likely to say, "If the heroine is twenty-five today, why wasn't her father in Korea?"

This is as far as I go with the planning on paper, because I find that if I do too thorough an outline, I will never write the book. However, it is all blocked out in my head, and I do know what bits of action or information—of the many odd items in my mental file—I will use in the novel. It may be no more than a tiny scrap, but it's enough for a springboard, and I can amplify it through research.

Research and reference

I do not write off the top of my head, and neither should you, no matter how well you know the background for your book. I have accumulated a random collection of reference books from which to authenticate backgrounds and places I have never seen. I have an old *Britannica* from which to bone up on the topography of Lebanon or the history of a Scottish clan; a good atlas (or almanac) which is essential to give you a general idea of distances between places, if there is any traveling in your story: Will it be possible to reach Grenoble in time for dinner? Flying from Rome to Wiesbaden in a private plane, what cities would your characters fly over and how long would it take? Hallwag-Berne, in Switzerland, publishes road maps for every European country, as well as street maps for every major city. Also, Michelin Publications, New York City, publishes street maps for European cities at a cost of about $1.50 each. And there are innumerable guidebooks with accurate names of cafés, inns, parks, public buildings, and other details for you to draw on. Other source material I keep on hand and use are airline schedules which give routes from one city or country to another; tourist folders put out by information offices of foreign countries, major airlines or cruise ships; AAA guides to restaurants and hotels; and magazines like *Gourmet* or *Holiday* to find the name of *the* restaurant in a city like Stockholm.

From your friends' descriptions of their travels abroad you can store up a good deal of authentic detail. I came by an Athens nightclub scene that way, and also an account of a marvelous sailing jaunt to a Greek island. It will help to have a small phrase book for the country in which your novel is set. You will need only the simplest words, but using them will add authenticity and flavor. If you use foreign words too much, readers may feel you are showing off. Maybe some readers will understand, but I do not chance that. Use only ordinary phrases for please, thank you, good morning, good night—and more only if to do so would be in keeping with your characters.

In writing a novel with a foreign background, I usually indicate at the start whether or not the heroine understands the language. That may be part of your plot: Does she know what the natives are saying? Amanda couldn't speak a word of Swedish —which was why she got the job. The villain *wanted* a girl who couldn't understand what was being said. If the girl does speak the foreign language, there must be a logical reason for her to have learned it. Persis studies Portuguese because of a dead godfather she loved, but Fran didn't speak a word of Arabic; it was not necessary to the plot.

Such research, though time-consuming, is worthwhile. Editors and/or readers often ask me, "How long did you live in Paris?" or "I didn't know you'd been to Greece." The fact is that my foreign travel has been limited to six weeks in Europe *after* I had written seven gothics, and I have yet to use any of the cities I visited as a background for one of my books.

After I've chosen the background, I make sure there is a logical reason for the heroine to go there. She arrives as a stranger, with no preconceived ideas so she sees what may be missed by the residents. She senses that something is going on, and puts together various clues almost unconsciously. I always introduce the hero quickly, and often have the heroine get off on the wrong foot with him. This creates a sort of subplot question in the reader's mind: How long will it take Sable to realize she loves rude, irascible Sholto?

The only way I ever deceive readers is by keeping the heroine from realizing how much she knows until the very end, when—after she is rescued from peril by the hero—she puts all the facts together and solves the puzzle. Sometimes I try to withhold a single fact from the heroine, and she learns it only during the wrap-up from the hero or the law agent. By then, the reader may suspect the evidence of that fact and may even have deduced what it has to be.

Embroidery and embellishment

That is my basic scheme. Now for the embroidery. There are certain things I use in almost every novel I write. There is often a cat (with personality), some emphasis and description of delicious food (I also write cookbooks), and some music, because I play the piano. At the age of sixty, I have met a number of people, picked up a number of tidbits to be used in fabricating a plot, and I have various friends who know things like gunnery, photography, horticulture, and the price of real estate in Virginia. Before I became a free-lance writer, I worked as a librarian, secretary, file clerk, office manager, and purchasing agent. I have gone to operas and ballets and a few expensive restaurants, and although I still make my own clothes, I know who could make them for you in Paris if you can't thread a needle.

It boils down to this: You must draw upon every scrap of knowledge and information you possess, and if what you have in your mental storehouse is not all Phi Beta Kappa quality, it doesn't matter. Remember, you are writing for people like yourself, and if you write convincingly, they will understand and enjoy whatever pleases *you*. Simply check and double-check whatever window dressing you add, whether it is the name of a square dance, the painter who did the hero's portrait, or a new word. Never shall I forget the love scene I read years ago in which the hero threw a *cord* of wood on the fire before seizing the girl in his arms!

Write what you know, add the embroidery carefully, and you'll have it made.

40

IDEAS FOR MYSTERY NOVELS

by Stanley Ellin

THE more things change, the more they remain the same. Which means, as any mystery writer will agree, that the tribal storyteller either delivered the goods to his Stone Age audience, or else went without his share of roast mastodon at dinner time.

The mystery writer today is the lineal descendant of that tribal storyteller. He must tell a story which has a beginning, a middle, and an end, and he must draw his audience into identification with a protagonist who faces immense obstacles on his way to a vital goal. And he does not have the escape route from these obligations that a luckier sort of novelist has. He cannot produce two or three hundred pages of fictionalized autobiography and expect his editor and audience to take it to their hearts. If the tribal storyteller tried that kind of trick, he'd be lucky not to have his skull parted from cranium to molars by a flint ax.

On the other hand, today's mystery writer, safe from such a fate, faces a problem his Neanderthal forebears didn't have. Since the caveman was the first storyteller, any story he told was likely to hold its audience spellbound by its originality. Now, a few thousand generations later, originality is considerably harder to come by. The method of narrating a story may be new and fresh, so the experienced writer, once on his way, won't have too much trouble in producing something different, but coming up with a new and fresh idea—the idea being the foundation on which he must build plot and treatment—can pose a tough problem.

What's new?

The basic idea for any mystery novel can be expressed in the simplest line or two, as it often is in the writer's notebook. This applies as well to the most elaborate literary works. No matter how much the pedant may shudder at such simplification, the idea for *Hamlet* as jotted down in Shakespeare's notebook might have been, *Tragedy of a young man who sets out to avenge his father's murder.* And, in fact, the idea for *Paradise Lost* is briefly presented by Milton in its opening words: *"Of Man's first disobedience, and the fruit/ Of that forbidden tree whose mortal taste/ Brought death into the world, and all our woe."* In his notebook, it might have been even further reduced to the phrase, *Adam and Eve story.* Let's not forget either that both the Hamlet story and the Adam and Eve story had been written long before Shakespeare and Milton did their versions of them.

Often, the novice mystery writer, bursting with confidence and creative vigor, is scornful of any such "borrowing." His head is swimming with vaguely formulated impressions of detectives and corpses, crime and punishment; he feels that at the drop of a hat he could come up with a hundred original story ideas. As he gets older and wiser and sadder, he discovers that when these ideas are formulated in the fewest possible words, they bear a startling resemblance to each other. And, even worse, to stories already in print. Once he sneered at the dolt who said there were only nine original plots in the world. Now he begins to wonder if there are even that many.

The question most asked of a mystery writer by his readers is, "Where on earth do you get the ideas for your books?" The answer, alas, must never be the truth. Tell a flatteringly awe-stricken lady, as I once did, that your first mystery novel was simply a twist on the old Hamlet story, and she is instantly crestfallen. "Oh—," she says, now seeing those feet of clay sticking out from beneath your trouser cuffs.

Indeed, as I later came to realize, it was not my story ideas which the lady admired, but whatever was ingenious in their treatment. She had been talking about birth and child-raising, and I had been talking about conception. And it is that period between conception and birth—a period of gestation which need take no longer than a split second in this case—that is the real subject of this article.

What if—?

It all boils down to those two words, whether the writer is aware of it or not. He experiences or witnesses or hears about some episode or situation, or, for that matter, recalls one from literature, and thinks, "I'd like to make a story of this." Here is the conception of the story idea. Then, as a born storyteller—and storytellers are born, not made—he intuitively feels the urge to reshape and develop this proto-idea, his raw material, into something exactly to his taste, and he asks himself, "What if I changed this, added that, took away the other?" He does, and considers the effect. "There's a story here all right," he says—and the new story idea is truly born. His story idea, and his alone.

The feeling of "rightness"

From my experience, that first flickering awareness that a certain episode or situation would make a good story is largely a visceral matter. One feels the rightness of the episode or situation as dramatic material. Here is the difference between the ordinary observer and the creative writer, because where the observer, the layman, tends to accept a situation on its own, the writer cannot resist tampering with it in his imagination. Like a chess master coming upon a game already in its twentieth move, he is curious to know not merely what the next move might be, but how the chessmen got where they now are. And to conjecture: What if, on the fifth move, the rook had been played instead of the bishop? What if that pawn there had been sacrificed? What if—?

It's also possible that the period of gestation between the first visceral recognition that a certain situation would make a good story and the first application of the *What if?* question can take weeks or months or even years. I had been fascinated by the Hamlet story long before I suddenly found myself wondering: What if Hamlet, well along his road to vengeance, unexpectedly discovered that the murder of his father was wholly justified? What if the father were a bloody tyrant who deserved his fate? And then I set to work writing my first novel on the basis of the answers I arrived at.

At that time, I wasn't conscious of the process I was using, but I grew more and more aware of it through the course of writing a series of short stories and books. There finally came the time when I used it deliberately, with full understanding that, when faced with the raw material for a story, I must immediately apply the *What if?* test to it. And must continue to apply it until a whole plot has been hammered out.

Writer's instinct

Up to then, I had not invented any private detective, preferring to write about different sorts of protagonists. Then the day arrived when I felt impelled to create my own Sam Spade or Philip Marlowe. As luck would have it, while still brooding over what form to give him, I was called to jury duty and found myself impaneled with eleven other unhappy citizens sworn to decide fairly the innocence or guilt of a policeman charged with taking graft. It was a miserable time for all of us, because not only was the cop extremely youthful and fresh-faced, but his pretty wife, their baby in her arms, patiently sat on a front bench in the courtroom through the trial, never out of the jury's eye-shot. In the end, the verdict was "Guilty" and even at the awful moment when it was read out in the courtroom, my writer's instinct was telling me that there was a story in all this, and it had something to do with the private detective I was trying to conjure up as the hero of my next book. Somehow, he must be involved with this stricken young husband and wife.

What if the wife hired my private eye to get the evidence that would clear her husband at the trial, and my detective, infatuated with the girl, desperately desiring her, set out to prove the husband's guilt, not his innocence? The cop in my story had to be innocent—the victim of a frame-up—to give the story substance. But that left my private eye a complete scoundrel, which would never do. So what if—?

In the end, I wrote a book called *The Eighth Circle* from all this and from a whole succession of *What ifs?* stemming from answers that kept opening new plot possibilities ahead. Through the entire preparation and writing of the book, whenever I was held up by any problem of characterization or plotting, I would simply pose myself that question of *What if?*, always finding this the shortest route to the problem's solution.

My latest book, *House of Cards,* was produced from the first dawning of its idea by this method. The Brontë kind of novel has always irritated me even while I was enjoying it. Always the same moony female being invited by the dark-browed, mysterious man to enter his mansion as governess to his children or as his wife or secretary or whatever; always the lush feminine handling of this plot structure. But who said that the ladies had the patent on it? What if I wrote it from the male angle? What if, instead of the guileless maiden entering the service of the handsome man of mystery, a guileless young man entered the service of a beautiful woman of mystery in her gloomy mansion? It was as easy as that. A couple of *What ifs?* and I was back in business.

"Where on earth do you get the ideas for your books?" the nice lady asked.

Everywhere on earth, of course. But please take notice, dear lady, it's only after they've gone through the *What if?* process that they magically become *my* ideas.

BIOGRAPHICAL NOTes

JOAN AIKEN has achieved success as a writer of both children's books and adult thrillers. She is the daughter of poet Conrad Aiken and lives in England where she was born and raised. Among her recent adult books are *Beware of the Bouquet* (1966), *Dark Interval* (1967), *The Crystal Crow* (1968), and *A Cluster of Separate Sparks* (1971). Her children's books include *The Wolves of Willoughby Chase, Nightbirds of Nantucket, Black Hearts in Battersea, The Cuckoo Tree, The Green Flash* (a book of suspense tales), and *Night Fall* (1971), for which she received a Mystery Writers of America Edgar award.

British crime writer CATHERINE AIRD combines the ability to turn out ingenious books and to analyze the process of creating them. Five of her detective novels have been published in this country by Doubleday: *The Religious Body; A Most Contagious Game; Henrietta Who?; The Stately Home Murder;* and *A Late Phoenix.* Her latest novel, *His Burial Too,* was published in England in May 1973. Two of her books, *A Most Contagious Game* and *Henrietta Who?,* were selections of the Mystery Guild, and her first book, *The Religious Body,* was adapted for television and broadcast in England on the BBC Saturday Night Theatre.

CECILIA BARTHOLOMEW is both a talented fiction writer and an outstanding teacher of writing. Her stories have appeared in such magazines as *McCall's, Ladies' Home Journal, Redbook,* literary quarterlies and western romance magazines. Her novels, *The Risk* and *A Touch of Joshua,* were published by Doubleday. For several years she has been a correspondence course instructor in creative writing for the University of California.

DESMOND BAGLEY started his free-lance writing career in South Africa in the early fifties, first as a part-time and then a full-time novelist. He also did radio broadcasts there on scientific subjects, edited a house magazine, contributed to various newspapers, and wrote scenarios. Later, as a full-time novelist in England, he achieved immediate success with the publication of his first adventure novel, *The Golden Keel,* which has been published in seventeen editions, hardback in eleven countries, paperback and book club editions in four others. The book has also run serially in newspapers and magazines in western Europe. Since then, several more of his adventure-action novels have appeared, including *The Spoilers, The Vivero Letter, Landslide, Wyatt's Hurricane, High Citadel, Running Blind,* and *The Freedom Trap,* which has been filmed on location in London and Ireland by Warner Brothers. Directed by John Huston, the motion picture stars Paul Newman. His newest novel, *The Tightrope Man,* is scheduled for publication in the summer of 1973 by Doubleday.

British author JOHN BRAINE writes prolifically in a variety of fields, but he is perhaps best known for his widely-read novel, *Room at the Top,* which became a successful motion picture. His other novels include *From the Hand of the Hunter, Life at the Top* (also filmed), *The Jealous God, The Crying Game, The View from Tower Hill,* and his newest novel, *The Queen of a Distant Country,* published in the United States by Coward, McCann & Geoghegan. He has contributed to such magazines and newspapers as *The New Statesman, Daily Express, Encounter, The New York Times, National Review,* and others and has done a television series in England called "Man at the Top."

One of the most productive and successful writers in the field of science fiction, Englishman JOHN BRUNNER has been making his living "almost entirely" from science fiction writing for the past fifteen years. More than fifty of his books, mainly science fiction, have been published in the United States (Ace Books, Pyramid, Ballantine, Pocketbooks, New American Library) and abroad (also translated into seven languages), with sales exceeding two and one-half million copies. Among his best-known titles are *Squares of the City, The Whole Man,* and *Quicksand,* nominated for the Science Fiction Writers of America's Nebula Award. His two most recent science fiction novels are *The Wrong End of Time* and *The Dreaming Earth.*

In addition to his novels, Mr. Brunner has contributed short stories and novelettes to the leading SF magazines in Britain and America. Many of his stories appear in anthologies. He also writes articles, reviews, verse and topical songs, one of which was recorded by Pete Seeger.

ELIZABETH CADELL's first novel was published in 1947, and since that time she has written over twenty-seven books, over half of them still in print. Among her most recent novels are *The Friendly Air, The Haymaker,* and her newest book, *Royal Summer,* a 1973 publication of William Morrow. Several of her novels—*The Third Surprise, The Yellow Brick Road,* and others—have appeared as condensed novels in *Ladies' Home Journal* and *Redbook.* Born in India and educated in Calcutta, London, and Darjeeling, she presently lives in Portugal. All of her books are published in England by Hodder and Stoughton.

BRUCE CASSIDAY, long-time Fiction Editor of *Argosy Magazine,* is also a successful author of stories, novelettes, and novels. His mystery fiction includes *The Floater* (Abelard-Schuman), *Angels Ten, The Seventh Miracle,* and *The Phoenician* (Pyramid Paperbacks). Among his juvenile books are *Blast-Off* (Doubleday) and *Guerrilla Scout* (Macmillan), and he has written a non-fiction book, *Practical Home Repair for Women* (Taplinger), now in its second edition. Mr. Cassiday is currently Executive

Vice-President of the Mystery Writers of America, serving his third term, and has served on that organization's Board of Directors for a number of years.

B. J. CHUTE began her writing career with stories and books for boys, and later moved to the adult magazine market, with stories in most of the major magazines. Two collections of her stories have been published: *The Blue Cup* (1957) and *One Touch of Nature* (1965); and five adult novels: *The Fields Are White, The End of Loving, The Moon and the Thorn, Greenwillow* (produced as a Broadway musical), and *The Story of a Small Life*. Miss Chute is a former president of the American Center of P.E.N., the international writers organization, and is an Adjunct Associate Professor in the English Department of Barnard College.

ALFRED COPPEL, a versatile full-time fiction writer, is the author of many novels, the most recent of which is *The Landlocked Man*, a modern love story (Harcourt Brace Jovanovich). His other novels include *A Certainty of Love, Between the Thunder and the Sun, A Little Time for Laughter,* and *Order of Battle* (all published by Harcourt). A long-time contributor to science fiction magazines, Mr. Coppel has written three science fiction novels, under the pseudonym Robert Cham Gilman: *The Starkahn of Rhada, The Navigator of Rhada,* and *The Rebel of Rhada* (Harcourt). As A. C. Marin he has also written three thrillers: *A Storm of Spears, Rise with the Wind,* and *The Clash of Distant Thunder* (Harcourt). He lives in California.

R. F. DELDERFIELD has been compared to Hardy, Galsworthy and Dickens, and his panoramic family sagas contain echoes of all three, but his work is uniquely his own. His 700-page novel, *God Is an Englishman,* quickly made its way to the best-seller list in this country; the second volume of the projected four-volume series, *Theirs Was the Kingdom,* followed in 1971 and was a Literary Guild selection. Among Mr. Delderfield's other highly successful novels are *A Horseman Riding By* and its companion in the series, *The Green Gauntlet, The Avenue,* and *Mr. Sermon* (all published by Simon and Schuster). In addition, *God Is an Englishman* and *Mr. Sermon,* as well as another novel, *Diana,* are published in paperback by Pocket Books. His last novel, *To Serve Them All My Days,* and a volume of autobiographical stories about his childhood, *For My Own Amusement,* were both published in 1972 by Simon and Schuster.

MONICA DICKENS, like her great-grandfather, Charles Dickens, is a best-selling novelist who has achieved acclaim in her native England and throughout the world. Her many different jobs—domestic, nurse, aircraft factory worker, reporter—and marriage to a United States Naval officer and their life in England and in the United States have brought her into contact with a wide variety of characters and situations which she has used in writing her successful books. Several of these reflect the same re-forming spirit that Charles Dickens revealed, especially her *One Pair of Hands, One Pair of Feet, Thursday Afternoons, The Nightingales Are Singing, The Winds of Heaven, Man Overboard,* and many more. Among Miss Dickens' best-known novels are *Cobbler's Dream, Kate and Emma, The Heart of London, The Landlord's Daughter, The End of the Line, The Room Upstairs, The House at World's End, Summer at World's End, World's End in Winter* (1973). She is a popular lecturer and has written a large number of articles for a variety of magazines.

DOROTHY EDEN was born in New Zealand and for many years has lived in London. Well-known for her period and historical fiction, as well as her suspense and modern gothic novels, she has written thirty-two books, the most recent being *Speak to Me of Love* (Coward, McCann & Geoghegan), a Literary Guild Alternate Selection. Among her other best-selling books are *Melbury Square, The Vines of Yarrabee, Waiting for Willa, An Afternoon Walk,* and *The Shadow Wife,* all of which have been published in paperback by Fawcett.

Miss Eden lives in the old London square which is the setting of her book, *Melbury Square.*

STANLEY ELLIN is one of today's most widely read and admired writers of mystery and suspense fiction. In addition to numerous short stories in such publications as *Ellery Queen's Mystery Magazine* and in anthologies, Mr. Ellin is the author of many novels, including *The Eighth Circle* (an Edgar award winner), *House of Cards, The Bind,* and *The Valentine Estate.* His most recent book, *Mirror, Mirror on the Wall,* was published by Random House.

JANICE ELLIOTT was born in Derbyshire, England, and read English literature at Oxford. In the past ten years, she has written nine novels, of which five have appeared in the United States: *The Godmother* (Holt, Rinehart & Winston), *Angels Falling, The Kindling,* and *A State of Peace* (all published by Knopf); and *The Buttercup Chain* (Pyramid paperback), a 1970 Columbia Pictures release and a British film entry at the Cannes Film Festival. Her most recent novel, *Private Life,* is a sequel to *A State of Peace.* She is also the author of two children's books, *The Birthday Unicorn* and *Alexander in the Land of Mog,* published in England in the spring of 1973.

MARGARET FORSTER's novels include *Georgy Girl,* which became a successful motion picture (she also wrote the screenplay), *The Travels of Maudie Tipstaff, The Park, Miss Owen-Owen, Fenella Phizackerley,* and most recently, *Mr. Bone's Retreat* (Simon and Schuster).

MARJORIE MUELLER FREER has written eight career novels, all published by Julian Messner, Inc. She has taught English on the high school, college, and adult education levels, worked in advertising, and written for magazines, radio and television, and for community, educational and college theatre. Currently, she is teaching creative writing in a secondary school and completing a series of books on writing for use in high schools and colleges.

ROSEMARY GATENBY's first mystery novel, *Evil Is as Evil Does,* was published in 1967 by Morrow. Next were *Aim to Kill* and *Deadly Relations* (both Morrow), the former being sold also for motion picture production and the latter becoming a Mystery Guild selection. All three were brought out in England in hardcover editions by Robert Hale, and have among them been translated into seven foreign languages. Mrs. Gatenby's newest book, *Hanged for a Sheep,* was published by Dodd, Mead in January of 1973.

HARRY HARRISON is one of the most prolific writers of science fiction, and a distinguished editor of science fiction publications and anthologies. He is an articulate and authoritative spokesman on behalf of this literary field. His work has appeared in practically every science fiction magazine, and he has had more than eighteen novels published, including his most recent books, *Stonehenge* (Scribners), *Montezuma's Revenge* (Doubleday), and *The Stainless Steel Rat Saves the World* (Putnam). He has served as editor of four science fiction magazines and has edited a number of science fiction anthologies, including the annual *Best Science Fiction* series. Mr. Harrison teaches a graduate course in science fiction writing at San Diego State University.

EVELYN HAWES is the author of three novels, *The Happy Land, A Madras-Type Jacket* and *Six Nights a Week* (published by Harcourt Brace Jovanovich), and a history of the Buffalo General Hospital, *Proud Vision.* Her stories and articles have appeared in *The Saturday Evening Post, Ladies' Home Journal, Redbook,* and other magazines.

A member of an illustrious literary family, JANE AIKEN HODGE (sister of Joan Aiken, q.v., and daughter of Conrad Aiken) has carved out a specialty in the field of historical fiction. Educated in the United States and England, she worked for *Time,* served as publishers' reader and book reviewer before turning her talents to writing books. Her published novels include *The Winding Stair, Watch the Wall, My Darling, Greek Wedding, Savannah Purchase, Marry in Haste* (published several years earlier in *Ladies' Home Journal*). Her most recent novel, *Strangers in Company* (1973), is a suspense novel set in modern Greece. Her full-length critical biography, *The Double Life of Jane Austen* (1972), has been widely acclaimed by critics and reviewers.

IRENE HUNT has been widely recognized as one of the most talented writers of juveniles since the publication of her first book, *Across Five Aprils,* runner-up for the Newbery Medal and winner of the 1964 Charles W. Follett Award. Her book, *Up a Road Slowly,* was awarded the 1967 Newbery Medal as "the most distinguished contribution to American literature for children." Her other titles include *Trail of Apple Blossoms* and *No Promises in the Wind,* 1970 winner of the Charles W. Follett Award.

EVAN HUNTER is the author of such best sellers as *The Blackboard Jungle, Strangers When We Meet, Mothers and Daughters, A Horse's Head, Sons, Last Summer,* and *Every Little Crook and Nanny,* many of which were made into successful motion pictures. Doubleday has recently published his sequel to *Last Summer,* titled *Come Winter,* which first appeared in *Cosmopolitan* as a one-shot, and which will be published in paperback by New American Library.

Writing under his pseudonym Ed McBain, Mr. Hunter is author of the equally popular 87th Precinct books, of which over twenty have been published, including such titles as *Fuzz, Ten Plus One, Like Love, See Them Die,* and *Lady, Lady, I Did It.* He has recently written a sequel to *Fuzz,* titled *Let's Hear It for the Deaf Man,* which was published in hardcover by Doubleday and which New American Library will bring out in paperback. Mr. Hunter wrote the screenplay for *Fuzz* (which is expected to gross more than four million dollars in this country), and is now busy adapting *Come Winter* for filming.

ELSIE LEE is the author of many successful gothic novels, including *The Governess* and *Ivorstone Manor* (under the pseudonym of Elsie Cromwell), *Silence Is Golden, Barrow Sinister,* and *Wingarden.* She has also written Regency novels (*Second Season, The Wicked Guardian*) and pure romance (*The Passions of Medora Graeme,* recently published by Arbor House). A well-known authority on food, she is the author of *Elsie Lee's Book of Simple Gourmet Cookery,* brought out by Arbor House (and issued in paperback by Dell), and selected as a Book-of-the-Month Club Dividend.

MARJORIE LEE's short stories and poetry have been published in a number of magazines, including *Cosmopolitan, Redbook, McCall's, Mademoiselle, Ladies' Home Journal* and *The Saturday Evening Post.* Her stories have been selected for reprinting in such anthologies as *Love and Marriage* (edited by Margaret Cousins), *The Ladies' Home Journal Treasury,* and others. Her four novels are *The Lion House* (Rinehart), *The Eye of Summer* (Simon & Schuster), *On You It Looks Good* (Morrow), and *Dr. Block and the Human Condition* (Putnam), and her four nonfiction books are *Games Analysts Play, Marathon 16, Sexual Marathon,* and *The Erotic Fantasies of Females.*

HANNAH LEES is the author of *Women Will Be Doctors, Till the Boys Come Home* and *The Sweet Death of Candor* (Harcourt Brace, 1969), as well as three mysteries and a nonfiction book. She has also written hundreds of short stories and articles for major magazines such as *Cosmopolitan, McCall's, The Atlantic, The New Yorker* and others.

NORAH LOFTS' name is synonymous with excellence in fiction, particularly the historical novels for which she is widely known in this country and her native England. Her novel, *Out of the Dark* (Doubleday), is an engrossing tale of a young English girl in the last century and was inspired by a real-life unsolved crime. Other best sellers (and major book club selections) by Miss Lofts include *A Rose for Virtue, The Concubine, The King's Pleasure, The Lost Queen* and *How Far to Bethlehem?* and most recently, *Nethergate,* all published by Doubleday. Scheduled for publication in 1974 is *Crown of Aloes.*

EUGENE MIRABELLI's recent novel, *No Resting Place,* received excellent critical comment on its publication, and it has been called the "best book about a contemporary marriage," and a novel which "should endure for a long time." His previous book, *The Way In,* was acclaimed as "a virtuoso performance," and an early novel, *The Burning Air,* was recently re-issued in paperback. Mr. Mirabelli teaches at the State University of New York at Albany and is currently at work on a screenplay and another novel.

PATRICIA MOYES has been called "the mystery writer who put the 'who' back in whodunit" with the writing of her Inspector Henry Tibbett books. These include *Dead Men Don't Ski, Death and the Dutch Uncle, Murder à la Mode* (which has been adapted and performed as a radio play), *Falling Star, Murder Fantastical, Johnny Under Ground, Death on the Agenda, Down among the Dead Men, Murder by 3's, Many Deadly Returns,* and *Season of Snows and Sins,* all published as Holt, Rinehart & Winston Suspense Novels. She is also the author of a children's mystery, *Helter-Skelter.* Many of her books have been serialized in publications in England, the United States, Canada, Holland, Italy, Germany, and Brazil, and they have also been translated into eleven languages.

Shifting American values and the legacies of power, both military and civilian, have been the dominant themes of ANTON MYRER's fiction. His most recent novel, *Once An Eagle,* was a Book-of-the-Month Club and Reader's Digest Condensed Books selection. *The Big War* was made into a major film by Twentieth Century-Fox, and *The Intruder* was subsequently published in condensed form in *Cosmopolitan*. An article, "The Giant in the Tube," appeared in the November, 1972 issue of *Harper's*; and in February 1973 Norton published *The Tiger Waits,* a novel dealing with the conflict between personal and professional demands in an American Secretary of State.

JOYCE CAROL OATES, National Book Award winner for her novel, *Them,* is the author of several other outstanding novels, all published by Vanguard Press: *Expensive People, A Garden of Earthly Delights, Wonderland,* and *Do with Me What You Will*; four collections of short stories, including her widely acclaimed *Marriages and Infidelities*; and a recent volume of essays, *The Edge of Impossibility: Tragic Forms in Literature.* Her work has also appeared in an impressive variety of publications, ranging from *Cosmopolitan* to *The Partisan Review,* from *Harper's* and *The Atlantic* to *Family Circle.* Her short stories have been frequently anthologized in such collections as *The Best American Short Stories* and *Prize Stories: The O. Henry Awards.*

ELLIS PETERS (pseudonym of novelist Edith Pargeter) has written a number of outstanding thrillers in addition to more than twenty books under her own name. Included among them are *Where There's A Will* (Doubleday); *Death and the Joyful Woman* (Doubleday), winner of an Edgar Award from the Mystery Writers of America as the best mystery novel of the year (1962); *Funeral of Figaro, Who Lies Here?, Mourning Raga,* and *The Knocker on Death's Door* (all published by Morrow). Her last thriller is *Death to the Landlords!,* also published by Morrow who have scheduled her newest one, called *The Hypocaust.* Viking will bring out her historical novel, *The Bloody Field.*

A practicing surgeon for many years, during which time he had written many successful short stories and novels, FRANK G. SLAUGHTER turned to full-time writing in 1946. During the past twenty years, Dr. Slaughter, one of the most prolific and best-selling novelists of this century, has had fifty-three novels and nonfiction books published, drawing for his backgrounds on historical, medical, and biblical subjects, with his most recent titles including *Doctors' Wives, Sins of Herod,* and *Convention, M. D.,* all published by Doubleday. In paperback, hardcover, book club and more than twenty foreign language editions, sales of Dr. Slaughter's books total more than fifty million copies.

The suspense novels by MARY STEWART have achieved spectacular sales as well as critical acclaim all over the world. Her books regularly appear on the best-seller lists in hardcover and have continued their impressive sales in paperback: The Fawcett Crest (paper) editions of her eleven novels have sold more than twelve million copies. *The Gabriel Hounds* (which sold more than a quarter of a million copies in hardcover) was a selection of the Doubleday Book Club, the Reader's Digest Condensed Book Club, and an alternate selection of the Literary Guild; *The Moon-Spinners* was made into a successful Disney film starring Hayley Mills; and *This Rough Magic* was a Literary Guild selection. Three of Mrs. Stewart's novels—*Madam, Will You Talk?, Wildfire at Midnight,* and *Nine Coaches Waiting* —were published in England in a one-volume *Omnibus,* with a preface by the author. Her novel, *The Crystal Cave,* sold over a hundred thousand copies in hardcover and was a Literary Guild selection. She has also made an exciting start as a children's book author with her highly successful fairy story, *The Little Broomstick.* Her next adult novel, *The Hollow Hills,* a sequel to *The Crystal Cave,* and also published by Morrow, has been chosen as a Literary Guild selection.

AMELIA WALDEN has had forty-six novels published by five different publishers: The Westminster Press, J. B. Lippincott, Mc-Graw-Hill, Appleton-Century-Crofts, and William Morrow. The subject matter of these novels has been diverse: suspense, sports, tycoons of industry, ghetto teen-agers, theatrical backgrounds (off-Broadway and the American Shakespeare Festival), espionage, public school teaching, international detectives, and jet-set crime. Her three newest titles are *Play Ball, McGill, Valerie Valentine Is Missing,* and *Where Was Everyone When Sabrina Screamed?* Some of her best-known earlier books include: *To Catch a Spy, How Bright the Dawn, The Spy Who Talked Too Much, The Case of the Diamond Eye, What Happened to Candy Carmichael?, Walk in a Tall Shadow, Basketball Girl of the Year,* and *A Name for Himself.* Many of these novels have been translated into French, Italian, and German.

To mystery novel writer HILLARY WAUGH, who has been writing whodunits for more than twenty years, "there's always another one." His most recent books are *Finish Me Off* and *The Shadow Guest.* Earlier titles include *Last Seen Wearing, Madame Will Not Dine Tonight, The Girl Who Cried Wolf, The Missing Man, End of a Party, Pure Poison, "30" Manhattan East,* and *The Young Prey.* Mr. Waugh has served as president of the Mystery Writers of America.

Novelist DAVID WESTHEIMER first achieved a major success in 1964 with *Von Ryan's Express,* which remained on the best-seller list for five months, was a Book-of-the-Month Club selection and was made into a major motion picture, starring Frank Sinatra. He followed this with *My Sweet Charlie,* which was well received as a novel, produced on Broadway, and subsequently filmed. This book was published in Italy, where it was a *Club degli Editori* (Italian equivalent of Book-of-the-Month Club) choice. Mr. Westheimer's most recent novels are *Lighter Than a Feather* and *Over the Edge,* both published by Little, Brown.

PHYLLIS A. WHITNEY, now at work on her fifty-second book, is published in seventeen countries around the world. Her writing achievements have been both in the field of juveniles and adult gothics. For eleven years she was a teacher of writing at New York University, and has taught at many writers' conferences. Her latest book for young people is *Nobody Likes Trina* (Westminster), and her most recent adult novel is *Snow-*

fire (Doubleday). Her novels—most of which have appeared in paperback under the Fawcett imprint, following hardcover publication—include *The Quicksilver Pool, Hunter's Green, The Winter People, Columbella, Sea Jade, The Moonflower* and many others and have sold over 6,000,000 copies. She is also the author of a basic how-to book on creative writing, *Writing Juvenile Fiction* (The Writer, Inc.).

SYLVIA WILKINSON's first novel, *Moss on the North Side,* was published in 1966; her second, *A Killing Frost,* in 1967; and her third, *Cale,* in 1970—all by Houghton Mifflin in hardcover and in paperback by Avon. Miss Wilkinson has taught creative writing at William and Mary and the University of North Carolina at Chapel Hill, and conducted a fiction workshop at the Boatwright Literary Festival. As a teaching consultant for Learning Institute of North Carolina, she visited a number of high schools to advise teachers on innovative teaching techniques and edited a book based on her experiences called *Change* (1971). In 1972–73, she worked with the Richmond Humanities Center as Poetry-in-the-Schools Consultant, and in the spring of 1973 as writer-in-residence at Sweet Briar College.

In addition to her writing and teaching, Miss Wilkinson also does paintings which have been widely exhibited. She is a sports car racing enthusiast, presently at work on a book on auto racing to be published by Houghton Mifflin.

MONA WILLIAMS has written numerous short stories, about twenty published novelettes, assorted poetry, and two movies, in addition to her novels. She is the author of three hardcover novels —*The Marriage* (Putnam's), *The Hot Breath of Heaven* (Putnam's), and *Voices in the Dark* (Doubleday). Her original paperback novels include *The Company Girls* (Fawcett), *The Passion of Amy Styron* (Paperback Library), and *Celia* (Dell). A number of her articles ("Waiting Out His Divorce," "The Cheaters," etc.) have appeared in *Cosmopolitan.*